Horatio Alger's Children

The Role of the Family
in the Origin and Prevention
of Drug Risk

Richard H. Blum and Associates

HORATIO
ALGER'S
CHILDREN

Jossey-Bass Publishers
London • Washington • San Francisco • 1973

HORATIO ALGER'S CHILDREN
The Role of the Family in the Origin and Prevention of Drug Risk
by Richard H. Blum and Associates

Copyright © 1972 by Jossey-Bass, Inc., Publishers

Published and Copyrighted in Great Britain by
Jossey-Bass, Ltd., Publishers
3 Henrietta Street
London WC2E 8LU

Library of Congress Catalogue Card Number LC 72–186580

International Standard Book Number ISBN 0–87589–120–9

Manufactured in the United States of America

JACKET DESIGN BY WILLI BAUM

FIRST EDITION
   First Printing: April 1972
   Second Printing: January 1973

Code 7211

The Jossey-Bass
Behavioral Science Series

General Editors

WILLIAM E. HENRY
University of Chicago

NEVITT SANFORD
Wright Institute, Berkeley

Preface

F amilies are important. Those of us involved in the study reported here care about how parents feel and how children turn out. Illicit drug use, insofar as it affects both parents and children, is also important. Parent's feelings, the destiny of the children, and illicit drug use are the three concerns toward which *Horatio Alger's Children* is directed.

In our project the research group assumed that characteristics of families and special features of the individual members of families are associated with the degree to which children use illicit drugs. To test this general expectation, we studied the drug use of children and adolescents, learned something of their childhood, and observed certain characteristics of their families. What we looked for specifically was derived from our own earlier findings about drug use, the facts and theory of the social and behavioral sciences, clinical psychiatric writing and psychoanalytic theory, and some old-fashioned, armchair hunches. As our study tools we employed interviews, individual self-ratings, observations in natural settings and in psychiatric treatment, and videotaped experimental situations. Our families were drawn from black and Mexican-American populations and from poor, middle-class, and upper-class white backgrounds. We also observed young, hippie families in San Francisco. Because we did not want to overlook major family and community concerns or positive suggestions about children's drug use and what might be done about it, we surveyed additional black, Latin American, and middle-class white families and community leaders to get their views. Finally, we tried to identify family and community actions programs which had been established across the nation in an attempt to prevent or alleviate family distress about the unhappy outcomes of drug use. among our youth. *Horatio Alger's Children* reports our findings.

To anticipate, my colleagues and I were able to identify a number of characteristics in children's histories and their families' features which were discriminating variables between those children with no drug use and children with high drug use. It is possible, on the basis of these characteristics, to estimate which children in which families will use drugs illicitly in a high-risk fashion. We believe that it is also possible to make some sense out of the drug-using conduct of children and youth since that conduct is linked to rather fundamental matters in childhood and parental conduct, priorities, and beliefs. We think that these findings will be of interest to teachers, other health and counseling professionals, and community leaders. The findings should also provide some guidance to parents involved in child rearing and to persons planning education and community action programs vis-à-vis youthful drug use.

I wish, first and foremost, to thank the 211 families who gave to us their time and opened their hearts and minds so that we might learn about the problems and joys of modern child rearing. I also thank the 282 parents and community leaders who lent us their wisdom and insight by discussing with us family and community needs and possible constructive approaches to youthful drug use. Second, I thank the many volunteers who participated as assistants and consultants in this endeavor. Through their work we were able to do some research, although still less than we feel is needed. Finally, I thank those who gave us financial support—initially the Bureau of Drug Abuse Control in the Food and Drug Administration of the United States Department of Health, Education, and Welfare, and, later, the Bureau of Narcotics and Dangerous Drugs of the Department of Justice. This work was performed under contract number J-69-14. The presentation contained herein represents the findings and viewpoints of the authors and does not necessarily reflect the position of the Bureau of Narcotics and Dangerous Drugs.

ASSOCIATES

Associate authors for this volume are Eva Maria Blum (coauthor of Chapters Eleven, Twelve, Thirteen, and Fourteen), Clara de Tobal (coauthor of Chapter Eleven), Emily Garfield (coauthor of Chapter Six), Rose Wax Hauer (coauthor of Chapter Six), David V. Hinkley (author of Chapter Ten), Mary Klein (coauthor of Chapter Six), Aubrey W. Metcalf (coauthor of Chapter Thirteen), Lillian Perry (coauthor of Chapter Six), and Jean Paul Smith (coauthor of Chapter Twelve). All other chapters are by me; some are also coauthored by me.

I wish also to acknowledge consultation assistance from John Weakland, Mental Research Institute, Palo Alto, California; Charles Richardson, Richardson Data Processing Services, Palo Alto, California; and Nancy Bayley, Department of Psychology, University of California, Berkeley. Research assistance was provided by Raquel Alvarado, Diane Bausek, Gerald Bausek, Diane Bodach, Joan Cameron, Ophelia Chafey, Florence Coe, Joan (Connie) Colgin, George Dragan, Kathy Gunning, Eirene Hardy, Rosemary Gutt, Elizabeth Hinkley, Elsie Hirscher, Kristine Hooper, Margaret Huntsberger, Therese Jordan, Peggy Joseph, Juanita McCloskey, Thomas McDonnell, Anthony Poso, Roberto Rosenkranz, Theodore Russell, Janice Pagen, Don Sangrey, Patricia Schmutz, Jackie Villarreal, Gloria Welsh, and Douglas York.

Stanford, California   RICHARD H. BLUM
January 1972

Contents

For information on which chapters were authored or coauthored by the associates, see pages xi, xv, and xvi.

THREE: CLINICAL STUDIES

FOUR: TAKING ACTION

Associates

Eva Maria Blum, *Institute for Public Policy Analysis, Stanford University (coauthor of Chapters Eleven, Twelve, Thirteen, and Fourteen)*

Clara de Tobal, *James Jackson Putnam Children's Center, Boston (coauthor of Chapter Eleven)*

Emily Garfield, *Institute for Public Policy Analysis, Stanford University (coauthor of Chapter Six)*

Rose Wax Hauer, *Institute for Public Policy Analysis, Stanford University (coauthor of Chapter Six)*

David V. Hinkley, *Department of Statistics, Imperial College, University of London (author of Chapter Ten)*

Mary Klein, *Institute for Public Policy Analysis, Stanford University (coauthor of Chapter Six)*

Aubrey W. Metcalf, *Langley-Porter Clinic, University of California Medical School (coauthor of Chapter Thirteen)*

LILLIAN PERRY, *Institute for Public Policy Analysis, Stanford University (coauthor of Chapter Six)*

JEAN PAUL SMITH, *Center for Study of Narcotics and Drug Abuse, National Institute of Mental Health (coauthor of Chapter Twelve)*

Since the first printing of this book, the Institute for Public Policy Analysis has been absorbed by the Center for Interdisciplinary Research.

Horatio Alger's Children

*The Role of the Family
in the Origin and Prevention
of Drug Risk*

Preliminary Considerations

1

Since the turn of the century, a great deal of investigation and thinking has been directed toward understanding how children develop, how the family environment is influential, and how various psychosocial problems arise and might be prevented or treated. It is beyond the scope of the present work to review or even note the contributions of those scientists, educators, healers, and others to whom the world must be indebted. However, to provide additional perspective, we do draw upon some facts and particularly relevant theories of scholars in the fields of child development, psychiatry, delinquency, pediatrics, and socialization.

DRUG USE AMONG CHILDREN, ADOLESCENTS, AND PARENTS

By now, a sizable body of literature describes the extent of illicit drug use among children and youth. These investigations sometimes go on to demonstrate correlates in social class, neighborhood and ethnic features, types of schools, parental positions on vital issues, personality of users, use of approved drugs, delinquency, and so forth. In our earlier two-volume work (Blum and Associates, 1969a, 1969b), many of these studies were noted. More recently, Dorothy Berg (1970) has compiled a list of studies, surveys, and polls on the amount and frequency of illicit drug use. The Staff Report of the Task Force on Drugs (White House Conference, 1971) has detailed the extent and kind of use, and a Canadian governmental commission (*Interim Report into Non-Medical Use of Drugs*, 1970) has provided a comprehensive review of use, correlates, and outcomes, with particular emphasis on marijuana—the most commonly used illicit drug. The National Commission on Violence (1969) has summarized data on the relationship between drugs and violence among young people. Ball and Chambers (1970) have considered the epidemiology of opiate use, following up the superb epidemiological studies of Chein, Gerard, Lee, and Rosenfeld (1964) in New York and Stevenson (1956) in Vancouver. Cahalan (1970) has provided an epidemiological study of alcoholism. The special problems associated with criminal law as it relates to drug use (marijuana, in particular) have been considered by Kaplan (1970) and Grinspoon (1969), both following Packer's (1969) seminal contribution. Marin and Cohen (1971) have offered advice for families, as have Saltman (1970) and Blakeslee (1971).

Statistics for the region in which our family studies were done are available from a group of studies. One source is the continuing survey of drug use in the San Mateo County (California) high schools and junior high schools (San Mateo County School Study, 1968, 1969, 1970). A second source is the junior and senior high school survey in Monterey County, California (Fries, 1969). A third source of data is a statewide California junior and senior high school survey by the California State Department of Education (1970). A fourth source consists of studies on college student drug use on the West Coast (R. H. Blum, 1969) and two follow-up studies (Garfield, Boreing, and Smith, 1971; Garfield, 1971). A West Coast university served both as a source of families for the present study and as a source of students for one aspect of the drug dealer study reported by Blum and Associates (1972a, 1972b). As of 1971, 69 per cent of the undergraduates at this university had used an illicit drug; 19 per cent had tried LSD, and 21 per cent were using marijuana regularly (weekly or more often).

The San Mateo County study for 1971, based on questionnaires given to over twenty-two thousand students in public and parochial schools, indicated that 59 per cent of high school boys reported marijuana experimentation and 44 per cent reported regular use (ten times or more during the past year); in contrast, 48 per cent of the girls reported experimentation, and 31 per cent reported regular use. Amphetamine use was at a peak for girls during their sophomore year (27 per cent) and for boys during the senior year (27 per cent). LSD use peaked for girls in the junior year at 15 per cent and in the junior year for boys too, at 21 per cent. Alcohol was used mostly by senior boys and girls— 84 per cent for boys and 79 per cent for girls. In the seventh grade, 18 per cent of the boys and 13 per cent of the girls had tried marijuana; 3 per cent of the boys and 2 per cent of the girls had tried LSD; and 5 per cent of the seventh-grade boys and 6 per cent of the girls had used amphetamines. Sixteen per cent of the seventh-grade boys and 11 per cent of the seventh-grade girls had used alcohol ten times or more; and 16 per cent of the boys and 14 per cent of the girls had smoked cigarettes. The Monterey County data (Fries, 1969), which included some Mexican-American families, showed that 46 per cent of the twelfth-grade students reported marijuana experimentation, with 16 per cent reporting regular use. In the seventh grade, 8 per cent of the students reported illicit experimentation, and none reported regular use. By the seventh grade, 66 per cent had tried alcohol, and 39 per cent had used tobacco. The most commonly used illicit, unsanctioned drug in the seventh grade was glue (used by sniffing), with amphetamines being the second most used.

Some data also exist for adult drug use in communities from which our samples were taken. One study (Blum and Associates, 1969a) showed that, for one community, two-thirds of the adults had used conventional social and proprietary drugs, prescribed painkillers, and psychoactive substances (either on prescription or over-the-counter psychoactives). One-sixth of the population had taken these as well as illicit or exotic substances.

In terms of correlates, the greater the lifetime experience with drugs, the more current use reported and the more drugs reported available at home. Some evidence also indicates that high drug-using parents handle their childrens' emotions more negatively and themselves more often disliked their parents than did low drug users or nonusing parents. High users were dissatisfied with themselves, their relations with others, and their work. They also seemed subject to cravings, extreme likes and dislikes, compulsiveness, guilt about their drug-taking habits, suspiciousness of drug contents, and fears of drug dependency. A tendency to proselytize about drugs, sensitivity to criticism for drug use, and fear of falling under the control of others because of drugs are also frequently encountered in high users. This group also used drugs as tools for a variety of personal purposes. In this adult sample, drug experience increased with education, incidence of divorce, youthfulness, and being white. Low drug use or nonuse was associated with church affiliation and actually attending church. Searching for embracing descriptions, we considered low drug users as conservative, high users of normal (legal) drugs as middle class, and users of illicit and exotic drugs as liberal disaffiliated.

In a study of marijuana use among adults in San Francisco, Manheimer and Mellinger (1969) report that 13 per cent of a random sample reported experience with marijuana and that experience is greatest among young adults. A final study that is relevant to our family study was conducted by Roney and Nall (1966). They investigated medication practices and learned that most medications were self-prescribed; the most widely used medications were taken for respiratory problems and the second most used were those for central nervous system distress (headache, nervousness, sleeplessness, depression, and so on). The average household had almost thirty medications on hand—most of which were not perscription drugs. About two-thirds of the families reported that their use of psychoactive substances was self-initiated and not on the advice of anyone. Wives and daughters most often found they needed something for nervousness, and wives took more drugs for pain and headaches than did any other family member. These mostly self-obtained and self-prescribed substances were more often used by better educated than by less educated families and individuals.

The high prevalence of illicit drug use among children and youth is a recent phenomenon, although the illicit use of drugs such as tobacco and alcohol on the part of children has long been with us. Since families do influence children, styles within the family should have something to do with the use or nonuse of drugs. We expect that since drug-use patterns have changed, styles of family life and child-rearing practices have also probably changed. Such a thesis does not ignore other changing forces in the environment, which also affect what children and youth do or how the family functions. Our hypothesis merely limits itself to the areas of the family, child rearing, and drug use.

When one thinks of influences upon changing American child-rearing practices, names such as Freud, Dewey, Gesell, and Spock come to mind. Yet, however persuasive these men may have been, their works are but elements in times which have seen rapidly increasing technology, urbanization, education, specialization, affluence, health advances, mobility, and communications. On another level, the times have been witness to agnosticism, pragmatism, relativism, liberalism, and the like. For the family, changing times have meant increased divorce rates. (For every two marriages in California, there is one divorce.) Thirteen per cent of the children in the United States are being reared in one-parent families. In addition, there are an increased number of remarriages, reduced birth rates (cut almost by half from 1910 to 1971), decreased proximity of kinfolk, considerable mobility (about one family in five moves each year), increased employment for women (now up to 40 per cent) (*Time*, 1970), longer lives for parents, greater life expectancy for infants, and reduced family functions as other institutions have taken over what were extended family responsibilities. For children, these changes have meant many things—not the least of which have been parental emphases on adjustment, happiness, competence, rights, health, and autonomy. In addition, the child now experiences an increase in the duration of time before full employment and a dilution of sources of power and influence. In other words, figures of authority and influence are found among preschool care centers, schools, clubs, recreation centers, health professionals, the mass media, and especially age-mates. As Bronfenbrenner has said (*Time,* 1970), "The battle today is not between children and parents, the battle is between society on one side and families on the other."

Bronfenbrenner (1958) described trends in infant care and child training (see also Davis, 1965) and concluded that mothers in all social classes have become increasingly flexible as to feeding and weaning, that middle-class mothers have become more permissive than are working-class mothers in regard to feeding, weaning, and toilet training, and that the practices of middle-class mothers have mainly been in response to what experts have recommended. Middle-class mothers have also become increasingly permissive in regard to letting the child express himself and in granting his wishes. Parents have also raised their aspirations for what the child should do and accomplish. In the middle class, relations between child and parents have become more egalitarian with greater parental tolerance and a freer exchange of affection than in the past. Davis (1965), reviewing Bronfenbrenner's (1958) findings, concluded that the middle-class parent is more responsive than is the lower-class parent to child-expert opinion. According to Davis, parents are eager and willing to learn; they want to do the best they can and, therefore, follow the advice of authorities. Implicit in this notion is that parental actions are not entirely predetermined by their own beliefs, emotions, and childhood experiences but, rather, that parents can exercise discrimination in selecting some of their child-rearing methods.

Davis analyzed research work dealing with what parents do and believe and elaborated on the current American theory of proper child rearing. Central to this theory are emotional warmth and feelings of being loved and secure. Material things are not so important; and, in some areas, heredity is also unimportant. Parents, to do a good job, believe they themselves must be emotionally secure and psychologically sound, that they must show affection and not deny love. Over half of the wealthy mothers and one-fifth of the low-income mothers have read Spock, found him helpful, and tried to follow his recommendations. Yet, says Davis—again citing the research evidence—of the many things that parents can give to their children, offering warmth or emotional security is less subject to control or choice than are mechanical things such as choice of foods and securing health care. The work of Spitz (1945) and Bowlby (1951) and the studies of Harlow and Suomi (1970) do suggest, as American mothers believe, that the child who is deprived of physical caring by a mother figure does indeed suffer. Sears, Maccoby, and Levin (1957) (see also Sears, Rau, and Alpert, 1965) indicate that warmth makes other techniques of mothering more effective than they would otherwise be. As far as specific items of infant care are concerned, Davis contends that particular practices and later personality and adjustment have not been shown to be related. (See also Orlansky, 1949.) We believe that most American parents emphasize a general style and atmosphere as crucial but would agree that the mechanics of infant and child care—as long as these mechanics are accomplished attentively with prime regard for well-being—are not of fundamental importance.

DISCIPLINE AND AFFECTION

Aside from affection, there is another variable which most American parents from any class would agree is critical. This variable is discipline. American parents agree that affection is entirely good, but there are fundamental disagreements in the philosophies and practices of disciplining children. Some parents believe that the important factor in the development and adjustment of the child is in the care that must be taken to avoid the exercise of discipline; some parents apply discipline as a matter of principle; others apply it as part of an authoritative style integrated with explanations, demands, and the like to achieve a successful outcome.

Bronfenbrenner (1969, 1970), in comparing Russian and American education and child-rearing practices, considered character education and moral development and concluded that moral standards are most successfully internalized (made into conscience) when both affection and discipline are high. (Existing research on character education and moral development has been reported by Bronfenbrenner, 1961a, pp. 71–84; 1961b, pp. 239–272; 1961c, pp. 90–109; Hoffman, 1961; Miller and Swanson, 1960; and Sears, Maccoby, and Levin, 1957.) Disciplinarian but unaffectionate parents raise children who respond only to power—that is, to punishment and external control. (Discipline, power, and control may be considered similar concepts.) When affection and discipline are low or when there is affection but no discipline, the child is likely to develop weak or inoperative moral standards. He may also distort matters of responsibility by blaming others, denying his own part in matters, avoiding recognition of what he has done, and so on. When parents are both affectionate and disciplinarian but their discipline takes the form of hurting the child's self-esteem or attacking his personal worth and capabilities, moral standards in the child may become rigid or self-punishing. Parents who have realistic moral standards and who are capable of evaluating extenuating circumstances are described by Hoffman (1961) as being able to communicate their disappointment in the child's failure to live up to expectations without having to attack the child's worth or withdraw love.

Any study of normal parents who come from the same environment and social class will probably find greater differences among disciplinary philosophies than among philosophies pertaining to affection. In our own work, we did not seek to describe either of these components as family attributes per se. Identifying and rating such dynamic features reliably is a perilous task. We did, however, seek information about beliefs and practices, which ought to correlate with the practice of discipline. For example, we sought parental views on such topics as the police, self-discipline with regard to obeying rules, the age at which various rules should be imposed upon children, and belief in God. As we shall see, many of these items are found to be associated with differences in childen's drug use. We did not weigh families on a scale that would identify—let alone quantify—discipline as a real entity; but we do propose that many of our findings make good sense if interpreted in the light of the basic and extensive work of other scientists. Our finding relates back to a major factor (discipline) which investigators such as Freud and, more recently, Spitz (1945), Sears, Maccoby, and Levin (1957), Glidewell (1961), Aronfreed (1968), and Whiting and Child (1953) have shown to be basic.

One assumes but cannot prove American families have changed more in regard to discipline than affection during the past fifty years or so. Had parents in the past been less affectionate and more disciplined than modern parents are, there might be no superficial measures of change in the moral behavior of their offspring (drug use, delinquency, precocious sexuality), as long as the environments in which the children lived had remained highly structured and enforced a set of agreed-upon conduct codes. That is the case because the unloved but strongly disciplined child remains responsive to moral requirements placed upon him by an environment that agrees upon, makes known, and, if needed, enforces its morality, as is often the case in small communities in America and also in underdeveloped foreign societies today (Blum and Blum, 1965). However, when controlling social structures break down and when disagreement characterizes the community itself, young people receive discordant messages as to what is proper, and the mechanisms for social control in areas short of strictly prohibited violations (homicide, incest, and the like) break down. Under such circumstances, the unloved but disciplined child can be expected to follow his impulses and self-interest.

Since large numbers of youth today do, in fact, live in situations where social structures (church, school, the military, places of employment, law enforcement, and the like) exert diminished controls, the use of drugs for pleasure—or the sale of drugs in pursuit of self-interest—could result from a reduction in external controls and not from changing child-rearing styles. We suspect that the drug use of some youth is a reflection of what happens when children are reared without internalized standards of the proprieties of pleasure, convention, or lawfulness. The same absence of constraint is necessary for the proliferation of most kinds of lawlessness (except acts of conscience such as civil disobedience, which are better conceived as intentional unlawfulness independent of restraint). At the same time, considering the emphasis on affection, the doting attention accorded to children today, and our cultural advocacy of kindness and love as nice things, we believe that the most common child-rearing trend in America has not been the withholding of love and the exercise of discipline. Possibly, affection and discipline have both been high and constant. If that were the case, there should be no change in the moral conduct of children except insofar as parental standards of morality have changed. Thus, if parents came to believe that illicit drug use or other unlawful behavior was totally acceptable, such parents might well engage in that conduct themselves and teach it to their children. Insofar as theirs was a minority view, these families would be risking censure from the rest of the community; but if such moral changes were determined by increasingly prevalent social forces, then whole groups or classes of such parents could provide a mutually reinforcing and accepting environment. Generally, one would expect such moral innovations from among liberal groups—that is, those who are urbane as well as urbanized. As in the case of acceptance of drugs in other times (Blum and Associates, 1969a), these persons are well educated, often artists or other intellectuals, who have been considered Bohemian experimentalists and whose innovations (divorce, premarital sex, agnosticism, draft resistance, overt homosexuality) have later become accepted if not approved practices for the upper and middle classes. In the area of drug use, we do have evidence of its moral acceptance by at least some parents; for example, 9 per cent of the parents of the heavy marijuana smokers and 2.4 per cent of the parents of light smokers in one university (Blum and associates, 1969b) were described by their children as smokers themselves. Chapter Eleven in this volume describes how the children of Haight-Ashbury hippies (a Bohemian group) are taught drug use at an early age.

One surmises that some component of children's contemporary illicit behavior is not due to any great shift in discipline or affection but, rather, demonstrates a change in the content of parental morality.[1] One could ask how it happens that parental

---

[1] Insofar as the criminal law is an expression of that morality, efforts to legalize marijuana may be seen, in part, as a movement to codify these changes—that is, to have the law catch up to the new upper- and middle-class standard.

morals change in content without necessarily implying any alternation in the handling or the amounts of affection and discipline meted out to children. We do not know. As the clinical material in Chapter Thirteen suggests, families may be more consistent over generations as far as their styles are concerned than observers have realized; thus, what grandfather did can be seen in what father does and in what the son plans to do.

Evidence pertaining to particular families indicates that there is a third style of child-rearing practices—that is, constant and low dosages of both discipline and affection. We might expect such child-rearing to lead to the environmental inheritance of misery and of sociopathy because those parents who have no control over or love for their offspring produce children with weak or inoperative moral standards. Robins (1966) followed up children who were seen in a child guidance clinic thirty years previously and found that, regardless of class factors, children from homes where fathers, mothers, or both were alcoholic and delinquent were very likely to become alcoholic and delinquent themselves. In our study of drug dealers (Blum and associates, 1972a, 1972b), we obtained evidence pertaining to drug use per se; children from homes where parents were criminal, addicted, or alcoholic (or all three) or from homes with low marital stability were themselves likely to be drug dependent and criminal. We also found examples of parents not only teaching illicit drug use to their children but also initiating their children in drug peddling as well. Thus, insofar as parents are themselves deviant, their children will probably end up the same way. This tragic destiny is escaped occasionally by a person who does marvelously as a human being, despite coming from such a background.

A fourth possible trend in child-rearing practices is that American families have remained fairly constant on warmth and affection but have become less convinced of the need for discipline than in the past. But abandoning certain disciplinary methods, while substituting others, is not a reduction in discipline per se: great grandfather may have used a switch in the woodshed, grandfather a hairbrush on the backside, and father the profound expression of disappointment coupled with no allowance or desserts for a week. After considering Bronfenbrenner's and Davis' data on increased permissiveness, the growing emphasis on reward rather than punishment, the stress on self-realization through lack of restraint, and the considerable increase in illicit drug use and delinquency among children whose parents are neither advocates of illicit drug use nor sorrowful figures incapable of love or control, we suspect that the major shift has been not only in the mechanisms of discipline but in its acceptance and utilization by parents who are trying to do what authorities have said is best. If that is the case, then those families in our sample who show what we propose to be correlates of the acceptance of discipline are traditionalists. They have maintained family child-rearing styles that were common in the past, whereas those families who display few disciplinary correlates are change oriented and ought to show tendencies toward liberalism, agnosticism, and the like. We shall see that this is indeed the case and that such differences are associated with offspring drug use in children. Indeed, our data on student drug use (Blum and associates, 1969b) indicate that illicit drug users more often than not come from homes characterized by high education, great wealth, liberal political opinions, little church involvement, and the like.

What we hypothesize in regard to child-rearing trends over time is a shift, not in affection, but in the acceptance and dispensing of discipline. In other words, a shift has occurred in the concentration and exercise of power and control in families. Our study does not constitute any test of such a historical proposition, but we believe our results make sense in that light. For a worldwide view of the history of the family, see W. J. Goode (1970).

PARENTAL AUTHORITY

Baumrind (1971) has carried out a study on family factors that illustrates discoveries relevant to drug use. She was concerned, in part, with socialization and social responsibility. Reviewing the literature, Baumrind concluded that close supervision and high demand for obedience (discipline) lead to responsible conduct rather than to rebelliousness. The least hostile children have parents who demand the most. Firm control is associated with the development of conscience. In her work, Baumrind found that the most socially responsible children had parents who exercise authoritative control (firm but not petty, setting high standards but explaining why, not deferring to peers or to the child but not viewing themselves as infallible). The sons, particularly, of parents who are either permissive or authoritarian (rigidly demanding, punitive, dogmatic, without give and take) were less socially responsible than children of authoritative parents. When parents were themselves nonconforming, their being authoritative was insufficient, and their children proved to be aggressive and resistant. These parents encouraged nonconforming behavior outside the home. Another finding that bears on conscience development comes from Hoffman (1971), who found that sons from father-absent families receive lower scores on all moral indices (judgment, guilt, values, conformity) than do sons from families where the father is present.

What does this evidence mean for drug use? Is it not likely that children of authoritative, conforming parents are most likely to follow parental standards with regard to drug use? Might we not expect that children of either permissive or nonconforming authoritative parents might be more likely than others to engage in disapproved and unlawful conduct (although for different psychodynamic reasons)? Should we not expect that children of nonconforming parents would be the same as their parents and, if exposed to drug-taking situations, would pursue these opportunities to the extreme? We do not know the answers to these questions, but our hope is that through research the answers will be forthcoming.

EMOTIONAL HEALTH

Westley and Epstein (1969) have conducted a study the methods of which closely resemble ours. These researchers were interested in the emotional health of college students in association with family patterns. They learned that "the way in which a family organized itself and functioned as a unit was both a consequence and a cause of mental health or illness of family members" (p. 6). Cooperation in the study was itself associated with the mental health of students; healthy subjects had families who cooperated the most; unhealthy subjects came from families that cooperated the least. Among their other findings are the following. (1) Emotional health of children and mothers was greater in families where there was activity with outsiders (community affairs, visits, sports, and so on). (2) Unhealthy family members had trouble expressing emotions; most could not express anger but instead denied it. They were less in touch with their own emotions. (3) Unhealthy students were confused and vague about their future goals. (4) Open or emotional communications or both were rare among members of unhealthy families; relationships were often rigid or cold; communications were evasive and limited to mechanics of living. The authors cite Ackerman (1958) and Jackson (1959) for confirming findings. (5) Problem solving was positive (openly faced, openly handled) in healthy families but not so in unhealthy ones. Indeed, families who had emotionally disturbed children did not face that problem either and seemed completely unaware of it. In contrast, even tiny problems were brought out in healthy families. Further contrast indicated those families that did face their problems had few of them; those that denied them had the most crises. The authors cite Koos (1946) in support of this conclusion. (6) The autonomy-dependency axis was the key factor in the emotional climate, and the mother most influenced that balance. (7) When both parents were emotionally healthy, so were their children; when both were disturbed, so were their children. (8) The relationship between the parents was most critical for the emotional health of their children. Parents who were affectionate, warm, and respectful in their own relationship produced healthy children. Parents who lacked these qualities in their relationship produced unhealthy children. (Sex was infrequent among disturbed couples). (9) When women married men beneath them socioeconomically and educationally and when men married above themselves, the chances for emotional ill health in parents and children were great. (10) Power in the family was also a central variable. For relevant work the authors cite Zelditch (1964), Blood and Wolfe (1960), Stodtbeck (1958), Clausen and Kohn (1960), and King and Henry (1955). (11) The healthiest family organization found by Westley and Epstein was one where there was a system of authority led by the father. Where the father was secure and took initiative in solving emotional problems and where the mother gave encouragement and respect for autonomy but was not dominant, then emotional health was optimal. The authors cite Komarovsky (1940), Herbst (1954), King and Henry (1955), Clausen and Kohn (1960), and Bronfenbrenner (1961b). (12) Families became chaotic when the father did not lead and when parents refused to exercise authority, compromised through democratic decision making with the children in power, or evaded responsibility. The authors relate this abdication to Western suspicion of authoritarianism and approval for conceptual democracy. They cite Miller and Swanson (1958) for similar findings. Children from father-led families were, in their sample, the most stable and assertive. By way of summary, the authors say that "the kind of family organization that is most . . . likely to produce emotionally healthy children has a balanced division of labor, a father-led system of authority, a mother who is upwardly mobile, a respect for autonomy, strength in problem solving, and a husband and wife who thoroughly accept both their conjugal and parental roles" (pp. 34–35).

How would one expect these observations to relate to drug use in children? Probably, emotionally healthy families would produce emotionally healthy children who, in regard to drug use, would not engage in behavior that risked drug dependency, arrest, or pervasive conflict with their parents. For conservative families, this would mean little or no illicit experimentation. For more liberal families this would mean that, in regions where marijuana use was normal for children, they would smoke marijuana but would avoid involvement in deviant drug subcultures, multiple illicit drug use, heavy use, or the use of any drug for escapist purposes.

POLITICS

Illicit drug use is a political phenomenon. Widespread moral concern and conflict attract the attention of the mass media and politicians and become vote-getting maneuvers. Youthful drug use is correlated with political stance, and therefore divergent proposals for legislation and public policy regarding drugs have emerged. Since, for normal students, drug experimentation and nondisabling use are imbedded in politics and social values more than in physical or mental health status, one expects the family factors that influence political development to be relevant for the development of drug views and habits as well. The considerable literature on political socialization reviews studies on within-family factors that contribute to political views (Lane and Sears, 1964; Hess and Torney, 1967; Bronfenbrenner, 1961b; Kohn, 1959, 1963). Researchers in the area of political socialization suggest not only that children usually follow parental party preferences and become active if their parents are, but also that the child's relations to the father are generalized (transferred) to political figures and authorities outside the system. In addition, positions and attitudes based on class membership can be altered when the father takes an unusual position vis-à-vis his class. Children with strong fathers "tend to be more attached to figures and institutions, particularly the President and the policeman, than the child whose father is relatively weak" (Hess and Torney, 1967, p. 101). Children who believe that their fathers are powerful become more informed and interested in political affairs than other children.

Lipset (1971) has reviewed studies on activism and has concluded that politically left children come from liberal or left families. He cites Flacks (1967), Keniston (1969), and others who confirm that the well-educated, affluent, progressive parent has children who are chips off the progressive bloc. Students who have active radical views believe they are more similar to their fathers than do students who are radical but inactive (Cowdry and Keniston. 1969). Finally, the fact that mother dominance and permissiveness loom large as determinants of left radicalism (Flacks, 1969) is also to be kept in mind.

What implications do these data have for drug use? We know that the use of illicit drugs by middle-class youngsters is linked to membership in high-status, progressive families; we would expect a high degree of involvement in drug use among children whose fathers are actively liberal and who have been taught to challenge tradition. One also expects a great degree of drug involvement among permissive families where the mother is dominant, where fathers are weak or absent, and where positive liberalism is complicated by reduced attachment to authority.

Children from such backgrounds should be aloof from the police, for example, or from authoritative law and order views. We are reminded, at this point, of the frequently derogatory opinion that professionals have of narcotics agents (R. H. Blum and J. Wahl, in Blum and associates, 1964). If, as fathers, such professionals were strong figures, they would transmit their views to their active and admiring children. If such fathers were weak, they would contribute to a disregard on the part of the child for the authority of both the father and the police.

CLASS

Class differences are important variables in the drug-taking behavior of children. Hess and Torney (1967) found that children of high-status families consider their fathers more powerful than do children of lower-class families. This, in turn is associated with a greater sense of political efficacy in higher-class children than in lower-class children. Lower-class parents are also more likely than higher-class parents to be authoritarian in their control, thereby producing external compliance if not inner conviction in their children. (Compare Baumrind's finding of decreased social responsibility and Bronfenbrenner's finding of a lack of internalized moral standards or weak character in children of highly authoritarian parents.) Lower-class children were also more positive than upper-class children about policemen, although they were preoccupied with this constraining-punishing role rather than with his peace-keeping one. Middle-class children tend to credit the police with little knowledge, and their parents regard being a policeman as an inferior occupation.

Since the youthful drug use that has received most comment is middle-class drug use, it is easy to see how a diminished regard for authority per se in the middle class could have supported increased drug-using conduct. The child of the middle class is schooled in the questioning of absolutes (including the father when he is weak). The middle-class child may side with the father (when he is strong) against the inferior police or deny the absoluteness of the law, by placing his moral or natural law against the positive or written law. The middle-class child is likely to be confident and willing to act on his beliefs because of strengths drawn from his high-status position and—sometimes— because of an identification with an admired powerful father. Such a youngster is obviously in a much better position to try something that has social-political significance such as drugs, than is the less reflective, less confident, less politically assertive, and more conventionally obedient working-class child.

The foregoing may help account for the conservatism in drug experimentation and in correlated social activism among working-class youth. These findings have no bearing, however, on the very extensive illicit drug use among the disorganized, disadvantaged poor. In this group drug use appears to take its most serious form in terms of dependency (addiction), ill health, social disability, and associated criminality and arrest. Alcoholism and heroin dependency are unduly concentrated in young, poor, urban males especially. (See Blum and Blum, 1967; Ball and Chambers, 1970; and Cahalan, 1970.) It is apparent from arrest statistics (Bureau of Criminal Statistics, 1969) that young Mexican-Americans in California, Puerto Ricans in New York, and blacks in urban centers (Robins and Murphy, 1967) are populations that are a special risk with regard to opiates. Also, the poor or, rather, particular sectors of poor people do not constitute a stable culture (as, for example, most of the world's peasants do), and they do not seek or share the conduct modes of the larger society (Banfield, 1970). Such sectors of the population risk suffering themselves, or visiting upon others, a variety of miseries, ranging from contagious diseases to crime. The report of the Joint Commission on Mental Health of Children (1969) calls attention to the fact that poverty is associated with infant mortality, brain damage, mental retardation, emotional crippling in young children, school maladaption apparent by the first grade, subsequent educational retardation, school drop out, and unemployment.

Some studies have shown that child-rearing practices are influenced by socioeconomic conditions (Hess and Shipman, 1965; Kohn, 1959; Maas, 1951; and Davis, 1943). Indeed, one may consider class factors as intercorrelated environmental circumstances that shape human beings (families and their children) just as do cultural or subcultural factors. Many investigators have considered how differently experience in one group versus that in another group shapes lives (Mead, 1950; Lewis, 1959). As for the special case of extreme hazard for the offspring of the disorganized American poor, descriptions may be found in Brown (1965), K. Clark (1965), Baldwin (1963), Shostak and Gombergue (1965), Seligman (1965), and Kardiner and Ovesey (1962). The gist of much of this work is that troubled and disorganized people make poor parents; destitute families in which the parents are without psychological strengths or social obligations to one another or to their offspring are hazardous situations for children. Moreover, when parents are themselves inadequately controlled and believe they gain nothing by developing self-discipline, then it is unlikely that discipline or other virtues can be employed for the benefit of children.

Clearly, both family style and class are associated with how the child turns out. Since certain disruptive social forces are intense and frequent in particular groups, the offspring of such groups are in particular jeopardy. An illustration of such a high-risk situation is when unskilled workers who are without the support of prexisting cultural solidarity move into disorganized slums of major cities. Insofar as offspring can move up into the working or middle class, this trend is reversible—as, indeed, it has been reversed by the third generation of nearly all American immigrants. However, when a reservoir of thoroughly troubled and trouble-making parents remains at the bottom and when this pool constitutes a large neighborhood, one sees the rather discouraging spectacle of disordered drug-using or even drug-dealing families.

MACHIAVELLIANISM

Christie and Geis (1970) have studied Machiavellianism and offer fascinating information about who is or is not Machiavellian and what the correlates of that coldly objective, pragmatic, and manipulative trait are. Christie and Geis, citing Braginsky's (1966) work on Machiavellianism in parents, report that when both parents are not Machiavellian (that is, when both are idealists, considerate, and otherwise nonexploitative), their children

are Machiavellian. Since low Machiavellian parents are responsive to the very early demands of the infant, they are, in a sense,
trained by the infant to serve his needs. One may guess that, as
the child grows, he senses his capability to manipulate his idealistic and considerate parents through wheedling, smiling, crying,
rewarding, and the like. One comes up with a theory of parent
rearing by children, which applies whenever child-centered
parents are easily conned by clever children. Perhaps such parent
rearing would occur whenever the mother is indulgent and the
father weak or whenever the family constellation is egalitarian.
In any event we would guess that if Braginsky's finding holds,
such a child learns very early that his pleasures and his desires
can be gained through any number of manipulative devices. If
we further posit that the pursuit of pleasure is easier for a child
to learn than is self-discipline, that permissive parents today are
idealistically motivated and essentially naive, and that it is not
too difficult for clever children to fashion a new ideology that
debases antipleasure strictures and converts delight into a new
morality saleable to flexible and well-intentioned parents, then
any pleasurable activity that does not run counter to parental
idealism is one which such parents could be manipulated into
accepting. Marijuana smoking is a good example of such a plea-
sureable activity which has, in a very short time, been converted
from a vice into a positive ideology. We should not discount the
role of the articulate younger generation in selling that new
morality. If so, the buyers have been idealistic, open-minded
parents already well trained by their children to accommodate
to the child's desires. Our notion does not argue for the new or
the old morality vis-à-vis drugs. This notion does imply that the
family in which the youngsters use illicit drugs in ways that are
not obviously damaging and in which the parents give either tacit
approval or open acceptance ("you can smoke weed only after
your homework is done, Chester") is (in the middle class, at least)
a family where the parents are low Machiavellians and the children high Machiavellians.

   In our studies, we have not tested for Machiavellianism;
but perhaps the correlates of Machiavellianism would be an emphasis on the part of the parents on the child's satisfaction of his

own desires and self-realization rather than an emphasis on the essentially restraining factors of adult development (becoming a contributing member of the community and the like). We would also expect low Machiavellian parents to be proud of their own flexible child centeredness, to ignore or pretend to ignore their children's illicit drug use if they do not approve, to condone social groups that are pleasure oriented, and to be less concerned about the prevalence of evil influences than about the fulfilllment of democratic ideals. Thus, one would expect such parents to worry less about communists and more about racists than would other persons. As we shall see, such expectations tend to be supported.

FAMILY PSYCHOPATHOLOGY

Much of the research on families has been clinical, centering on the description of processes within the group that lead one or several members to chronic distress. The pioneering work in this area was that of Jackson (1959). His work relates to the interpersonal emphasis of Sullivan (1953), Bateson, Jackson, and Haley (1956), Group for the Advancement of Psychiatry (1954), Haley (1962), Watzlawick, Beavin, and Jackson (1967), Jackson (1968), and Farina (1960). Alkire (1969) has shown that disturbed children have powerful mothers, whereas normal outgoing children have powerful fathers (defined in terms of eliciting communication from the child). For the disturbed fearful child, communication among all members of the family was very poor. The conclusion, over several categories of families and disturbances, was that, in families with disturbed children, role reversals occurred where mothers acted like fathers and vice versa. This reversed dominance was associated with particular communication patterns within the family. These findings echo those of Westley and Epstein (1969), who also found poor communication in families with emotionally unhealthy children.

The implication of these findings for drug use is not that drug users' families are likely to have poor communication, role reversal, and pathological processes but rather that when illicit drug use exceeds its normal experimental or social forms and becomes a devious means for communicating rebellion or hostility or for emotional escape, then a pathological situation probably exists within the family. Conversely, if the findings on family dynamics are correct, one would expect some form of maladaptation among children in these families but that maladjustment need not take the form of drug use. If drug use does occur, then one might surmise that the drug-taking behavior of children from a pathological family background would quickly become extreme. Our intensive clinical videotape work with very high and very low drug risk families did include family dynamics. As we shall see, the families of high drug-risk children differed from low-risk families; both roles and communication figured as important factors.

Further
Considerations

✻ 2 ✻

Scholars, clinicians, and laymen
familiar with the field of child development would probably
agree that affection and discipline are central aspects of family
life. They would also concur that morals, mental health, and
social values are significant factors which are probably related to
differences in drug use among children. Yet, before we can expect
these or any other features to be differentially associated with
drug use, we must ask whether there is any evidence that the
families of illicit drug-using children differ from the families of
nonusers.

THROUGH THE CHILD'S EYES

There is evidence that families of drug users do, indeed,
differ from families of nonusers in predictable ways. The work of
Chein, Gerard, Lee, and Rosenfeld (1964) on heroin users in the
slums showed that drug users' families have greater weaknesses
than do other families. Robins' (1966) work showed the correspondence between parental drug dependency (alcoholism) and

23

sociopathy and alcoholism in the offspring. Our own work, including both the normal population study and the student surveys, tests, and clinical observations, also points to differences between these two kinds of families. The self-reports of students indicate that drug-using offspring feel greater disagreement and distance between themselves and their parents than do nonusing offspring. Emotional emptiness characterized the relationships between heavy drug users and their parents in the composite clinical picture (Eva Maria Blum in Blum and associates, 1969b). The self-reports of offspring from other families indicated the existence of warmth and discipline. Drug-using students come from families where social, self-prescribed, or medical use of psychoactives is acceptable and where parents (by virtue of being liberal) appear to sanction the autonomy of their young.

Bewley (1970) has reviewed English studies and found that, for sedative users, separation from parents had been the majority experience prior to age sixteen. Amphetamine users had also experienced abnormal separations and were typically from families that were mother-dominated and that had histories of disturbed relationships, psychiatric illness, alcoholism, and criminality. The Monterey County school study (Fries, 1969) reported that illicit users more often came from homes with unstable or tragic marital relations and that alcoholism among the parents of the illicit users was more prevalent than it was among the parents of nonusers. Love, rigidity, and financial security were matters to which the students often alluded in describing familial assets or liabilities which were linked with their own conduct toward drugs. Using a Family Adjustment Test, Kleckner (1970) found that drug-using students scored higher on feeling homeless and had a more negative view of their families than nonusers. However, Steffenhagen, McAree, and Zheutlin (1969), studying college students, found no indication of family disorganization per se as a discriminating feature; they did note that their sample was taken from a middle-class population in which family disorganization of the sort that characterizes low-income, heroin-using families does not often occur. Finally, the statewide California study of junior and senior high school students (California State Department of Education, 1970) found that one-half of the nonusers felt that they communicated easily with their parents, whereas only about one-fourth of the drug-using students felt this way.

Junior high, high school, and college students do describe their families and their relationships to them differently, depending on whether these students are illicit drug users. The degree of difference that emerges among these self-descriptions is likely to be a function of the degree of involvement with drug use, although the research has not always examined for a continuum. What youngsters describe is consistent enough (and easily verified by matters such as divorce and alcoholism) to lead us to accept the fact of family differences among groups that vary in their illicit drug involvement. For the low-income levels (especially slum populations), the differences are dramatic, involving factors such as family disorganization, sociopathology, and psychopathology. For middle- and upper-class users, family differences are not so striking and are only superficially visible. The factors involved are usually not pathological but center on communication, conflict, the quality of emotional life, and the drug use, political stance, and social values of the parents.

The evaluation of a child or youth by a psychiatrist or psychologist is not a direct look at the family but may be used as a special lens for viewing the family situation. If the general psychodynamic notion that disturbed children are likely to come from upset family situations is correct, then psychodiagnoses, which find drug users to be more psychologically ill than are nonusers, would provide inferential evidence as to the source of the illness—that is, evidence as to the distressful character of certain family situations. We shall not push that clinical assumption too far; nor is it our task here to test it, as a few general studies are already available. Westley and Epstein (1969) have carried out one such study. Another study was conducted by MacFarlane, Allen, and Honzik (1954). We cannot review in any detail the growing literature that suggests the existence of personality disorders among some illicit drug users. It is necessary to view the findings with caution, for either normality or maladjustment may be found, depending upon the sample used. As in the study of alcoholism, one must be careful to distinguish between drug effects, the impact of a drug-involved life, and features attributable to preexisting personal or family conditions. Much clinical research suffers from failures to control sufficiently for such matters. In addition, bias easily affects results if the clinician already knows the drug-use status of his patient or has a pathological theory in mind to account for drug use.

Among studies showing or implying the great frequency of psychological distress or psychiatric illness among users are those of Chein, Gerard, Lee, and Rosenfeld (1964), Scott and Willcox (1965), Brehm and Back (1968), Kleckner (1968), Ungerleider, Fisher, Fuller, and Caldwell (1968), Hawks (1969), Steffenhagen, McAree, and Zheutlin (1969), Westley and Epstein (1969), Pittel (1969), Noble (1970), and Calef, Gryler, Hilles, Hofer, Kempner, Pittel, and Wallerstein (1970). Against these works and as part of our counsel of caution, we call attention to works such as those by McGlothlin, Cohen, and McGlothlin (1967), Hogan, Mankin, Conway, and Fox (1970), Goode (1970), and Blum and associates (1964, 1969b). In such studies personality differences as such have indeed been found to differentiate between illicit users and nonusers at the college level, but evidence for clinical pathology is weak or absent. Most differences are matters of interests, esthetics, traits, and aptitudes (introversion, mysticism, suggestibility, regard for others, impulsiveness and the like). Possibly such differences may be linked at a low level of correlation to parental personality and family styles, but this is not known at the present.

The argument for family differences and, specifically, for greater interpersonal malfunctioning and psychopathology among certain drug users than among nonusers is worth keeping in mind as one investigates the family characteristics of both groups. We think that it is reasonable to expect such differences among heavy users of drugs, those who suffer bad outcomes, or those who are otherwise painfully deviant in respect to their illicit use. It is essential to keep in mind that illicit drug use is, by now, a statistically normal thing between ages fourteen and twenty-four. Furthermore, clinical observations not only entail special methodological difficulties, but reports by children about their families are colored by factors other than their family experience viewed objectively. For example, membership in a peer group where family criticism is a fashion or even a necessity for membership can lead to derogatory reflections about parents as a learned language of dissent or a set of learned perceptions. Also, well-educated people tend to be critical of themselves and others, sensitive to minor malfunctions (J. Davis, 1965; Koos, 1954), and, as members of the middle class, chained to aspirations (for themselves and others), which keep rising beyond achievements (Banfield, 1970). Indeed, mental health status is found to be correlated only at weak or zero levels with intellectualized concerns, even if these concerns deal with interpersonal functioning and purport to be appraisals of the real world (A. Davis, 1943; Fiedler, 1949). Thus, if youngsters' views of their families are shaped by the politics of adolescence (concepts of the generation gap, of the authenticity of confrontation, of adult hypocrisy, or of a beautiful new generation in opposition to an ugly establishment), one must not be surprised when descriptions are unrelated to actual levels of adaptive functioning.

NEUROPHYSIOLOGICAL-BIOCHEMICAL LINKS BETWEEN PARENTS AND CHILD

The conduct of children can be linked to family characteristics by inheritance or by the prenatal interaction of genetic and environmental factors. We are limited here to calling attention to the mechanism without engaging in any review of the literature that bears on such transmission. At one time, alcoholism, for example, was considered to be inherited; yet both the scientific literature and an environmentalist bent now discount such probabilities. That is not the case with schizophrenia, where genetic factors clearly do operate—albeit in interaction with environmental ones—and one might argue that alcoholic symptoms in a schizophrenic person therefore have a genetic base. Evidence from animal studies (Nichols, 1960) indicates that addiction liability can be bred in rat strains, as can other traits such as nervousness or particular learning aptitudes. We are not aware of any studies on human beings that show drug dependency or other drug-related disorders to have genetic features, although such possibilities cannot be excluded. We would very much doubt that primarily social behaviors such as the illicit—but not crippling—

use of drugs have genetic origins. Fischer, Griffin, and Kaplan's (1963) study showing that tobacco smoking is linked to inherited taste specificities is, however, the kind of investigation that makes one qualify overly confident expectations. (For further discussion see Kalow, 1967; Fuller, 1970.)

In other areas, one finds hints of an association between offspring's biochemical characteristics and the characteristics either of parents or of developmental experiences. Karczmar and Koella (1969), for example, consider an inverse relationship between norepinephrine or serotonin or both and long maturation, with prolonged maternal contact as part of a syndrome of high curiosity and exploration in offspring. Should these hormone levels in turn be related to drug preferences or problem liabilities (a highly tentative proposition, which awaits investigation), one would have to consider possible genetic-environmental interactions contributing to certain forms of drug-using. The work of Lambert, Hohansson, Frankenhaeuser, and Klackenberg 1969) reports a positive association between mothers' catecholamine excretion levels of noradrenaline-adrenaline and childrens' excretions. These are in turn associated with intellectual levels and with fathers' disciplinary efforts through spanking the child. Fathers' noradrenaline excretion levels were negatively correlated with fathers' and mothers' frequency of spanking the child. Noradrenaline secretions were also positively correlated with the age of both parents at the birth of the child.

These and other provocative investigations produce evidence that hormone levels in children can be associated with parental discipline, intellectual level, task efficiency, curious or exploratory behavior, and early maternal contact. Further, constancies may be found in hormone excretions (or postulated neurophysiological substrates) among mother, father, and child in relationship to the behavior of each.

How do these findings relate to the use of illicit drugs? No tie has yet been shown, with the exception that the actions of substances such as amphetamines and LSD have themselves been shown, or posited, to involve catecholamine substrates. Studies have been conducted in this area, such as those by Funkenstein, King, and Drolette (1957) on catecholamines, stress, and mental illness, and the investigations of Klerman, DiMascio, Greenblatt, and Rinkel (1959), suggesting that psychoactive drug preferences are associated with action-inaction tendencies that might, in turn, be tied to neurophysiological variables. Since the time of these pioneering works, however, such inquiry remains one of the most attractive and untouched fields in psychophysiological terms. We make this point here to emphasize the many possible mechanisms which may account for associations between parental behavior and children's drug use. Our present work, which focuses primarily on moral, social, and psychological dimensions (although admitting some health and disease variables), should not, for all its positive outcomes, lead us to overlook other ways in which parents influence children's behavior. We suspect that in the future there will be more studies like those of Lambert, Hohansson, Frankenhaeuser, and Klackenberg (1969) on psychophysiological mediators. Such investigations will prove most helpful in elucidating the circumstances and the transmission of emotions that are associated with learning, which may be central to the growth of personality and subsequent extreme drug conduct.

EXTERNAL FACTORS

Many other factors have been shown to affect youthful behavior. These factors may emerge in the future as variables which are mediated by the family and which affect drug use (especially extreme drug use), but which are at this time only theoretically pertinent. Also, factors already shown to be associated with varying rates or kinds of drug use have not, to date, been analyzed as to how their impact occurs or, more importantly, how that impact may interact with family factors to produce particular drug attitudes and practices in youth. We outline some of these factors here, not for the purpose of careful review and evaluation, but in order to remind the reader of their existence as we proceed to look at the family data.

Peers. The evidence shows that youthful illicit drug use begins as a group activity and that, for most users, it continues as a social behavior. Peers supply one another drugs, provide the justifications for and interpretations of drug experiences, teach use and cautions, and constitute the drug-using constituency that advocates liberalization of the law, purity in substances, honesty in dealing, and so forth. We do not know the extent to which peer influences interact with family influences. For example, the friends of student A may provide a setting for use, while his family standards provide internal limits on drug involvement; for student B, friends may constitute the sole source of guidance and instruction in drug use because his family is a weak and sometime thing. In contrast, student C may choose his closest friends from among nonusers because he has assumed his family's antidrug morality and he prefers friends who share similar sentiments.

Over the last generation, peers have become important in the use of tobacco. The McArthur, Waldron, and Dickinson data from 1958 (a study begun in 1938) showed that parental smoking habits were the single best predictor of offspring's smoking; in contrast a 1970 study (Lieberman) showed that the smoking habits of peers were the best single predictor. Perhaps, apparent peer influence reflects a permissive trend whereby more parents allow smoking and the subsequent inevitable association of their offspring with others who do likewise. The comparison may be unfair since McArthur used Harvard students, whereas the Lieberman survey used a nationwide sample of over 1,500 teenagers, from thirteen to eighteen years old, in scattered metropolitan areas. Perhaps, a self-selection factor is at work here just as in other areas of drug use where youth tend to associate with others who behave in ways similar to their own. Haire and Morrison (1957), however, offer data to the effect that between ages twelve and eighteen peers outweigh parents as a source of influence, albeit on issues that are not as central to family morals and emotions as drug use. Boehm's (1957) findings go even further. Comparing Swiss and American children, Boehm showed that Americans are other-oriented, whereas Swiss children are attuned to a conscience that meets cultural standards for character. In comparison to the Swiss, Americans value getting along with others, which is necessarily a matter of accommodating to the group. In regard to American peer groups then, it may be that if the group is not self-selected, the drug-use views of the group prevail. To some extent this is the case. In our study of college students (Blum and associates, 1969b), illicit use varied from campus to campus, increased as nonusing students were exposed to using students, increased for abstainers as their environment was peopled with users, and was predictable in advance of the onset of use on the basis of the drug habits of the admired associates of nonusers.

Our best prediction, then, would be that students in a setting where drug use is prevalent would themselves use drugs unless they came from most unusual families in terms of an antidrug stance or within-family strengths capable of developing strong antidrug values. We shall see that this may well be the case as far as the prevalence of drug experimentation is concerned; when we come to measuring middle-class, high-risk drug use, knowing the characteristics of the family allows us to make almost completely accurate predictions. Perhaps this indicates that peer influence and, indeed, the choice of peers or of settings where they congregate are limited to areas of conduct which are discreet rather than dramatic in their unconventionality. For intact families, at least, peers are ordinarily not influential as far as the violation of family and cultural standards is concerned.

A study by Wolfe (1969) showed that dormies (live-in prep school students) used significantly more illicit drugs than did townies (students who live at home). As we examined our data for illicit drug use in a sample of college students living at home, we found that they had less illicit drug experience than did residents on campus, where illicit use was prevalent. The implication is that, at either the high schol or college level, students who live at home are insulated from opportunities to use drugs or the influences of drug users. It may well be that the decision to live at home is made by students who are, in any case, different; perhaps they have less money or prefer continued family involvement. Clearly, family influence continues to exert itself in the face of a tempting peer environment.

School. We have already noted that drug use differs with the college. We suspect the same is true for high schools if one were to separate small from large, rural from urban, or parochial from public schools. We cannot say to what extent self-selection of particular places, institutional ethos, or common determinants in the larger environment account for these differences. Hess and

Torney (1967, p. 101) do show that, for political beliefs, "the public school appears to be the most important and effective instrument of political socialization." This is particularly the case for the lower class and, we infer, for middle-class families where the father is politically disinterested or weak in terms of family power. However, Hess and Torney did not compare schools but, rather, looked at family and school influences. Insofar as political stance is part of the large social ideology of which drug use is a component, ideological experience in different kinds of schools ought to orient youngsters differently toward drug use. We are not speaking here of formal drug abuse education, which is recent and unevaluated, but rather of the whole complex of views transmitted by teachers and otherwise reinforced by books, peers, and the like.

One should not attribute to schools influences that are, in fact, those of the neighborhood and pupils whom the school serves. Coleman (1966), for example, found that (when class-cultural factors were excluded) differences in schools accounted very little for differences in learning; differences in facilities, curriculum, and staff had only small association with achievement. (Pupil-teacher ratios, for example, were not strongly influential on achieving.) Family background, as represented in the quality of fellow students, was shown to be a strong correlate of achievement. As Coleman and his colleagues (1966) wrote, "Schools bring little influence to bear on a child's achievement that is independent of his background and social context" (quoted in Banfield, 1970, p. 143). The attitudes of the pupil, his self-concept, and his sense of control over his environment (passive versus active, fatalistic versus initiative taking) were particularly important in achievement. We have no way of knowing, without direct studies, whether these same family backgrounds and pupil attitudes correlate with drug use as it differs from child to child and from school to school. One suspects, however, that it would.

Dropping Out. In our studies on drug use (Blum and associates, 1969b) and drug dealers (Blum and associates, 1972a, 1972b), we found that dropping out of school occurs more often among drug users and dealers than among other students. Schools differ in their drop-out rates, but the evidence links this rate to factors such as class and race. For example, 65 per cent of school drop-outs in 1969 came from families with incomes under five thousand dollars a year (Joint Commission on Mental Health of Children, 1969). Among certain minority groups, drop-out rates from high school run as high as 70 per cent; indeed among some migrant groups, most may not ever have dropped in. Among Harlem students in the eighth grade, 85 per cent are functional illiterates; it is no wonder that such students would want to leave school. Yet one study of drop-outs (Cervantes, 1969) showed that, in a working-class group, within-family and personality factors may be determining factors. For example, families of drop-outs are less cohesive than other families, have few family friends, have family associates who are likely to be in trouble, and do not appear to disapprove of or control the choice of children's peers, even if these be troubled and troublesome children themselves. If we assume that the high drop-out rate among poor slum children is in turn linked to family factors, then we return to the problem of the disorganized family (nonfamily) rather than to the problem of schools as the primary determinant of children's conduct. In other words, one would link drug use and drug dealing of the drop-out primarily to the general constellation of events of which family, class, neighborhood, peers, and the youth's personality are all a part.

ENVIRONMENTAL STRESS

We may conceive of the child in the disorganized family as suffering chronic stress; the same may be said of the person who experiences other painful situations such as degrading poverty. As Banfield (1970) notes, however, for some persons the slum can be exciting, congenial, and tolerant, as well as a place for criminal opportunity and the unfettered pursuit of certain pleasures— heroin addiction included (Preble and Casey, 1969). Insofar as environmental events are painful, especially when the environ- ment furnishes extreme chronic stresses such as undernourish- ment, rejections, and illness, one may assume that mental health is diminished (J. Davis, 1965). When that occurs the use of pain- suppressing drugs makes sense.

The evidence is reasonably strong (Blum and Blum, 1967) that alcohol use is more likely to result in dependency when it occurs for escapist reasons or when it carries an emotional loading than when it is a moderated pleasure-seeking activity occurring in structured situations. The Chein, Gerard, Lee, and Rosenfeld (1964) data on teen-age initiation of heroin use also suggest greater personal inadequacy and anxiety among these youngsters than among nonaddicts. Thus, their use of heroin is likely escapist in nature. A different pattern for heroin now seems to be emerging (Bentel and Smith, 1971; Sheppard and Gay, 1971; Gay, 1971) for middle-class hippies who have used amphetamines and who need depressants as downers. Even so the concept of stress may be invoked, for not only is the need for depressants urgently felt, but, more important, the life of the hippie caught in the speed scene (R. Smith, 1971) can be very stressful indeed. Furthermore, our studies on dealers indicate that for many users, especially those in the lower class or those involved in a criminal or addict life, chronic drug use provides suppression of distress rather than new pleasure. Environmental stress is most likely to occur in these groups, for as Gurin, Veroff, and Feld (1960) found, emotional health increases with socioeconomic status. Again it is reasonable to expect that the family is a force that helps resist or exaggerate the stress of other environmental factors. In this way, the family intervenes to abet or prevent escapist or other pain-reducing, self-prescribed, psychoactive drug-using conduct.

AGE

J. Davis (1965), reviewing age in relationship to mental health, found that older people are under more stress than other people because of poverty, isolation, illness, and lost or diminished self-esteem and may, in consequence, suffer diminished mental health but for the fact that older people apparently are more likely to have a frame of reference that softens the negative impact of environmental stresses. Consider that drug use leading to dependency (whether heroin, alcohol, or barbiturates) is a phenomenon of youth. Rarely do we conceive of onsets in later life, although, of course, the sad consequences of any early onset

can be seen then (Wiseman, 1970). There may, however, be artifact in this notion; perhaps our times are so attuned to the
youthful that drug use in the elderly is ignored. Then again, it
may be that, whatever the stresses, the elderly do not try out new
solutions, or if drugs are at hand, they cannot afford them. Yet,
escapist drug use among the young may occur because they do not,
as older people do, have a frame of reference (patience, tolerance,
wisdom, whatever) which allows them to handle painful experiences without recourse to chemical remedies. If it does so, a strong
family would serve as buffer against stress, and parental support
could be considered a substitute for the wisdom of the aging.
Without such parents, the great vulnerability of the environmen-
tally stressed youngster is understandable.

RELIGION

College-age drug users are less religious than are nonusers,
whether this is defined in terms of active affiliation, belief in God,
or church attendance. This diminished religiosity is in keeping
with a high social status, education, and liberalism in the family.
Conversely, religiosity defined in terms of conventional affiliations and beliefs probably serves as an insulator against a variety
of disapproved or immoral enterprises since its presence signifies
internalized conventional moral standards or involvement in
social groups (such as a church) which supervise conduct. Another
factor may be operating here as well. J. Davis (1965) has reported
that reduced religious participation is correlated with low mental
health scores. No doubt, such correlations are complicated by
other matters. For example, socially involved people tend to have
higher mental health status than do isolated individuals. One
presumes, then, that socially active people, more than isolated
people, would be involved in religious activities. Even so, the
constellation of beliefs and activities associated with being religious may immunize not only against the unconventional but
against stresses or emotional ill health per se. One would guess
that the family that is both affectionate and disciplined would
probably accept authority at several levels—that is, the authority
of the father as well as of a loving God would be accepted more

readily than in an antiauthority family. If so, one would expect
children's drug use to occur more in nonreligious families than
in religious families, either as a function of a healthy but unconventional (liberal) outlook or in association with family disorganization, pathology, and stress. One must not expect one-to-one
correspondences between any one or several predispositional factors and forms of drug use.

DRINKING AND ITS CORRELATES

Excellent work has been done on alcohol use and problems.
This work gives us many clues that are useful in approaching and
understanding the youthful use of other drugs as well. We know
that drinking and other drug use are correlated (Blum and associates, 1969b). The teetotaler, for example, is hardly likely to
begin marijuana use. In short, it would be a mistake to separate
alcohol use from use of illicit drugs. We should ask, then, what
alcohol predictors can be found in the family. Robins (1966) has
already shown that alcoholic parents are likely to produce sociopathic (and potentially alcoholic) offspring. Knupfer (1963), Cisin
and Cahalan (1966), Jones (1968), McCord and McCord (1962),
and others have shown how ethnic group, urban location, age,
personality, and like factors are also predictors of drinking. Cahalan (1970) has conducted a two-stage drinking study that includes a prediction component. Attitudes toward drinking are
powerful predictors of drinking problems. For example, the more
alcohol does for a person (the more levels on which it is rewarding), the more drinking there will be. Also, the more permissive
the climate of drinking, the heavier the use. Thus, if parents
provide such a permissive climate—or if peers do—more drinking
is expected. Such drinking permissiveness occurs most, by the
way, among young high-status men (where one also finds heavy
illicit drug use). Cahalan found that young men who had environmental support for drinking and who were school drop-outs were
more likely than other men to have drinking problems. The more
impulsive and nonconforming these men were personally, the
more problem drinking there was. When such personality traits
are found in people who consider drinking both useful and im-

portant, a very high risk of alcohol problems is found—a risk, by the way, which is greater in persons under thirty than over thirty.

The importance of work such as Cahalan's cannot be ignored. Generalizing from his work to our own endeavor, we would anticipate that high-risk drug users would more often than not come from families who use and value alcohol and where there is a permissive and supportive climate for other drug use (social, self-medicating, prescription, or illicit). In such families parental styles of use most likely serve as examples and encouragement for the offspring, and child-rearing practices, values, and goals probably do not emphasize self-control or conformity. We shall see that, for the middle class, these predictors of drinking problems fit with remarkable accuracy the portrait of the family whose children belong to a high-risk illicit drug group. This fact does more than demonstrate the importance of looking at drug use as a general, rather than specific, feature; it raises the question of whether those youth who are now involved in dangerous illicit drug use may not eventually become involved with alcoholism.

DELINQUENCY

Illicit drug use by youth is by now so common and has engendered such widespread public concern that one may forget that, in the terminology of the law, illicit drug use is nevertheless delinquency. Whatever else determines illicit drug use, it is still a willing violation of the law. There is no reason to disregard the massive literature on delinquency as a source of understanding for at least some aspects of illicit drug use. Indeed, there is good reason to expect that youths who are willing to use drugs illicitly will also show greater tendencies to violate other laws. Work with delinquents has long shown the role of the family and related personality features to be critical (Aichhorn, 1935; Merrill, 1947; Erickson, 1950; Glueck and Glueck, 1960; Glover, 1960). The factors that are characteristic of delinquent children and subsequent adult criminals are the same as those mentioned for drug users—namely, disorganization (broken homes, absent or irresponsible parents), lack of discipline, the presence of criminality or drug dependency in the parents, failures in affection, warping childhood experiences, association with delinquent peers, and the absence of immunizing affiliations such as church or community-approved groups. Such factors are rarely adequate explanations, and one must confess ignorance when it comes to idiosyncratic variations such as the model child from a terrible environment or the serious offender coming from fine surroundings. Psychodynamic studies can be helpful in explaining these peculiar developments and in pointing out how individuals who are genetically and psychologically different uniquely respond to their own personal worlds even when those worlds seem similar from the outside.

This dissimilarity among individuals and their responses to the world makes the convenient classification of environmental events unsatisfactory as anything but a crude tool for predicting mass phenomena or for understanding individuals having specific characteristics with known correlates (Meehl, 1954). Family studies can try to bridge the gap between broad social enquiries and intensive psychodynamic ones. Our approach, however, since we are interested primarily in the mass phenomena of youthful drug use and its etiology, leans toward the broad social enquiry. With regard to delinquency per se, we would predict that the families of children in our high drug-risk category will (with socioeconomic status controlled) be more criminogenic than others; that is, there will be greater delinquency in the parents, greater drug use (alcohol included), greater disharmony as measured by expressed dissatisfactions, and the children will be more delinquent in these families than in other families. These differences can be expected to be mild at best—at least among the middle class where we are drawing upon families that are respected, intact, and successful so that real variation is small indeed compared to the people outside.

HEALTH

Use of drugs may be seen in terms of morals, politics, and delinquency, rather than as a health issue. This does not discount the fact that some users suffer illness as an outcome, but at least in college such outcomes are rare (Blum and associates, 1969b).

Up to now, we have not considered drug use as a disease (Cahalan, 1970; Chafetz, 1966). Nevertheless, there are features of drug use that may be health linked at group and at individual levels. There are, of course, consequences such as abscesses and hepatitis from intravenous injections. But these clearly play no role in predicting use except in the sense that those who are more involved with drugs are more likely to use newly available illicit drugs than those less involved. In other words, chronic marijuana smokers are much more likely to try heroin than are marijuana avoiders. At the level of low socioeconomic status and correlated disorganized family patterns, there are clear links between health and drug use. We have already noted how children of the poor have more brain damage, mental retardation, blindness, and other disorders than children of the wealthy. Necessarily there will be a correlation between their subsequent heroin use (up until 1970, also a phenomenon of the poor) and ill health—but only in those special settings that "culture" heroin. At yet another level are associations of etiological interest. For example, our findings in the normal population study indicate that youthful high drug users tend to adopt the sick role and have greater experience than others with medication and medical care in adult life. Here, one finds correlations among illicit drug experience and the use of prescribed psychoactives (or pharmacologically psychoinactives with only symbolic utility). At a psychosomatic level, we found more childhood and adult eating problems in high drug users (including both legal and illegal drugs) than in low users. High drug users were also more likely than low users to eat, drink, and use drugs because others were doing so. (This finding is reminiscent of Schacter's (1971) exciting discoveries about the inadequacy of internal hunger cues and the stimulus bound perceptions of obese people.) High users in our study had more accidental overdoses than low users and used drugs for suicide attempts—a phenomenon that did not occur at all in the low-drug group. At this point, one sees real health issues. In other words, etiological factors responsible for drug use become demonstrably linked (even if not causally) to outcomes that are dangerous to health and life. In certain instances, there is a limited one-to-one tie; the rare patient who becomes a morphine addict subsequent to being administered that drug in a hospital is an example (Lindesmith, 1968). Another example is the nonaddict who cons his way into a methadone program to become a methadone addict under medical supervision. This phenomenon is iatrogenic drug dependency, though it is, no doubt, powerfully motivated by psychological forces in the patient. Iatrogenesis may also result from physicians' prescription practices. Doctor and patient characteristics unrelated to medical diagnosis can partly predict what kind of patient will receive what kind of psychoactive drug from what kind of doctor (Cooperstock and Sims, 1971). That of course is legitimate—however irrational it may be, but, nevertheless, the distinction between licit and illicit drug use becomes blurred in this area as the correlative studies show.

Each of the foregoing is of etiological interest. None of these phenomena, however, gives any indication of particular syndromes in which dependency upon specific substances can be traced to such things as biochemical idiosyncracy, metabolic malfunctioning, concurrent disease, or the like. Researchers may one day discover such links, as they seek to account for findings like those of Beecher (1959), who showed that most normal people dislike morphine effects on first injection but about 10 per cent unaccountably find it pleasant. Perhaps, one day there will be biochemical elucidation. In the meantime, and for our purposes in what is essentially a psychosocial study of families, our notions must be limited to the nonmedical realm. Even so, we can expect that high drug-risk children will show different health histories from controls and, specifically, that they will have more psychosomatic disorders and feeding difficulties. In addition, their mothers probably report more distress during pregnancy than do other mothers. As will be seen, these notions receive only partial support.

SUMMARY

Illicit drug-using youth differ from nonusing youth when the two groups describe their own families and parent-child relationships. Clinical psychiatric histories also show such differences, which indicate greater family troubles among heavy illicit users than among low users. However, socio-economic factors and case finding methods can work to produce these differences unless such variables are controlled. A different way of thinking of family impact on youthful drug use is biological and considers the possibility that genetic-environmental interaction from the time of conception may produce some of the parent-child similarities that obtain for drug use, drug risk, or for some forms of hormone and metabolic functions. Our family data do not bear upon this relatively unexplored area.

There are many factors that affect youthful behavior outside the family. These factors may affect drug use and drug reactions but also may be mediated by the family. Peer, religious, and school influences as well as environmental stress are factors—or concepts—which have been considered. There are also elements of youthful conduct that have been or can be expected to be correlated to levels and styles of illicit drug use. These include dropping out of school, drinking, and delinquency. Family factors shown to predict this kind of behavior ought also to predict illicit drug conduct. Consideration has also been given to health as a concept linked at several levels to the family role in youthful drug use.

The briefest consideration of the work that has been done shows that youthful drug use is related to a number of well-investigated areas. One can reasonably expect that family factors, which contribute to these related behaviors, will also be found to be predictive of low and high drug risk. As with other conduct forms, family styles and influences can be expected to vary with class, education, and other embracing biosocial characteristics.

Some Modern
Problem Parents

❧ 3 ❧

As we began our family studies, we had a number of ideas about how the families of children low in drug risk would differ from those with children high in drug risk. We also tried out various schemes for observing families and classifying the drug use of their children. We spent some time refining our notions, developing interview and observation schedules, training interviewers for reliability, and developing a standard approach to families. During this period there were a number of pretests of instruments, ideas, and approaches which culminated in a dress rehearsal—a final pretest. Since, on a clinical rather than statistical level, the pretest yielded findings of interest, we report them in this chapter. We also present the major items of procedure and our scheme for classifying families as low, moderate, or high risk.

LOW RISK AND HIGH RISK DRUG USE

Basic to the pretest and all our other family observations was our measure of children's drug use—the criterion variable on the basis of which families were classified into high, middle, or low risk. Our measure was derived from the lifetime experience of each child, as reported in direct, private interviews using a drug history form. This self-report was supplemented or modified by reports of the siblings and the parents of each child, all of whom were seen individually. Our initial conception of risk was based on a set of a priori assumptions. The heavy use of any psychoactive substance which had any reported adverse effects was a risk. Also, the one-time use, without medical supervision, of any substance that was a potent pharmacological agent and that could lead to adverse effects even upon a single administration was a risk. The occasional use of psychoactive substances that were considered to be mild in ordinary administration but were nonetheless illegal was also a risk; and, finally, any form of repeated personal or social (medically unsanctioned and unsupervised) use of psychoactive substances that had in fact led to a bad effect as defined by the user or by an official agency was considered evidence of risk taking in the child.

Our definition of risk embraces medical, social, and legal outcomes, which have in common only the fact that a young person uses a psychoactive drug without medical approval. Our definition also embraces estimates for the future as well as events of the past; that is, we consider some kinds of drug use risky even if no unhappy outcome is reported by the child or his family. We preferred the notion of risk to the notion of abuse, acknowledging that risk is an arbitrary estimation procedure. The concept of risk was used because there is no popular agreement on the meaning of abuse and because abuse carries a perjorative connotation implying that a youngster is doing something very bad indeed. (See our related discussion, "On the Presence of Demons," in Blum and associates, 1969a.) Finally, while the notion of abuse ordinarily excludes the use of approved drugs, even if these drugs are potent and could lead to unhappy outcomes, it nevertheless includes experimental or occasional use of mild illicit substances where the danger of any kind of unhappy outcome is slim. (See "Drug Outcomes" in Blum and associates, 1969b.)

For the pretest classification we used a simple scheme, which considered a family high risk if any child in that family showed (1) compulsive use of alcohol or tobacco or both; (2) any use of LSD, opiates, cocaine, or special substances; (3) regular illicit use of barbiturates, amphetamines, tranquilizers, and marijuana; or (4) any bad effects from the use of any of these. The middle grounders were those with occasional illicit use of any of these drugs; and the low risk families were those showing no use, by any of the children, of any substances (other than alcohol or tobacco) without medical prescription.

After the pretest, we switched to a new method for classifying families. To create a measure of risk on the basis of experience reported in the lifetime drug history, we assigned scores—or weights—to the kinds of use reported for each of the psychoactive drugs employed privately, socially, and illicitly. Each child in each family received a cumulative score based on the number of points assigned. The drugs for which scores were possible were alcohol, tobacco, tranquilizers, sedatives, stimulants, cannabis (marijuana or hashish), hallucinogens, opiates, cocaine, and special substances. This latter category was used mostly for sniffing substances (gasoline, glue, paint thinner, nitrous oxide) but also for other odd materials such Asthmador and amyl nitrate. For each of these drugs or categories thereof, there was a set of enquiries and a set of scores that varied in number from drug to drug. (See Table 1.)

For white, middle-class families, we used the same scoring procedure, but we normalized families. That is, we divided the sum score of each child by the number of children in that family who were thirteen years of age or older. We excluded children under thirteen because we found, reviewing all 125 families in the pretest and white, middle-class study, that no child under thirteen had used any illicit drug other than alcohol or tobacco. In addition, the young children in our white, middle-class sample had not described any bad outcomes or heavy use of approved drugs, nor had their parents or siblings described these for them. For classifying low-income white families and black and Mexican-American families, we used a different procedure, which is described later.

One theoretical possibility was that the number of children thirteen or over in a family might itself be a factor discriminating

Table 1

Weights Assigned to Psychoactive Drug Use in
Calculating Degree of Family Drug Risk

Drug		Items Weighted
Alcohol	11	(total possible score = 13)
Tobacco	5	(total possible score = 6)
Amphetamines	5	(total possible score = 12)
Sedatives	7	(total possible score = 13)
Tranquilizers	5	(total possible score = 11)
Marijuana-hashish	3	(total possible score = 5)
Hallucinogens	4	(total possible score = 11)
Opiates	5	(total possible score = 14)
Cocaine	4	(total possible score = 12)
Special substances	2	(total possible score = 5)
Total	**51**	

Highest possible score including alcohol and tobacco = 102
Highest possible score excluding alcohol and tobacco = 83

high and low risk families. If, for instance, families with mostly
older children had higher risk scores than other families, then
our classification procedure would suffer from a hidden artifact,
or bias. We examined score distributions for families classified
by number of children aged thirteen and over and learned that
the number of older children did not contribute significantly to
individual scores. We therefore accepted our normalizing procedure.

After gathering data in both the pretest and the white,
middle-class study, we instituted another procedural change.
In our first definition of risk we included heavy drinking or tobacco smoking or reports of any bad effects from these such as accidents and arrests. We wondered whether a total score (including
alcohol and tobacco) was necessary or whether we could simplify
our scoring and use illicit drugs only (including, of course, the
illicit use of medically available substances such as barbiturates
or morphine). To resolve this issue, we ran a correlation (Spear-

man Rho) to see how families ranked when the total drug risk scores (including alcohol and tobacco) of all siblings were used as a basis for classification in comparison with how these same families ranked when alcohol and tobacco scores were excluded from the calculation of drug risk. The correlation obtained was .90. We then ran the same test for siblings thirteen and over (normalizing again) to find out how families ranked when alcohol and tobacco were included and then excluded from scoring and classification. The correlation coefficient was .92. We concluded from this very high correlation that risks, as derived from a measure of alcohol and tobacco use levels and outcomes, did not contribute much to family ranks and so could be discarded in classifying families. The correlation itself suggests either that alcohol and tobacco use vary little among youngsters (thus contributing little to final rankings) or that youngsters' risk scores for alcohol and tobacco are very close to their risk scores for the illicit substances. In any event, after the pretest, all classifications of families were based on illicit use scores only.

To improve upon the classification procedure used in the pretest—where, as noted, any regular use of illicit drugs by any one child qualified a family as high risk—we abandoned that a priori classification and grouped families in the white, middle-class study on the basis of their relative standings in the final distribution of risk scores for all families. We took the score of each family and ordered the families from high to low (now excluding alcohol and tobacco). The lowest scoring family (low risk) had a score of zero; that is, no child had any risk score at all. The highest family scored 150, which means that their children thirteen and over averaged a risk score of fifteen out of a total possible high risk score of eighty-three. (Our normalized scores are multiplied by ten to avoid fractions.) We divided the distribution into approximate thirds; the actual cutting points were made wherever there were breaks in the score continuum.

SELECTING PRETEST FAMILIES

Class differences affect many if not most measures of children's emotional health, delinquency, and moral values, including (as best we know) illicit drug use. Consequently, in all our family work we sought to control for socioeconomic levels. For the pretest, we wanted families who were middle class, white, and residents in similar communities. We also sought only those families that were intact—that is, families where neither husband nor wife had been divorced and where both were resident at home. Because we wanted a chance to look at family child-rearing practices in action, we needed families where children were still at home. Also, because we had to give families a chance to qualify as high risk, we looked for families where at least one or more of their offspring had gone through the teen years. In the region where the study was carried out, the majority of high school and college youngsters had experimented with illicit drugs; a seventeen year old who had grown up in the area could be sure to have had the chance to qualify as a risk himself.

For the pretest, local families were contacted who were known to fit our criteria: yearly income level of ten thousand dollars or more, family intact, and at least one college-age child and one or more young siblings living at home. Further, families were approached selectively with an eye to obtaining a final pretest sample balanced as evenly as possible between children with high and low levels of drug use. Our families were asked about their willingness to participate in the study; they were also guaranteed anonymity, gratitude, and an interesting experience. With that, we went to work. We saw ten families who, on the basis of interviews with their children, were found to have no children who received risk scores on any approved drug or used any illicit drug. (For the pretest classification we had used the alcohol and tobacco scores as part of the risk-calculating method.) Six families had no risk score for approved drugs but had one child or more who had tried marijuana or used it occasionally. Eight families were considered high risk—that is, families where real troubles were reported for some drug, or where marijuana, illicit barbiturate, amphetamine, or tranquilizer use was regular (once a week or more), or where there had been one use or more of hallucinogens, opiates, cocaine, or special substances, or where any combination of these conditions had occurred. After completing our pretest and coding the data, we found that our sampling re-

quirements had not been met in two families, who ended up in
the middle-risk category since they were not intact—one parent
being dead or both parents being divorced or separated. We also
found that one family had not met the middle-class income criterion of ten thousand dollars a year or more; this was a high
risk family.

PRETEST RESULTS

Pretest results were of two kinds. One result involved experiences, which led us to revise our interview and observation
schedule and alter our classification procedures. The other kind
of result involved trends in the data. Because our sample was
small, we did not attempt to use statistical tests and did not affirm
that our findings were real—that is, represented phenomena not
likely to have occurred simply because of chance variation. Nevertheless, the differences that did emerge were provocative and, as
we shall see, were often supported by results from the larger study.

Low risk families more often than high risk families (excluding the middle grounders) were politically conservative
church going, and church affiliated; indeed, all low risk families
were traditional church-going families, who believed in God.
Political as well as religious disaffiliation were most common in
high risk families, where parents rejected all major political
parties and did not attend church. Low risk and high risk families
also demonstrated differences in political thinking. The families
were given a list of groups and asked to rank the groups according to how threatening they were to the country. High risk
families tended to indicate that the military was a most threatening group, while low risk families ranked hippies as very
threatening. Communists and black power advocates were homo-
geneously viewed as major menaces by all groups.

With regard to drug use, only high risk parents had themselves used an illicit drug. Among these parents, there was high
use of medication in general, including sedatives and tranquilizers
in particular. Smoking and drinking, however, occurred most
heavily in the conservative, low risk families. In these families,
serious real problems were inferred on the basis of reports of

parental poor health and job problems. Parental dissatisfaction with their children and the parents' poor relationships with their own parents occurred more often in high risk families than in other families. Mothers in the high risk group were also more dissatisfied than other mothers with their actual lives as compared to their aspirations. These same mothers were better educated but held jobs less often than mothers in the low risk group.

Difficulties with feeding, obstetrical care, infant health, and allergic reactions occurred in all groups, although differences in distribution anticipated later findings in the major study. Similarly, children in all groups had experienced school and social problems, although disciplinary behavior and running away occurred most often among high risk children. In terms of descriptive values, religious interests and self-discipline capability prevailed among children of the low risk group, whereas pleasure seeking, independence, and left political interests prevailed among high risk children.

Family organization showed the most dramatic differences in the pretest. Low risk families were father-led or authoritative families, where the father supervised studies, had the last word on health practices, major purchases, and the like. Actual arguments and disputes (by a count of the events during the week prior to testing and a count of rule disputes) occurred more often in high risk families than in low risk families, as did chronic bickering between parents and children on major items. The concept of discipline as a required element of child rearing was not emphasized by parents in high risk families, but it was in the low risk families. There was less freedom of choice for children in the low risk family, and in these same families older children followed their (preprogramed) courses without fuss. Our inference is that the children felt the choices were their own.

Parental goals and values differed considerably among families. Happiness figured as a major value for children to achieve for the high risk families, whereas religion (morals and spirituality) and the earned respect of others prevailed as achievement goals in the low risk families. On a forced ranking of twelve values to be appreciated or attained, God ranked highest among low risk families, whereas self-understanding and maximizing one's human potential were foremost in the high risk families. Freedom to do what one wants was ranked last in the low risk families. In regard to goals set for their children, the major difference occurred in the area of personal development; high risk parents stressed that their children should become loving people. Parents were asked to evaluate their success and failure in child rearing as determined by whether the children had achieved the value goals that the parents had hoped they would attain. Low risk parents believed they were successful in bringing up their offspring to be obedient, self-controlled, popular, and unfrustrated. High risk families felt they had produced flexible children prepared for a world of change. The low risk families gave themselves more credit than high risk families as measured by their belief that their children had turned out to be what they, as parents, had desired. As far as developmental failures are concerned, the low risk families believed they had not produced children who were prepared for a world of change or who were able to spontaneously expand their creative potentials. High risk parents felt their aspirations had not been met in that their children were, in fact, frustrated and without satisfactory self-control. When discussing how these various failures had occurred, high risk families were more likely to blame the child, whereas low risk families expressed a sense of weakness vis-à-vis the forces in the environment such as peers and television.

As concerns law and authority, all low risk families made a point of explicitly teaching their children respect for the police and the law. This was not the case in high risk families. When asked about laws that need not be obeyed or that were unjust, the high risk parents specified archaic laws and drug laws; low risk parents either said that all laws must be obeyed or singled out antisegregation, civil rights, or traffic regulations as laws to be appropriately disregarded. Only in high risk families (and, indeed, in most of them) did parents and children contend that policemen were intellectually, personally, or morally deficient.

With regard to drug laws, only in high risk families (and here we add middle risk families as well) did parents say that it did not matter whether children tried marijuana, that drug use was understandable or acceptable, and that, as parents, they were not worried about their teenager's drug use. Paradoxically however, it was only in the high risk family that—to use a hypothetical case—parents said they would in fact call in the police, if pot were discovered in a youngster's room. Such crises among low risk families would be handled internally through discussion and punishment. As for LSD, only in high risk families did any parents say they would be indifferent to the child's use or leave the choice up to him.

A number of ratings were made of family interaction. The design of the pretest and the later studies called not only for private interviews with each family member and for interviews with the two parents together without the children but also for an all-family meeting at a dinner to which the interviewer was invited as a guest. As many of the family members as possible took part in this ordinary family meal. Low risk more often than high risk children were rated as obedient. In their interaction with the child, low risk mothers were rated as cooperative, encouraging, and humorous, whereas low risk fathers were rated as having a calm temperament and as having a tendency to teach or instruct. Only in high and middle risk families was the television turned on during dinner or interviews. Home observations showed that low risk families had, by physical count, less medicine in the bathroom medicine chest (but more over-the-counter substances outside that chest), less hard liquor, and fewer cigarettes on hand than did high risk families.

Children in each family were asked their views on drug issues as well as their personal histories. When asked about the differences between families with children who use illicit drugs and families where the children do not, children from low risk families (that is, children who were not themselves illicit users) emphasized the disunity of using families and the strictness of nonusing ones. They also spoke of purposeful training—that is, education not by fact but by instruction in nonuse. When discussing their own estimates of drug behavior among their peers, nonusing children were found to be less well informed about the drug conduct of their peers. In addition, the only children who did not know any dealers were from low risk families. Only among high risk children was there discriminating information about the

drug conduct of peers as well as acquaintance with a large number of suppliers. This is, of course, understandable since these
children, as users, were in touch with other users, used drugs with
peers, and needed to have access to suppliers.

Immunizing against drugs. These limited observations
argue that children from low risk families are insulated from
drug access, even though they live in neighborhoods and go to
schools where such access is easy. From our preliminary data, we
inferred that insulation from drug familiarity and access occurs
in consequence of peer selection by the children and under the
guidance of parents. It is also a result of the fact that the children's activities are centered on the family more than on outside
events or people and is a consequence of the internalization of
antidrug standards, which lead the children either not to see drug
opportunities or to reject them. There is also the rather slim
possibility (given the proselytizing of users) that being square or
straight reduces the number of overtures made to the nonusing
child.

Pseudodemocracy and rebellion against authority. The pretest findings on attitudes toward the police, discipline, goals,
values, and so on lead us to speculate that high risk parents are
themselves rebellious against authority or, at least, unresolvedly
ambivalent about it. They are unable to take a strong stand on
major issues, find it hard to make decisive value judgments that
require the exercise of power over their children, and prefer to
escape from the obligation of being an authority figure—an untenable position if authority is distrusted in general or if there
has been no identification in childhood with an admired authority. Parents can avoid becoming authority figures by concentrating energy in abstract or peripheral issues, which can be shared
with children, which are moral, but which do not require the
parent to intrude upon the child's development in areas where
conflict is sure to emerge. In short, the parent avoids interfering
with what the child wants to do. Thus, these parents attend almost solely to issues external to the family—be these business

matters, bridge clubs, or humanitarian endeavors such as ecology, race relations, or the Vietnam war. In the context of escape from the exercise of authority, these endeavors may, however, constitute taking care of someone else's business and not taking care of family business if such issues deflect the parents from shaping children via discipline, as opposed to affection alone. Expressing concern about issues external to the family can itself be diagnostic of antagonism to authority, when the primary factor is hostility toward power figures rather than a substantive analysis of the social problem itself. Relevant here is Hess and Torney's (1967) finding that political attitudes learned within the family as an outcome of the child's view of the father are generalized to external political authorities. By no means do we intend to underrate the importance of the abstract issues, but our clinical impression is that parents who are rebellious to authority and unwilling to be authoritative in handling their own children do project strong power-hating components, which are directed toward social issues without being essential to their examination.

Uneasiness about authority can be conceived in terms of the response that parents expect from their children via projection. If a father has an unresolved dislike for his own father because of the authority role of the latter, that father also expects his own children to feel the same way; in other words, he expects his own children to reject him. The father (or mother, for that matter) lives in fear of the child's censure. Such sentiments are expressed directly, and one hears these parents say that they want their children to like them and would do nothing to alienate the child. One version of this attitude is emphasizing the importance of loving. Hating is never discussed but is the sword suspended overhead. One hears an authoritative father speak humorously but genuinely about how his child must learn to get along with him and not vice versa. A father with authority ambivalence, however, cannot accept unequal or hierarchical parent-child relations.

One ideologically appealing way of handling such difficulties is to set the family up as a microdemocracy—a pseudodemocracy, however, since small children are not equally responsible members who understand the common good and negotiate self-interests through rational compromise. In this pseudodemocracy, the children are instructed in rights, privileges, and equality, which allows the parents to abdicate decision-making powers, responsibility, and unequal status. The parents' concern with being liked, their egalitarianism, and their desire to be friends to their children place the parents on the footing of peers—an observation initially made by Metcalf (1971). Being peer rather than parent to the child has another appeal since it helps parents stay young through vicarious identification with their children, in a society where youth is enshrined and the wisdom of elders is challenged. When the family members are all children together, who can accuse the parents of being either tyrannical or old-fashioned?

Overidentification. A further development can occur when the parental role of leader and disciplinarian is rejected and when parents and children are equals. In such situations, children may be viewed as better than their elders, as knowing more, or as having unclouded eyes for truth. The wisdom of the child is exalted, which leads parents away from teaching and guiding roles to humoring and deferring to the child. The parent may try to put himself in the head of the child and imagine how he, the parent, looks through those eyes. Discipline becomes punishment not training because power, when exercised, has a hateful component. "It hurts me more than it hurts you" can be overidentification. The parent has put himself inside the child and essentially disregards the child who is really there. The imagined pain is something the parent cannot bear, so he seeks to avoid all conflicts that might require the exercise of power.

In these situations, there sometimes comes a day when things have gone too far and something must be done. Yet some parents remain impotent and cannot act. In one family, a young teenager was a problem, displaying extreme drug use, truancy, and an uncontrolled temper. The family called the older sister home from college—herself immature and but marginally adjusted; she was to be the parents' consultant, and the younger child was placed in her hands. The sister unexpectedly advised that the thirteen-year-old should not be burdened with having to rule the whole family (the diagnosis she made) and suggested the parents do that job themselves. The parents then packed off the older sister and sent the problem child to a residential school instead—a school known for its permissiveness. This gesture failed too, and so the child was boarded with another family. That also failed. The next step was to give the child free rein; the parents paid for travel and expenses, while the by now fifteen-year-old teenager roamed the country on her own. In other families, we have seen instances where the child was expelled from home or other places of authority and exiled to mental health or juvenile facilities. In such cases, the parent can never be the direct instrument of discipline, even when far harsher effects are achieved by his abdication. This behavior is only superficially paradoxical, for by this stage the child may indeed be hated—an emotion ill concealed by the verbal veil of love. These observations do not imply that low risk families cannot be harsh or cruel, even though we did not observe it in our middle-class sample pretest. We expect that pattern most often in the affectionless family or in the disorganized lower-class family where brutality can go unremarked.

Uncertainty and ideology. In psychodynamic association with rebellion are uncertainty and perhaps reliance on shifting nonauthoritarian environmental standards for guidance. Insofar as parents themselves grow up without accepting tradition, conviction, or an authority-derived faith, they cannot be sure how to act with their children. There is genuine doubt as to what rules one should follow when trying to rear a child. Consequently, on matters little and big, there is ambivalence, mind changing, and, we suspect, inappropriate emotion as the parent faces child-rearing problems he fears are of his own making. This results in great conflict with the children who respond, whether anxiously, angrily, or manipulatively, to the uncertain inner states and shifting outer edicts of parents. It is especially true that older children have a harder time than younger ones. Although the romantic, naturalistic doctrine "let the child blossom" may apply to younger children, by ages eight, twelve, or fourteen (depending on the child's energy and the parents' patience), a child can be a rather boisterous bull in the china shop. The discomfort quotient of parents is then finally pushed to its limits, and the previously unfettered child is reined in. We learned, for example, that in some high risk families, the older children have more rules imposed upon them than do younger ones. But this, quite obviously, is difficult to do with the older child, and it is understandable how the newly fettered youngster can become angry. His unhappiness is increased when he compares himself unfavorably with his younger siblings.

Ideological correlates of these inner positions follow. The better educated parent (high risk) is likely to espouse tolerance, open mindedness, and an acceptance of change. He voices a scientific view of things: there is no truth, only successive approximations, and values are relative. His stance allows evolution, if not revolution. The low risk parent, to the contrary, rests on faith, conviction, and dogma derived from the hierarchy of authority —God, the law, tradition, grandfather, father, and the self as living embodiment of the order of things. One suspects that responsiveness to "expert" child-rearing advice has been more on the part of open-minded parents who accept change and need guidance since the admission of uncertainty—scientifically or socially—is their credo. Permissiveness, then, is doubly reinforced when the uncertain parent also rejects authority.

Belief in God is one area of least certainty for high risk parents and the most certain area for low risk parents. Low risk parents insist that their children accept God; the question, in their eyes, is hardly one of "believing in Him" since "He exists." After the child reaches his teen years, attending church becomes relatively unimportant since the foundation of belief is already built and since, at least in sophisticated suburban regions, the convention of church going may be dissipating. The opposite occurs in the high risk family, where, under religiously liberal parents, the young child can make up his own mind about God. By the time the child is ten, he may have a complete disregard for the issue, but his parents are now concerned that the child has not sampled adequately from the cultural bazaar or that the child's ignorance might affect his later status. The parents then begin to insist that the child at least be exposed to religion and try going to church. If the child senses that church without God is hypocrisy and that the pressure to attend is mindless conformity, it may be too late. Another example occurs with regard to bathing. Our pretest comparison of low and high risk families suggested that in early years there was less freedom of choice about when to bathe in the low risk families than high risk families but more freedom in the teen years. Once a child is taught to be clean, he will, by adolescence, carry on routinely. Conversely, if the child is not required to be clean in early childhood, he will, by his teen years, have some rather strong habits. By that time, he may have some strong smells as well, which drive the parents to reconsider their permissive doctrine and begin to insist on bathing. As with religion, it may be too late. The teen years are torn with arguments, wailing, and recriminations. Retarded enforcement of outward form without instilled inner principles accompanied by an actual uncertainty about the principles in question is a prescription for chaos.

Rejection. When the uncontrolled child exceeds all limits and discipline is finally required, the parents necessarily feel upset, helpless, and confounded. In their own eyes, they have put their best effort and their love into a child who has not understood how he is supposed to act; perhaps he has not received a message confusingly sent (Bateson, Jackson, and Haley, 1956; Weakland, 1960). Everyone and no one is to blame for such situations. The child has failed to be the responsible equal his parents envisioned. When that happens extreme anger and rejection of the child can occur. Police are called if drugs are found, or the parents chastise themselves for child-rearing failures. The low risk families, faced with far less conflict and disappointment, can afford to be cooler than this about matters. When things do go wrong, they blame neither child nor themselves but are likely to talk in terms of being overwhelmed by external forces.

Ideologies are corollaries. The high risk families have a psychological and interpersonal orientation; problems are defined and are solved at this level. Indeed, pretest parents in the high risk category had more experience with psychotherapy than did low risk parents—a characteristic that was not considered to be a measure of sickness in this sample. Low risk families are not psychologically oriented, and when bad things happen they externalize the blame to evil forces in their surroundings. Most anything that constitutes a change from the status quo is in this category: communists, civil rights workers, black equality advocates, and, of course, hippies. Naturally, people who are not afraid of power but who use it effectively and confidently will use it to combat their enemies. Their heroes are presidents, churchmen, and others in the brotherhood of power. Their causes are, we suspect, sometimes mythical, but solidarity is nonetheless their property.

CONJECTURES

Sex-role diffusion. In some high risk parents, we saw uncertainty about sex roles—that is, about what constitutes proper and gratifying conduct and emotions for being male or female, father or mother. Insofar as the man rejects authority, he may defer to his wife as well as to his children. He can also be forced to pursue acceptance and esteem situationally. In other words, he emphasizes personal merit alone (achieved status) rather than enjoying his lot in the order of things (ascribed status). We have seen such men in high risk families.

We also found high risk mothers who rejected authority, a factor evident from their dating days when they avoided strong males. A gentle fellow was preferred, perhaps because their own fathers had been weak or distant. The mother may strive for satisfaction through aggressive hobbies but still suffer from unrealized aspirations. Only in high risk families did we find mothers whose current hobbies were shop and mechanics or competitive athletics. Low risk mothers tended toward gardening and reading.

Most likely, emotional distance becomes useful in such circumstances. If one is uncertain, if roles are unclear, or if one's own merit is always at risk because it rests on the judgment of the changing world, then total investments in other people are dubious. These would include the intense sexual investments of a marriage. Further, along ideological lines, these highly educated women presumably value reason more than do other women (low risk mothers, for example). For the educated woman, intellect is the guide, whereas instincts are not. Again, the tendency is toward abstract concerns, and the translation of feelings into issues is one step removed. One's everyday activities within the family are intellectualized and modulated by hesitancy. High risk mothers may spank their children but do so thoughtfully, after much deliberation and with self-recriminations. Low risk mothers spank their children without hesitation because it come naturally. Perhaps, turning on the television during dinner or during our interviews points in the same direction. Television is a distraction and defense against feelings, a defusing of interpersonal intensity. The high drug use in high risk families serves, we believe, similar functions.

Self-doubt. We believe that high risk more than low risk parents are unable to trust their emotions and are uncertain how to behave as parents, as male or female, or as husband or wife. If so, they lack a basis that would enable them to take stands on bread-and-butter family issues or to react spontaneously. Having no particular article of faith while holding themselves and others psychologically responsible, they must rely entirely on their own ratiocinations or on the newest pedagogical fashion.

Is it surprising that self-doubt and heightened sensitivity to one's own causal role are accompanied by religious agnosticism in high risk families? If there is no final authority, if all things are relative, and if man's mind is the highest form of life, the ultimate responsibility of the individual as well as anguish are the results. High risk parents have accepted, as their ethic, the most spectacularly successful enterprise of this century—the positivistic, pragmatic, scientific model. The open mind, an interest in new evidence and new theories rather than the old, the rational rather than irrational approach are the canons of belief for an educated elite. The occupational success of this educated elite is, indeed, a demonstration of the worth of the model. But, as in science, experiments fail, and when the experiment is both crucial and failing, it casts doubt upon an entire theory. If child rearing can itself be considered such an experiment, how must the parent feel when things go wrong? When the inevitable troubles occur, such parents must surely view them as disasters because they challenge and undermine basic assumptions. Are the new ways already old and doomed to fail? Many may feel that the best they can do is to get out of the way as gracefully and as soon as possible so that those better able to understand changing times can salvage the mess they have inherited. And these new experts are the parent's own children, at twelve or sixteen or eighteen years of age.

Except for rare cases, we saw no parents who were virtually crippled by their own sense of failure. The parent who is faced with serious troubles in his child or the one who is overly sensitive to the quite normal problems that occur during the child's development usually does not arrive at a shattering conclusion of total failure. In extreme cases, parents blame their offspring for having failed them—that blame sometimes being couched in the false neutrality of a diagnosis such as the child's own neuroticism, minimal brain damage, or disposition toward being his own worst enemy. In the case of a child's drug use, it is often most convenient for the parent to blame the drug itself for what the youngster does. The demon is in the drug, and only through ingestion does it become resident in the child.

INDIVIDUAL VERSUS COMMUNITY PERSPECTIVES

The pretest observations we made may imply a breakup of traditional value systems in high risk families—a phenomenon of change that is a generational process evident over many centuries (W. J. Goode, 1970; Ullman, 1966). Associated with change is an emphasis upon private experience and, subsequently, upon the rights of the individual (Dorsen, 1970). In line with this thinking is the notion that the individual has a right even to those experiences that are induced or accompanied by drug use. As private experience is exalted, so the moral law supersedes the positive law since the former is written in the conscience of each and is derived from personal experience. The moral or natural law has indeed worked strongly for human goals, emphasizing equality over privilege, kindness over cruelty, social interests over vested interests. Yet the natural law can also exalt the selfish or self-centered. If private experience has dominion, then what can counter the attainment of personal desires, be it sex, drugs, excitement, quitting school, or what-have-you? If parents are not buttressed by traditional moral standards based on a faith in the order of things, they can only rely—insofar as they might wish to counter such hedonism at all—on arguments drawn from a new faith in pragmatism and science. As concerns drug use, such parents can speak of adverse effects in terms of risks to one's health, reputation, or civil freedom, but laws as such (God's or man's) are not the currency of that realm.

Low risk and high risk families have different attitudes toward private pleasure and toward laws or morals as they pertain to vice. The issue is pervasive. In the high risk family, each person functions first and foremost as an individual in his own right. Each individual is autonomous, and his attention is directed toward his own interests, well-being, and realization of his potentials. The parents' goal is to facilitate the growth of the child's self. In low risk families, however, each person is defined as a group member whose personal meaning is derived from the part he plays in the whole. It is not the independent coexistence of each individual but rather the interdependence of all members that counts. The family is a tightly knit group whose differentiated tasks all contribute to an orchestrated outcome. The concept of *family* plays a most important role and has an effective integrating and directing influence.

It is not surprising that when it comes to peer influences, the child from the low risk family is more resistant or less involved with peers than are other children. Those peers with whom the child does become close are also woven into the family fabric. Often, the children and their families will share church or club activities. Independent interests mark the children and families in the high risk group, and while they too may be very active socially, their actions are not taken in concert. For the low risk family, what is done, what is believed, and what is learned are all reinforcing. Moreover, such families are able to transmit to their offspring a coherent set of community goals and standards that are, at bottom, family goals. These offspring are as their parents were—solid, albeit conservative, citizens. High risk families transmit their beliefs as well but with less certainty as to the outcomes. These families provide society with its innovators, its skeptics, its liberals, its radicals, or, as the case may be, with its well-born outsiders (Lipset, 1971; Keniston, 1960).

COMMUNAL DIRECTION

Let us argue for the present that societies that are bent on retaining unified social order or that strive to establish new solidarities try to control child-rearing practices. In Red China today each person is asked to dedicate himself to the struggle and to the people at the cost of his own personal pleasure, choice or advantage. The Soviet Union followed the same methods of control. The New Soviet Man (Bauer, 1955), the model Red Guard, and the tradition-protecting Bantu (Mutwa, 1965) all share a common enforced morality that constrains the young from Dionysian styles or a critical examination of the dogma's narrow path. The question is whether group cohesiveness depends upon the suppression of individual interests. Does effective organizing and proselytizing for a certain order require, as Freud held, the conservation of energy through sublimation? Can it be that the effective transmission of rigid values depends upon the older generation's ability to control the sources of pleasure of the young, thereby restraining the flow of instinctual desire long enough to ensure that social ethics have been internalized?

Let us look for a moment in the opposite direction, at what happens when pleasure is sanctioned and when parents avoid frustrating and inhibiting the child. Does the child then become a creative, loving person? And, if he does or does not, will he be fit to live in society?

Low risk parents have as explicit goals the rearing of responsible citizens who are respected and obedient to parents, the law, and God. These standards and the self-control of the child are priorities which low risk parents feel they must achieve; their failure—as they see it—is in not developing children who are also flexible and creative. Conversely, high risk parents do not expect self-control in the child, even though they are disappointed when this characteristic is missing. The child-rearing methods of high risk parents from demand feeding through toilet training through progressive schools, are geared to the child's readiness and interest. The child's state dictates his direction, and by puberty he has probably learned that his desires are the touchstones of virtue.

We could expect this child, unschooled in boredom, tenacity, and displeasure, to be easily discouraged when events of the world are not geared to his readiness and interests. Such a child could be expected to protest the irrelevance and unresponsiveness of institutions that serve their own interests but are inattentive to his. Should protest fail, such a child might readily embrace obtainable and primitive satisfactions, only two of which are drugs and sex. Or, he might further retreat from the controlling institutions that are intolerable to him and create his own communities where the problems of school, business, or other traditional enterprises are not posed.

Our comments have carried us far beyond the data of the pretest and into matters of conjecture hardly subject to experiment at all. We found, however, that the issues that came to our attention during our initial observations are fascinating and important, especially since child rearing is not a matter of concern merely to particular parents and children but to the future of society as well. The issues raised here are considered in later chapters where we review findings from the clinical inquiries.

When comparing the philosophy and styles of high risk and low risk middle-class families, the reader probably is, as we are, sympathetic to both approaches. All the families in our study are striving to do their best for their children in accordance with their own beliefs. On the one hand, there is the belief in the certainty of God and the law. There is family strength, with a reliance on discipline, togetherness, and with trust and pride in the old ways. On the other hand, there is the appeal of science, with a trust in experimentation, pragmatism, discovery, the honesty of doubt, and the hope for individual happiness, equality, and creativity. In such a contrast, one sees at once the difficulty encountered when we sought to classify our families according to drug use. Drug *abuse* is indeed a pejorative term and implies abuse of pleasure, moral failing, unleashed instincts, selfishness, and a transgression of the old rules of self-discipline and community respect. Drug *risk* is a term in the new style, offering no moral or legal judgment. It implies uncertainty to be resolved via experience and experiments with pragmatic judgments rendered which are concerned only with demonstrably harmful drug outcomes.

SUMMARY

In a pretest, we studied twenty-four families with similar biosocial characteristics, selected for their income level, intact family structure, and college-age as well as younger children. Interviews with the children yielded drug histories, which became the basis for classifying the families into low or high risk. Analysis of the data was impressionistic because the samples were small. On the basis of the analysis, clinical conjectures were set forth to guide our approach in later videotape studies and in evaluating data in later chapters.

The trends of the pretest suggested that two constellations of beliefs and practices exist: one is traditional and authoritative; the other is permissive. Traditional families have fathers in authoritative roles, emphasize obedience and self-control in their children, and create tightly integrated, interdependent family units. In these families there is low risk of unhappy drug outcomes. In general, traditional families appear satisfied with their child-rearing outcomes. Permissive families emphasize the child's flexibility and freedom. These families often face a number of problems as their children grow up and start doing things their parents had not expected. Under such circumstances, conflict and disappointment occur. Moreover, there is greater use of illicit drugs by these children than by other children.

High risk families appear to use more prescribed medications and have more alcohol and tobacco on hand than low risk families. Their children are more knowledgeable about illicit drug use and sources. Children from low risk families appear insulated from the influence of drug-using peers, even though they live in neighborhoods and go to schools where illicit drugs are readily available. We have speculated on personal, familial, and ideological features that may be associated with these differing forms of conduct and interest.

White Middle-Class Families

❧ 4 ❧

The present chapter reports findings based on a study of 101 white, middle-class families, classified into high, middle, and low risk categories according to the drug use of their children. The prerequisites for using a family in the study were that all families live in the same area, that both mother and father live at home, and that high school-age siblings or younger children live at home. Families were selected by taking a complete sample of all undergraduates who attended a major university and who listed local addresses in the student directory. These students were randomly contacted and screened to ensure that they and their families met the foregoing requirements. Of the 126 students interviewed, 123 gave us permission to contact their families. Seventeen families refused to cooperate; three families were leaving the country; and two did not meet our criteria.

Interviews and ratings were conducted by using a pretested schedule for which interviewers had been trained for reliability. To avoid bias and because the student interview included a drug history, no single interviewer saw both the student and the student's family. Further, to prevent interviewer bias based on a knowledge of the children's drug use, the drug history taken from each sibling in the family over the age of five was delayed until all other sections of the interview and observations had been completed. Families were not classified until all interviews were completed. To test the reliability of the interviewers' ratings of the families on behavior and appearance, three interviewers viewed a videotape experimental session with 13 of the 101 families. In this way, the extent to which the original interviewer agreed with himself was checked against his rating of the same family in the videotape session and against the ratings of the other two viewers of that session who were, in turn, compared with one another. On fifteen rating areas (which involved over twelve hundred possible agreements or disagreements), there was agreement 83 per cent of the time between the original interview and the videotape experimental session. The family interview and the videotape experimental session provided quite different content and settings, so that the reliability measure contains evidence for the consistency of the behavior of families as well as of the reaction of interviewers. In some cases, interviewers may have remembered previous ratings, but, considering that each family had hundreds of inquiry items plus twenty rating areas and that there was an average lapse of one year between the family interview and the videotape session, we discounted the significance of the memory component. When the three videotape viewers were compared with each other on the rating areas for the thirteen families, the percentage of agreement was as follows: rater number one agreed with rater number two 86 per cent of the time; rater number one agreed with rater number three 85 per cent of the time; and rater number two agreed with rater number three 88 per cent of the time. It is noteworthy that the first of the videotape raters was a clinical psychologist and that the two family interviewers (number two and number three) were trained as such but were not clinicians. (There were over twenty-seven hundred possibilities for agreement or disagreement on the videotape materials.)

Interviews took place in the home except in rare instances when a working parent preferred to come to us. Included were individual sessions with one parent (generally the mother) who was asked about herself and also about each child, a family-together session, a dinner-together session, and individual interviews with each resident sibling. (An individual interview form was left to be filled in by any missing person—usually the father.) When siblings were away from home, the interview form was sent to them for self-completion, accompanied by assurances of privacy and anonymity. In five cases, refusal for the dinner-together session occurred, and in such cases ratings of person and interaction are missing. Families were usually seen over a period of four weeks, which involved at least three different home visits. With a family of four, an average of eight hours was spent with one or another family member.

All interview data were coded and handled on a computer. Two major tests were run on each set of enquiry or rating items. One test was run for each category of coded response to examine the significance of differences, which indicates when families in one group vary from those in another group to a degree greater than would be expected by chance. An analysis of variance was also run, which indicates the degree to which the array of all replies or ratings following a given query (all coded responses) differ from group to group relative to within-groups differences. In certain cases, additional tests were run—namely the Wilcoxon, Chi Square, and a Pearson product moment correlation. Further statistical analyses, using discriminant analysis procedures, are reported in Chapter Ten.

In Chapter Three, we discussed our method for classifying families into low, middle, or high drug risk. Childrens' drug use was scored, and a family average was obtained for all children at or above thirteen years of age—the empirically determined age of illicit drug use. Families were ordered by their scores, and cutting points were made at approximate thirds. There were thirty-three families in the low risk group, twenty-nine in the moderate group, and thirty-nine in the high risk category.

There were 2071 enquiry and rating areas. These involved questions, ratings, descriptive choices, and forced choice rankings. For each of these, the low risk group was compared with the middle and the high risk groups, and the high risk group was compared with the middle and low risk ones. Our analysis concentrates on low-high differences; but, when an interesting difference distinguishes the middle group from the others, then it is noted.

An overview reveals that of the 2071 separate enquiry areas, in 452 a test of the significance of difference between proportions showed that one or more reply or rating area differed significantly ($P = < .05$) when low risk families were compared with high risk. There were 286 such differences when low risk families were compared to the middle group, and 373 differences when the middle group was compared with the high risk group. As expected, the most extreme differences occurred between low and high risk families, rather than with the middle ones. Analysis of variance on 762 enquiry and rating areas yields significance, indicating that the overall distribution of replies or ratings among the three family groups does differ. Thus, about half the enquiry areas as well as particular aspects of rating and response may be said to differentiate low, middle, and high drug risk families. Some but not all these differences are given in detail.

FAMILY DESCRIPTION

Low risk families differed from high risk families in that the former, at the time of the interview, had more children living at home. Looking at the children's family status, we saw that the high risk children often come from families where there have been separations or divorces. Children in low risk families differed from high risk ones in that the high risk more often had their own apartments when they were away from home (as opposed, for example, to living with relatives). Further, many more crucial (potentially stressful or traumatic) events were reported by siblings in high risk families than were reported by children in low risk ones. Marriages in the high risk families had been shorter, on the average, than in low risk families. This is partly attributable to divorce since there is a trend—although not significant—for mothers in the high risk more than the low risk families to have had divorces (five out of thirty-nine in the high risk group as compared to one out of thirty-three in the low risk group and three out of twenty-nine in the middle group). All families, however, were particularly stable maritally. (Short marriages were not attributable to the parents' ages since the parents, and especially fathers, in the low risk group tended to be younger than in the high group.) Family income was higher in the high risk group with over half the families earning more than twenty-five thousand dollars a year. For the entire sample, reported incomes were high, with only three families earning less than ten thousand dollars annually and four out of five earning fifteen thousand dollars or more.

Mothers. All mothers but one in the sample were the biological mothers of the older college student who was initially selected for participation in the study. Thus, nearly all of the siblings in the study were reared by their biological mothers in intact families. Mothers in high risk families did differ from low risk mothers in that they often had four-child families, but they did not differ in the overall number of children. The high risk mothers were better educated than low risk mothers, who had often begun but not finished college. The religious affiliation of mothers also differed; more low risk than high risk mothers were Catholic or Mormon. Looking at church attendance we found that it was also greater for low risk than high risk mothers over the twelve months preceding the interview. Low risk mothers had often experienced religious involvement as teenagers, and, at the time of the interview, low risk mothers were more involved with church-related activities than were high risk mothers. Political party preferences did not differ between high and low risk mothers. Among the moderate risk families, however, more said they were liberal Republicans than in either of the other family classifications. Actual candidate choice in the last presidential election did differ; low risk mothers voted for Republican candidates or for George Wallace more often than high risk mothers. Among the leisure interests of high risk mothers, do-it-yourself activities occurred more often than among low risk mothers. High risk mothers were also more interested in travel and less interested in reading or creative writing than were low risk mothers. There is evidence that high risk mothers had greater leisure and interest in pursuing adult education.

Reviewing the mothers' life histories, we found that most mothers in all families had held jobs of some sort. Low risk mothers had begun their employment earlier than high risk mothers, but there was no significant difference in the age of first self-support. Most mothers in the entire sample felt that as children they had gotten on well with their own parents but somewhat less well as teenagers. Almost all believed they had been normal young people. No mother in the entire sample had ever had a nontraffic arrest, but there were differences in their traffic offense histories. Recent moving violations were more frequent (four times so) among high risk than low risk family mothers.

As concerns their drug histories, the differences are clear. High risk mothers were regular drinkers more often than low risk mothers; among high risk mothers, alcohol problems also occurred and were identified by affirmative responses to questions as to whether anyone else was worried about their drinking or their use of alcohol for escape. Illicit drug use was rare in the sample but did occur, without differentiating among groups. A few mothers had used nonprescription barbiturates and amphetamines. One mother mainlined speed (a moderate risk mother), and three had tried marijuana (two of them low risk mothers). The only mother currently smoking marijuana was in a high risk family. Two mothers had tried hallucinogens (one a low risk mother who used it regularly in the past). Three mothers had used illicit opiates, and two had used cocaine.

Health and pregnancy histories of these mothers differed little. Almost one-half of the mothers were regularly taking medication, and one-third had undergone psychotherapy. There were, however, more abortions and still births among high risk mothers than low risk mothers, as well as a trend toward more food difficulties (overweight and underweight). In relation to social views, mothers were asked to force-rank a list of twelve groups according to the degree to which these groups posed problems for the nation. Hippies were more often ranked by low risk than by high risk mothers as posing the greatest difficulties.

Fathers. High risk fathers more than low risk fathers were in professional and artistic occupations rather than white collar, business jobs. High risk fathers were better educated than low risk ones, holding more advanced degrees and having become self-supporting later in life. Low risk fathers were often Catholic or Mormon, whereas among high risk fathers, there was a trend (not significant) toward atheism or agnosticism. Low risk fathers had more recent immigrant backgrounds than high risk fathers. However, when grandparents had been born abroad, Eastern European origins were the more common among the righ risk than low risk fathers.

The sample did not differ among its subgroups in regard to fathers' political affiliations or preferences. High risk fathers reported more leisure time than did low risk ones. High risk fathers (in contrast to their wives) are more likely to read and show more interest in travel than low risk fathers. When asked to reflect on the primary sources of pleasure, fathers in high risk families often cited recreational pursuits; low risk fathers said their families gave them most pleasure.

Drug use histories show that high risk fathers drink alcohol more often than low risk ones and more often use it for escapist purposes. High risk fathers have used barbiturates and tranquilizers more often and in greater amounts than low risk fathers. Only one father, in a high risk family, reported ever having tried marijuana or an hallucinogen. A few had used amphetamines without prescription; one father tried cocaine, and some have had prescribed opiates.

As to social views, low risk fathers differed from high risk ones in evaluating the groups that posed the greatest problems for the nation. Communists and segregationists received moderate rankings from high risk fathers, whereas low risk fathers ranked communists as very threatening and segregationists as less so. Labor unions were considered to be less menacing by high risk than by low risk fathers whereas the military was viewed as troublesome by the high risk fathers and not by the low. The suburbanite mentality was considered a national problem by high risk fathers more so than by low risk fathers.

THE MOTHER DESCRIBES HER CHILDREN

The plan of the interview called for the mother in each family to describe the health, adjustment, and drug histories of each of her children. At the outset, a difference emerged. The biological mothers in low risk families in each case described their children. However, in the high risk families—because of the presence of a stepmother, the absence of the biological mother, or an egalitarian insistence by the father that he join in this motherly role—we found biological fathers were often involved in our request. All in all, 112 siblings were described for low risk families, 106 for the moderate group, and 125 for high risk families.

Mothers were asked whether they had planned for their babies. There was no difference between high and low risk families, but the moderate families had more accidental babies than the others. Low risk mothers more often than high risk ones said they were sick during most of their pregnancy. High risk mothers, more fearful of aborting, took more special precautions to ensure a full-term birth than other mothers. Even so, premature babies were more common among high risk mothers than among other mothers, as were abortions and stillbirths. Caesarian sections were least common among moderate risk mothers, whereas post-delivery complications associated with prematurity occurred, as would be expected, among high risk families' neonates.

An adjective check list yielded a few differences in overall maternal characterizations of the neonates; *obstinate*, for example, was seldom applied by moderate family mothers, whereas feeding problems were often indicated by low risk mothers. Insufficient breast milk was another complaint of the moderate risk mothers. High risk mothers were unsure whether their babies had been quiet and nondemanding, whereas low risk mothers were particularly sure that their babies had been especially skillful, overactive, and presistent from the start. In contrast to moderate risk mothers, high risk mothers emphasized how sociable their babies had been. Low risk mothers also appeared to have worried more than other mothers about possible emotional problems in their overactive babies. More than others, these low risk mothers also noted that their babies resisted weaning and were not interested in new foods. An emotional loading on feeding was suggested by high risk mothers as they described, more than others, deprivation of food as a punishment for finicky eating habits in their young children. As for eating rules among low risk families, children were encouraged to try everything. Some low risk families required that everything on the plate be eaten, whereas in high risk families the mealtime rule more often was that the child must finish everything before getting dessert. Children from low risk families were (or their mothers were) troubled more often than other children about being underweight, whereas those from high risk families were concerned about being overweight. Serious illnesses in infancy occurred least often among moderate risk families, whereas serious illnesses from ages two to twelve occurred most often among the high risk children. Between the ages of two to twelve, allergies appeared least often in the low risk children and most often in high risk ones. No consistent findings were obtained on childrens' nervousness (nail biting, bedwetting, nightmares, and the like). High risks, especially in comparison to moderates, were seen by mothers as having least infant nervous problems, whereas nightmares were a difficulty among low risks. During adolescence, only the high risk children were described as suffering from headaches.

Puberty was reportedly reached earlier by the offspring of low risk families than by other children, but maturational problems were least noted by moderate risk mothers. Doctors' visits during the twelve months prior to the interview were fewest in the low risk families; these families were also least likely to give vitamins. Uncertainty as to whether children had been receiving over-the-counter medication during the month prior to the interview characterized high risk mothers. During that period, low risk children had least often received stomach remedies or other nonprescription medicaments. Low risk families had also been the most reluctant to give alcohol to soothe an infant.

High risk mothers more than low risk mothers described their teenage and post-teenage children as having had trouble when drinking alcohol (being sick especially). In regard to marijuana, the replies of mothers ranked quite neatly with the risk classification of their families; 3 per cent of the low risk, 17 per cent of the moderate, and 42 per cent of the high risk children were said to have tried it. About one-half of those parents said that their children had told them about it. When we compared these parents' estimates to actual use, as reported in private interviews with their offspring, we found that 18 per cent of the low risk children reported one use or more of marijuana or hashish as compared with 44 per cent of the moderate risk children and 75 per cent of the high risk. This indicates that only one-sixth of the low risk mothers were correctly informed, as were two-fifths of the moderate mothers and nearly three-fifths of the high risk parents. Since so few low risk children were believed by their parents to have used drugs, one cannot reliably compare mothers' descriptions of use; yet, the distribution of upset as compared to understanding mothers is the same for all three classes of mothers. In regard to hallucinogens, no low risk child, only 1 per cent of the moderates, and 11 per cent of the high risk children were known to have taken these substances. Parents had learned by means other than by being told (for example, bad trips had come to their attention).

We were interested in learning about readiness and responsibilities. We found that low risk families often delayed allowing their children to baby-sit. Low risk mothers required their children to be rather old before leaving them without a sitter, and, especially in contrast to moderate children, low risk children began participating in family chores earlier. More than one-half, for example, of the low risk children began chores before the age of six. More high risk than low risk families waited until the child was nine years old. Yard work in particular was more often assigned by low than by high risk families. Sunday school was often required by the low risk families.

As concerns television watching, a trimodal distribution complicated things. During the school week, one segment of the high risk children spent the least time watching television; another segment spent about three hours a day (more than the low risk children); but then, among the low risk sample, we found some children watching television four hours or more each day. During vacation time, a high risk group watched it least; low risk children watched it moderately more; and a segment of moderate risk children watched it most.

We also asked about other habits and behavior. Thumb sucking was described as most prevalent among the high risk children, and mothers in this group were much more likely than other mothers to do nothing about it or, if they did, to substitute a pacifier. Masturbation and childhood sex play was much more often denied by high risk than low risk mothers; that is, far fewer of their children than other mothers' children were said to have done such things. As for other "mischief," low risk children less often than other children were truant, rowdy, discipline problems in school or negligent in their school work. Aside from school misbehavior, we inquired about a variety of pranks—delinquencies in fact—and consistently found that the moderate risk mothers less often than other mothers knew about truancy, curfew violations, rowdiness, theft, vandalism, alcohol problems, drug use, traffic violations, running away, or other misconduct. In these areas, the differences between high and low risk children occurred in regard to running away, traffic violations, and illicit drug use— high risk children having done more of each than low risk children. Actual troubles with the police were rare and did not discriminate among groups. As a matter of record, we noted that of all the children in the entire sample known to have used illicit drugs ($N = 134$), only two were known by the parents to have been apprehended by the police. Both these children, as our classification would predict, were in the high risk group. The only misbehavior that was more prevalent among low than among high risk children was property damage (breaking a window, for example).

We asked about separations and learned that the children of low risk families had less often than high risk children been away from home for more than two weeks. We also inquired about interests and found that low risk children were often interested in (or would consider) being a policeman, whereas high risk children were opposed to the idea. Interest in drugs was noted by high risk mothers, and opposition to them was noted by low risk mothers. Being part of the radical left was noted by high risk mothers for their children, whereas low risk mothers indicated their children were opposed to the radical left. As for personal religious experience, there is a bimodal distribution with both interest and opposition noted in low risk children and disinterest noted in the high. Mothers of moderate risk families described their children as having greater interests than other children in creative arts or in making money, but trying new things was not a characteristic of moderate risk children. Considerable interest in sports was attributed to the low risk youngsters.

Mothers were asked to compare each of their children to other children of the same age. Low risk children were said to be above average at meeting deadlines, at being matter of fact, and at feeling satisfied with who they were. Youngsters of moderate risk families were in their mothers' eyes and compared to high and low risk children, less curious and more average in their sensitivity to pain. High risk children were believed by their mothers to be less cautious and less likely to be bored than low risk youngsters.

We asked mothers to appraise themselves with reference to their strictness. Low risk mothers more often felt satisfied with the degree of strictness or leniency they had applied. They also described themselves, more than high risk parents, as being sure about what they were doing. Moderate risk mothers said they were least relaxed in their child handling. Low risk mothers as compared to high risk ones said there was no particular age which had been most difficult; for the high risk mothers (especially in contrast to moderates) early childhood (from two to eleven years old) emerged as the most difficult period for the parents. Mothers were asked what had given them the most pleasure in bringing up each child; negative statements appeared most often among the appraisals of the high risk mothers (for example, coping with extremes of mood).

FAMILY ORGANIZATION

One section of the interview was conducted with both parents present. We enquired about leadership, policies, values, and the like and thereby took advantage of one of several chances to assess parental interaction and agreement. We recorded not only what both parents said but also whose opinion carried when it came to making a statement for the record. There were few differences in what the parents said about decision making at any level, nor were there behavioral differences in whose word actually carried. When asked who was the boss in the family, the low risk wife was nominated more often than husbands and to a greater extent than in high risk families, although this was a minority reaction. In discussing child discipline, low risk parents, in contrast to high risk ones, agreed that "a lot" of discipline was necessary, along with attending to the child's preferences. In these discussions, the mother deferred to the father's opinion. The remark "Let the child choose for himself" occurred more often in the high risk than low risk families. As regards conduct where discipline was most necessary, the child's own safety was often specified by high risk mothers, whereas respect for the rights of others was cited by the low risk mothers. Free choice (undirected, nondisciplined) was most often advocated by high risk fathers as regards the child's choice of friends.

In a review of disciplinary events in the family during the week prior to the interview, the high risk families were found to differ from low risk ones in that they more often handled a problem by depriving the child of privileges. On these disciplinary occasions, only children in high risk families were described as having reacted with anger. A list of items was presented to parents, and they were to indicate at what age free choice was allowed for both boys and girls—that is, at what age the child was entrusted with decisions. There were a few clear-cut trends, and analysis of variance showed that the distribution of replies was consistently different; in particular, certain modal ages emerged as significant. For example, for low risk boys, fourteen years old was the turning point for food choices and bedtimes, whereas high risk children were allowed to make these choices earlier than fourteen. At age eighteen, low risk children could decide about church attendance; but high risk children were again allowed to make this choice earlier. Fourteen was also the year in low risk families for self-direction on study habits; the mode for high risk children coming later. Free choice for involvement in political activity was later for the low risk children than the high risk children. At age eighteen low risk boys decided for themselves on household chores, and at fourteen or fifteen they decided when to bathe—the mode for high risk boys being earlier than this for bathing. More freedom in hair styling was given to high risk than to low risk boys; the mode was for low risk families not to allow such choice until age eighteen. Dating choice trends also appeared to be free in high risk families; the mode for low risk children was at sixteen, but for high risk children it was "anytime." The free choice modal age for marijuana use in high risk boys was eighteen; for low risk children, it was "never." Most families in all classes opposed LSD use, but only in the high risk families did parents say that free choice depended on the child.

As for girls, high risk families much more often than other families allowed girls to choose their friends "anytime." High risk families set a modal age at thirteen for bedtime free choice, and at ten or twelve let girls decide for themselves about church. The modal age for low risk girls was eighteen on church attendance, but their parents more often than others said that believing in God depends upon the child. Free choice for studying had a mode at fifteen for low risk girls, which was earlier than for high risk girls, as was the choice of joining the family on vacation. Political activity choice, however, came earlier for the high risk families than for other families. Eighteen was the modal age in high risk families for decisions about helping with chores. Fifteen was modal for bathing for low risk girls, but high risk families favored individualized choices, saying it depended upon the child. The same was said by high risk families about going to the doctor. Similarly, high risk girls were allowed to decide how to wear their hair "anytime" more often than were low risk girls. Free choice dating was more common "anytime" in the high risk families than in other families—the modal point being age sixteen for low risk girls. Only in high risk and moderate families did we find parents who said they did not know what the proper age is for free choice of sexual intercourse. Only in the high risk families was the use of LSD an "anytime" choice or dependent upon the girl.

We observed the parental exchanges about these age readiness rules and recorded disagreements, agreements, and final authority in the discussion. There were few differences, but we did find in high risk more than in low risk families that the father carried the day for his more liberal decisions as to when children could choose their own friends. Only in high risk families did fathers defer to mothers on judgments about politeness and respect—in other words, when the child could choose to be rude (an item which itself did not discriminate among families). Fathers had their way in the low risk families in discussions on bathing rules.

Parents were given a list of twelve statements about basic values and were asked to rank them according to how important they were for their children to learn. Each parent ranked the statements independently. We found that low risk mothers, in contrast to high risk mothers, gave high rankings to belief in God and low rankings to the child's freedom to do what he wants. The high risk mothers, especially in contrast with moderate mothers, gave priority to the child's understanding of himself, to the maximizing of his own potential, and to loving his country. Low risk mothers, to the contrary, tended to give a low ranking to getting along with others. High risk fathers gave belief in God a low ranking, and low risk fathers gave it a high ranking. High risk fathers gave priority to their child's being able to maximize his own human potential, to becoming a respected citizen, to being a real success, and to being free to do what he wants. High risk fathers gave a low ranking to having regard for law and order. Low risk fathers gave low priority to their child's learning how to get along with others but gave high ranking to the child's loving his parents.

The parents were then given a list of child-rearing goals. They were asked to rank the ten items from most to least important. Low risk parents gave a low ranking to avoiding frustrating the child and to helping the child become a loving person. Trends (nonsignificant except for overall analyses of variance) were for low risk parents to emphasize teaching the child self-control, whereas high risk parents tended to emphasize expanding the child's creative potential, turning the child into a respectable citizen, and preparing the child for a world of change.

We asked parents what children ought to be taught about policemen and the law. Moderate family mothers were noticeable for their indifference or neutrality. High risk and moderate fathers were the same. A discussion of the obligations of lawfulness and of teenage drug use ensued, but no differences among classes of families emerged. We did see, however, that the high risk mother tended to be at a loss to describe how she would react if a child of hers were to tell her of his intention to take LSD. High risk mothers were also more rational in their hypothetical responses to learning that their child was giving away or selling drugs; that is, these mothers would learn more about it and find out why. High risk fathers were also more intellectual than other fathers in responding to this same hypothetical situation, although a subgroup of them indicated they would have an extreme emotional reaction of disapproval (as opposed, for example, to low risk fathers' admonishments and tightening up on the rules).

Parents were then given a list of controversial issues, which were said to be disputed among parents and educators. Parents were asked to agree or disagree with the issue statements presented. Low risk mothers more often than others (especially in contrast with moderate risk parents) agreed that parents should punish small children when they use naughty words. On other items, no differences occurred, nor were fathers from the various risk groups in disagreement. We asked parents what advice they would give to new parents on how best to raise children. High risk mothers and fathers, replying separately, were most often uncertain about what to advise. Low risk mothers emphasized being natural, loving, and sincere. Low risk fathers stressed the importance of communication between parents and children. Upon completing the interviews we asked parents what else we should have discussed with them or which items were given insufficient attention. High risk parents said we should have paid more attention than we did to adjustment (for example, the family's inability to put down roots or the effects on the children of never having a stable group of close friends). We then turned the conversation to drug problems in general, asking what parents would like to see done in their community. Low risk parents more than high risk ones spoke of the need for increased parent participation in educational drug programs. High risk parents spoke of the need for reform of the drug laws.

INTERVIEWS WITH OFFSPRING

Out of the 343 siblings over age five in our total of 101 families, we completed interviews for 330. Fifty-one interviews were sent to siblings living away from home, and, of these, forty-six returned the completed form. Seven interviews were not completed at the parents' request (a refusal to question the younger family members or a retarded child). Only one sibling refused to participate. Of those children in or through college, more high risk youths had majors in arts and humanities than did low risk youths. Among the low risk children, only 7 per cent said they were not religious or were without religious affiliation, whereas 49 per cent of the high risk children declared themselves unaffiliated. Politically, low risk youths declared themselves to be independent-conservatives, whereas high risk youths were often left of center, new left, or Marxist.

We asked youths to consider differences among families and to compare very heavy users, moderate users, and nonusing age-mates whom they knew well. Among high risk children, a close acquaintance with heavy drug users and their families was common. Family unity and family love and interest were discriminating themes that were often suggested by the low risk children; high risk children often proposed that family factors played no distinguishing role in drug use. High risk youngsters often said that parents should have no goals regarding children's drug use. Low risk children more often than did high risk children said their parents did not want them to use illicit drugs. Indeed, the majority of all parents were seen as subscribing to an antidrug stance. Low risk children also said their parents wished them to abstain from alcohol, whereas high risk children indicated that their parents approved of moderate drinking. Only among moderate and high risk families were parents said to accept or not worry about tobacco smoking.

The drug histories provided the scores upon which the classification of families and children were based; thus, these histories necessarily reflect differences in the three groups. Alcohol and tobacco were not included in the scoring system. (See Chapter Three.) High risk children reported more current alcohol use and more problem use (escapism, blacking out, and post-drinking amnesia) than did low risk children. High risk children in six families reported that their fathers were alcoholics, and some children in high (five) and moderate risk (four) families reported that their mothers were alcoholics. No low risk parent was said by any child to be an alcoholic. Past smoking experience and current smoking were common among high and moderate risk children who also reported tobacco dependency (hard to stop, increasing use, or heavy use). As regards the use of amphetamines, sedatives, tranquilizers, hallucinogens, opiates, cocaine, and special substances, the past and present use of high risk youngsters differed dramatically from the infrequent or nonillicit use of low risk children.

Our concept of risk, our scoring, and our classification system rested upon outcomes as well as the kinds and degrees of illicit drug use. Table 2 ranks the bad results experienced by 2 per cent or more of the using population from each drug or drug class. The table also includes alcohol and tobacco outcomes that did not contribute to risk and classification scores.

Table 2

Risks as Bad Outcomes from Drugs Ranked by Prevalence Frequency

Drug	% of Youngsters Reporting One Time or More Use (Total Sample N = 293)	Outcome	% Users Reporting
Alcohol	97	Loss of self-control	8
		Trouble with friends or relatives	4
		Unconsciousness	3
		Physical injury	3
		Concern about overuse or dependency	3
		Car accident	3
		Chronic trouble thinking	2
		Sexual difficulty	2
Amphetamines	18	Bad trips	19
		Loss of self-control	6
		Trouble with friends or relatives	4
		Chronic trouble thinking	4
		Serious study problems	4

Table 2 *(cont.)*

Sedatives	37	Chronic trouble thinking	3
		Worried about overuse or dependency	2
Tranquilizers	23	Worried about overuse or dependency	4
Marijuana-hashish	46	Trouble with friends or relatives	8
		Loss of self-control	8
		Chronic trouble thinking	7
		Worried about overuse or dependency	7
		Serious study problems	6
		Hallucinations	5
		Unconsciousness	3
		Sexual difficulty	2
		Serious mental disorder	2
Hallucinogens	12	Flashbacks or hallucinations (undesired)	28
		Trouble with friends or relatives	14
		Serious study problems	8
		Chronic trouble thinking	6
		Loss of self-control	6
		Serious mental disorder	6
		Worried about overuse or dependency	3
Opiates	8	Trouble with friends or relatives	13
		Unconsciousness	7
		Serious illness	7
		Chronic trouble thinking	7
		Serious study problems	7
Cocaine	2	Trouble with friends or relatives	17
	(N = 6)	Loss of self-control	17
		Serious study problems	17
Special substances	7	Chronic trouble thinking	100
		Physical injury	5
		Serious mental disorder	5

The outcomes shown in Table 2 and other outcomes reported by less than 2 percent of the using population suggest that risks occur in association with private and social psychoactive drug use.

Children were asked about their siblings' drug use. Since each child's own score contributed to his family's risk classification, one would expect that illicit use was a family affair—that is, one would expect that siblings of users were themselves users. That is the case for all drugs except alcohol. Children were also asked at what age they should be allowed to decide for themselves on a variety of items. We found that children in high risk families set an earlier age (including "anytime") than did low risk children for choosing friends, bedtimes, church attendance, belief in God, how much liquor to drink, political activities, keeping their rooms, wearing their hair, where to go for leisure and fun, whom to date, sexual intercourse, use of marijuana, and when to respect police. Moreover, the boys of low risk families were found to advocate a later age of readiness than did their parents. Only in the area of studying did high risk boys consistently propose late decision making on their own. Girls' opinions were also stronger than were their parents' opinions on rules and readiness. High risk girls advocated earlier ages than did their parents for free choice of friends, church attendance, belief in God, drinking, political activities, keeping their rooms, wearing their hair, where to go for leisure and fun, what careers to choose, whom to date, whether to smoke cigarettes, whether to engage in sexual inter-course, and when to respect the police. High risk girls, favor, as their brothers do, late free choice on studying.

Direct enquiries as to parental views on sexual activities showed that more high risk than low risk children believed they had done things which their parents would disapprove of. Low risk children believed that their views on sex were like their parents' views, whereas high risk youngsters believed their views were more lenient than their parents' views. When asked about parental views on masturbation, more low risk children than high risk children said their parents considered it an abnormal act. In regard to other child-rearing practices, low risk children tended to agree that small children should be punished for saying naughty words, that teenagers should be grateful to their parents, and that no child should be permitted to strike his mother.

The possibility was posed that families could uncon-sciously elect one child to be the problem or bad child of the family. The children were then asked whether this had occurred in their family. More high risk than low risk youths said that this had occurred in their families; indeed, one-third of all youngsters agreed with the proposition. Youths did not differ in their descriptions of who ran their families or whom they talked to about their problems. Youngsters were given the list of goals that were important for children to learn and were asked to rank the items from one to twelve. In contrast to high risk youngsters, low risk youth gave high rankings to belief in God and to loving one's parents. High risk youngsters gave priority to treating all men as equals. Low risk youngsters gave low rankings to maximizing one's own human potential, to being free to do what one wants, and to prizing health and strength. High risk youths tended to give low priorities to belief in God and to being a respected citizen.

We also asked the young people to rank order a list of goals which people could have in bringing up their children (the same list the parents were given). Low risk children gave high rankings to turning the child into a respectable citizen, to teaching self-control, and to teaching the child obedience. High risk children gave high priorities to helping the child become a loving person and to encouraging and expanding the child's creativity. Low risk children gave short shrift to the latter goal and to avoiding frustrating the child. High risk children gave a low ranking to turning the child into a respectable citizen.

THE WHOLE FAMILY

We had dinner with almost all families and after dinner chatted and watched while the family gathered round, if they did so. We tried to persuade everyone to be at home for the dinner but not to have a dinner for company. Our interviewer participated (unless requested not to) by bringing a cake, pie, or other dessert. High risk boys (usually the second and third boys in a family) were absent at this affair more often than were low risk boys. Also, only in the high risk group did families refuse or otherwise claim inability to arrange a mealtime invitation. Mothers in all risk categories had cooked most often, but low risk mothers also served the meal more often than did other mothers, although this was a minority pattern. Meal content differed somewhat; low risk families served more starches and desserts than did other families whereas wine was most often served by the high risk families. Prior to dinner, high risk families served drinks more often than did low risk families. Smoking just before and during dinner was also more common in the high risk families than in other families. In the high risk families eating problems occurred in that a family member refused to eat or finish food.

Parental behavior toward the children was rated by an interaction rating list. No differences were observed between low and high risk fathers. Moderate risk fathers, however, were more positive in rule enforcement, in child supervision, and in expressing trust and respect than were other fathers. High risk mothers acted with love or offered rewards (but with an uncertain impact on the children) more often than did low risk mothers. High risk mothers were also more passively aggressive (expressing displeasure or anger by inaction, being sullen, uncooperative, or silent) than were low risk mothers.

Children of high risk families tended to fight, to be angry, or to be disrespectful more than did other children. High and moderate risk children were often demanding or whining. Low risk children, to the contrary, were often obedient and got along well. Parental moods did not differ much among the classes of families, with the exception that moderate risk mothers were most tense. Parental relationships themselves did not differ (as rated during mealtimes), nor did the activity levels of parents or children. Physical appearance differed only in that moderate risk mothers tended to be plump, whereas high risk mothers tended to be trim.

HOMES

Low risk homes stood out as being more attentively cared for than were the other homes. The atmosphere of low risk homes (particularly in contrast to moderate homes) was described as being inviting, warm, cared for, and relaxed. In low risk homes, housekeeping was systematic. Only high risk homes were rated as sloppy, and even in high risk homes that were well cared for, the children's rooms were often sloppy. In the high risk families more often than in other families, servants helped care for the home and prepared meals. No differences in the standard of price of the family automobile was noted; however, the second cars of the high risk families were newer than were other second cars. Moderate and high risk families had more television sets than did low risk families.

As regards over-the-counter remedies, low risk families had fewer sleeping preparations than did other families, but families did not differ for aspirin, cough syrups, and many other common substances. A prescription chart was employed by the interviewer to guide enquiries about the presence and application of medications. Prescribed sedatives were more abundant in the high risk homes than in other homes, as were antibiotics or antiinfective agents. Antiallergy substances or antihistamines were also more prevalent in high risk homes than in other homes, by the householder's count. High risk families were more likely to have one or more members currently taking a given preparation than were low risk families (even when the drug was present in both types of homes).

COMMENTS

The advantages and disadvantages of quantitative or objective research on families are revealed in the data. The canons of statistical inference make evident that low risk families differ from high risk ones, that moderate risk families differ from either extreme but tend to be like low risk families, and that the differences corroborate what other investigators have found, what other theorists have propounded, and what was proposed on the basis of the pretest findings. It is remarkable that such differences occur within a sample that is very much of a piece, having been drawn from white, wealthy, well-educated, healthy, suburban California families whose children attend the same university. The most forceful message we can derive from the findings is that illicit drug use among children serves as a very strong pointer to major differences among families—differences that seem to be linked with essential values.

Our data come in bits and pieces. It is arbitrary in consequence to rely on differences significant at $P = <.05$ but pass over nearby items where P = <.10, even though the former involves a minority of members in any family category and the latter a majority. Seeking objectivity is not without hazard. Recording what one is told is not the same thing as believing it since people often shape their replies so as to give a socially desirable answer or to comply with what they think the interviewer wants. Thus, hardly any differences occurred in what high or low risk parents said about when a child is ready to decide for himself; yet their sons and daughters over thirteen were very clear about who was ready to do what and when in their families. The strength of the replies of the children belies a seeming similarity in this area between high and low risk parents. In the same way, children's comments about values worth learning and goals for child rearing strongly discriminated between high risk and low risk families, whereas the parents' replies yielded a weak discrimination. Was that because the parents did not really know how different their own values were from their children's, or was it because parents were muted somewhat by the interview and moved toward some invisible norm?

Despite the fact that youthful illicit drug use is very much a matter of family status, views, practices, and habits, we know very little about how parents manage to shape children. Some of that shaping must be fairly simple learning—whether by exposure, identification, or repetition. When parents use drugs medically and socially, their children also use drugs. Further, some parents do not disapprove of illicit use—at least not the use of mild drugs. We still do not know enough, however, for most parents in our sample were straight as compared to their children. We can offer explanations, but one still does not know how establishment parents can have children who have progressed beyond family standards.

The data are consistent but by no means entirely so. Consider, for example, that low risk fathers tend to stress communication with children and that their children are usually in agreement with them on sex, drugs, religion, politics, and age readiness rules. Yet, when it comes to knowing about childrens' illicit drug use, proportionately more of the high risk fathers learned about their children's use in one way or another than did the low risk fathers.

These twists require interpretation that becomes conjecture and, subsequently, a step away from hard fact and objectivity. The diminished knowledge of children's drug use among low risk parents (3 per cent knew while, in actuality, 18 per cent of their children had tried marijuana) could be accounted for on the grounds that these children do not communicate things that would disturb their parents. Also, low risk children use infrequently and probably stop using drugs to avoid feeling guilty or risking the disappointment their parents would feel.

Another curiosity arises in that high risk children more than low risk children believe their parents accept masturbation as normal; yet, high risk mothers denied that their children had masturbated more often than did low risk mothers. Perhaps, high risk children oversimplify their parents, believing that their parents are lenient but failing to see the moral core that is hidden behind the obligatory permissiveness. The existence of this moral core is made evident by the correctness of these parents' lives, by their stress on reputation as a child-rearing goal, and by their moral outrage when they do learn of their children's illicit drug use. At the same time, these parents display a general inability to cope when the child steps beyond the bounds of parental intentions. The misinterpretation of parental intentions is demonstrated rather clearly by the fact that high risk boys downgrade the importance of becoming a respectable citizen, which is unusual because here they have not simply progressed beyond their parents' values but apparently have never adopted the parental values as their own.

The business of learning at home and becoming what the parents seem to want may be a component that leads the children of freedom-encouraging parents to become drug-exploring adolescents. But as the correlates of risk suggest, the process is more complicated than that since other determining forces operate in subgroups we have not identified. (Unusual youths who use opiates or cocaine are examples.) Correlates of high risk that call for interpretation are: (1) high levels of activities that take the mother outside the home (aspiring mothers); (2) high levels of traffic delinquency in mothers (lawless or risk-taking mothers); (3) the mothers' indifference toward the police and the laws; (4)

a prevalent alcohol problem in mothers and fathers; (5) the early death of the paternal grandfather; (6) the fathers' pleasures outside the family; (7) difficult pregnancies in mothers; (8) food problems in mothers; (9) the prevalence and acceptance of thumbsucking in infants; (10) allergy histories; (11) high incidence of medical care; (12) high levels of disciplinary difficulties in school; (13) frequent and long separations from home when children are young; (14) the child's lack of caution, inability to beat boredom, and anger when disciplined; (15) unsureness and occasional negativism about child-rearing in mothers; (16) fathers' occasional deference to mothers in supervising children in regard to courtesy; and (17) an emphasis on being rational or on intellectualizing when faced with family or community problems.

We suspect that such variables imply more than values and habits and are probably related to dimensions of affection, leadership, attitudes toward authority, confidence, realism, maturity, and the ability to express and enjoy emotional life. Much is missing because we have not dealt with differences in the data that were trends rather than hearty probabilities; in addition, the observations made here do not lend themselves to elaborations of the theories and conjectures previously set forth. (In subsequent chapters, we review intensive observations on some of these same families.) Unexpected results were the lack of major differences between high and low risk families in visible authority structure, the lack of differences in the delinquency of the children, and the discrepancies between child and adult views. Our findings also produced many similarities where we expected differences.

Thus far, we have focused on the family, on the parents, and on parents in relation to children. Interviews with the children showed that high risk children differed from low risk children in ways that were most compatible with differing religiosity, permissiveness, drug habits, and individual adjustment and happiness versus the controlled community-oriented positions of their parents. Yet, as with their parents, one wonders about idiosyncratic features. (We explore these idiosyncratic features in Chapter Five.) We have leaned on the high risk families in that most of our comparisons pointed out their traits rather than the differing traits of low risk families. That bias in attention, however, is not intended to convey disapproval. Both low risk and high risk families are composed of fine people whose values and styles are derived from American life. Perhaps, the permissive and troubled family seems to be momentarily under fire, but their goals of raising citizens who will be free and creative are not under attack. The traditional, tight knit, and controlling low risk family is not without its problems. Keeping in mind their tendency to approve antidemocratic values such as segregation and their opposition to fitting their children for change, we see that low risk families also constitute a social force that has troublesome components.

Little attention has been given to moderate risk families. Moderates had more accidental babies than did other families; mothers had insufficient breast milk even though their infants had the least illness; moderate risk mothers knew least about the possible delinquencies of their children but knew more about drug use among their children than did low risk mothers; and moderate risk mothers seemed least relaxed about child rearing. Moderate mothers described their children as having strong interests in the arts, but these tendencies are taken to be aesthetic since moderate risk children were not curious or interested in doing new things. Finally, moderate parents affirmed their neutrality vis-à-vis what their children thought about the police and the law. Such differences present a mixed bag that does not allow us to formulate any notions or typologies that make a special case out of the middle ground.

We predict that some of the moderate children who are now using drugs illicitly (at least 23 per cent occasionally use marijuana) will abandon illicit experimentation to become respectable, religious, and politically involved citizens. Most of the moderates have already stopped illicit experimentation. The prediction is compatible not only with the current drug use and backgrounds of moderate risk children but also with a portion of the interview enquiring about acquaintance with drug dealers (a rather good measure of involvement in the illicit drug life). The moderate youngsters, like the low risk ones, differed significantly from high risk youth in not knowing any dealers at all or in knowing only a few. Few moderate risk children are likely to become seriously involved with drugs. Those moderates who have been unusual users are the most likely candidates for heavy use. (One out of eighty-eight, for example, used amphetamines regularly; one tried cocaine; and six tried hallucinogens.) Another possibility (depending upon social circumstances such as the availability and public acceptance of marijuana use among adults) is that some of the moderates may continue occasional marijuana smoking while pursuing the straight and respectable life. Six of the eighty-eight youths in the sample had been regular users at one time; if marijuana were to become socially acceptable in the middle class, they might continue use without becoming involved with extremely powerful substances. At the moment, since we do not anticipate a wave of approval of adult marijuana use, our best guess is that most moderate children will become straight adults and that moderate families are actually somewhat liberal versions of low risk families.

The ordinary marijuana cigarette is less potent than ordinary doses of LSD, amphetamines, heroin, or other powerful substances. But since drug involvement means having taken more than a single dose, the problems of risk in association with complex psychopharmacological variables are raised. These variables include frequency of use, manner of administration, dosage, concurrent physiological and psychological states, and presence in the drug (or the body) of other substances that might potentiate or antagonize. These issues concern us because part of our original definition of drug risk rested upon them. For example, a higher risk score was given to a youth who was taking marijuana regularly than to a youth who had taken it only once. But our outcome data lead us to ask about risks. For one thing, we must not take the conceptual category of high risk too seriously. Table 2 indicates that, except for the special substances (glue, gasoline, paint thinner, hair spray), most youths who use alcohol or illicit drugs do not experience, or at least report, any serious adverse effects. Self-reports are, of course, not totally reliable because people forget things—especially less recent events. In addition, the drug taker may be a poor diagnostician of his own mental or physical status while under the influence of the drug. Bias can also mislead. For example, marijuana advocates might underreport ill effects, whereas youths who are suffering from an underlying emotional disturbance (be it hallucinations or depression) have been known to blame these effects on drugs. (In such cases, the effects become bearable as something external to the person and presumably as a matter of choice or control.) Table 2 suggests, however, that for children favored with health, good nutrition, opportunity, and love, unpleasantness can nevertheless occur. Marijuana (or hashish) has not, after all, been used very long; only 15 per cent of white middle-class youngsters have used it once a week or more often for six months or longer; yet bad outcomes do occur at a somewhat greater rate than is obtained for alcohol.

SUMMARY

On the basis of children's drug histories, families were classified as low, moderate, or high drug risk. All families were white middle-class residents of the same area and had at least one college-age child. High risk families differed significantly from low risk families, with the moderate risk families falling in between (but more similar to the low risk group). High risk families are less religiously involved and put less emphasis on child rearing, belief in God, and self-control than do low risk families. High risk families give greater freedom to children, form less cohesive family groups, show more evidence of alcohol use and the use of medications, and generally demonstrate more permissive attitudes than do low risk families. The evidence is not strong for differences in leadership or affection, although one may infer that high risk families have less enjoyable emotional interaction and put more emphasis on issues and intellectualizing than do low risk families. Differences occur in pregnancy, infant health, early and late feeding, allergy and medical care histories. Among high risk parents, alcohol problems occur, which suggests that physical and emotional health over a lifetime may play a role in predisposing to various degrees of drug use risk in adolescents.

For the most part, high risk drug use is apparently part of a constellation of beliefs and practices which lead the children to express in action the child-rearing goals and personal beliefs of the parents. In becoming what parents want them to become, some children offered unexpected surprises and problems which the parents could not handle equaniminously or directly. The low risk families are more satisfied and have far fewer problems than do high risk families. Low risk parents believe they have accomplished their child-rearing goals. Their children, unlike high risk children, sometimes give stronger voice to parental standards than do the parents themselves.

Lest oversimplified notions of goodness and badness enter into the evaluation, one should keep in mind that all the parents possess decent and admired values from the American culture. The high risk parents have emphasized the child's adjustment, individuality, freedom, exploration, and change. Low risk parents have given priority to discipline, family togetherness, love of God and country, and support for authority and the status quo. Reviewing the data that formed the basis for our classification of families, we observed that most drug-experienced youths have used illicit drugs in a mild or irregular fashion rather than in a regular, intense fashion. Even so, bad outcomes were reported which justify some concern (but not alarm) about adolescents' unsanctioned drug use.

Individual Factors
Predictive of
Drug Risk

❧ 5 ❧

Family factors account for most of the differences between high and low risk drug use among offspring. Nevertheless, on the basis of the proportion of children (normalized) within middle-class families that had certain traits or histories, we saw that the children themselves differed from low to high risk. In some cases, the moderate risk children were unusual, being extreme on special traits. In this chapter, we shall examine some of the individual factors which, independent of family ranking, discriminate individual youngsters with high risk scores from individuals with low scores. In this procedure, we are dealing with descriptions of individuals and not families, and our classification procedure is one of individual drug use not averaged drug use. The interview and rating materials upon which this chapter is based come from parental descriptions of each youngster and from interviews with the youngsters. Since illicit drug use was not found under the age of thirteen, comparisons here are limited to teenage children and offspring in their early twenties.

Two types of findings will be presented. The first type includes factors that have already emerged as significant discriminators of high and low risk families. In these cases, the findings from the family study and the comparison of individuals are perfectly complementary. The other type of finding includes a difference that discriminates high risk individuals but does not discriminate whole families. These findings may be taken as idiosyncratic features that blossom in an individual analysis but remain concealed in family comparisons. This can occur when high risk families contain some children who have low risk scores and whose histories or traits differ from those of high risk siblings. Both factors—the family as a whole and the features of its individual members—contribute to the prediction of drug risk, although family factors account for most of the variance and are the best predictors.

In presenting the findings, we have marked with an asterisk every difference which discriminated between high and low risk children as individuals but which did not discriminate (at P = < .05) between high and low risk families. The data are analyzed for three groups, based on the distribution of individual drug risk scores. There are 103 youngsters in the high risk group, 92 in the moderate group, and 95 in the low risk group. Statistical tests used were the difference between proportions and an analysis of variance. N variation occurs because the individual interview was missing for some offspring.

FINDINGS

One or more significant differences (P = < .05) occurred in the parents' replies or rating codes among 80 of the 184 enquiry and rating areas, when high versus low risk features were compared. There were 159 significant analyses of variance, which allowed the inference that overall reply patterns or ratings within an area differed among the three risk groups. Among the 80 areas where significant differences were observed for one or more of the codes in rating area, only thirteen areas discriminated between high and low risk individuals which had not discriminated families. Of 184 interview and rating areas in the whole family interviews, 82 areas yielded one or more coded differences, significant at P = < .05. These overall findings confirm the reality of differences between high and low risk children and show that these differences apply to families as a whole.

Child description. When reviewing the differences between high and low risk individuals, as described by their parents, we saw that low risk children were unplanned babies more often than were high risk children. Mothers of low risk individuals complained of vascular-circulatory disorders during pregnancy less often than did mothers of high risk individuals. Moderate risk children were also least characterized by respiratory ailments when ill as infants. Low risk individuals, as infants, were healthy more often than were high risk ones.* As infants, low risk individuals were often described as especially skillful, and their mothers were least in doubt about their sociability.

Low risk infants were described as having problem reactions to and disliking new foods, whereas high risk infants were described as being selective in accepting new foods. Moderate risk individuals, as infants, reportedly tended to become allergic to foods, and suffered from small appetites or from eating too much * less often than did high or low risk infants. Moderate drug users, then, were as infants likely to be moderate eaters as well. High risk individuals were punished by food deprivation more often than were low risk individuals, although this was rare in any case.

In regard to toilet training, low risk individuals were without problems, and moderate ones were easy. Serious illness between the ages of two and twelve and frequent illnesses during infancy characterized high risk children. During infancy and the teen years, moderate risk youngsters were least likely to experience respiratory illnesses. As teenagers, moderate risk individuals also had fewer accidents leading to broken bones than did the other groups. Although plant and dust allergies were rare in the whole sample, they were most often reported among low risk children.* Moderate risk individuals responded least often with animal allergies.* Low risk children constituted the group most likely to be hospitalized for serious infectious diseases, but high risk children spent the greatest total time in the hospital.

Between the ages of two to twelve, high risk children were bed wetters more often than were other children, and, as teenagers, high risk individuals had headaches. Moderate risk children suffered from nightmares or from fears and wakefulness in the night less often than did other individuals. Puberty came later for high risk individuals (age 16) than it did for low risk youngsters, and maturation problems were most often ascribed to the high risk group.

Over-the-counter remedy use varied between high and low risk individuals. In the month prior to the interview, fewer low risk children than other children had taken aspirin, vitamins, laxatives,* antiallergy compounds,* or stomach remedies. Uncertainty as to what high risk children had taken occurred. High risk individuals had received tranquillizers * and, though rare, had been given alcohol as a medicament when infants * more often than had other individuals. Contemporary alcohol problems occurred most often in the high risk sample, where youngsters were sick or drunk. High risk individuals were more often known by their parents to have used illicit drugs than were moderate risk children.

Mothers were asked whether they were now worried about any child. Mothers of high risk children were worried * more often than were mothers of moderate or low risk children (although the majority of all children, including high risk ones, were not the subject of worry). Low risk individuals were the subject of maternal anxiety less than were moderate risk individuals. Although the rate of worrying differed, the ostensible reasons did not differ very much. Emotional and behavioral problems were the most prevalent reasons for worry, but drug problems were not mentioned except in two cases (both high risk).

In regard to responsibilities, we found that some low risk individuals were never allowed or asked to babysit their siblings. Also, the time that high risk children spent on chores was most likely to be unknown.* Television watching time during school and vacations was less for high risk children (compatible with family emphasis on achievement through study in these well-educated families). Sunday school attendance began earlier for low risk children than it did for other children.

As for habits and problems, we found that low risk parents had difficulty recalling whether the child masturbated. When masturbation was acknowledged and responded to by parents, moderate risk youngsters were more likely than were others to have their conduct ignored. On other items, high risk individuals were truant, violated curfews, and acknowledged alcohol and drug use more often than did low risk individuals. Low risk children were least likely to be involved in truancy, violating curfews, rowdiness, theft, vandalism, alcohol and drug use, traffic violations, and running away. Although highly uncommon, running away did occur in high risk children. Traffic violations characterized the majority of high risk individuals and the minority of low risk ones. Taking books out of the library without signing for them was also more common among high risk children than it was among low risk youngsters. High risk youngsters had most trouble with the police and were likely to oppose the idea of becoming police officers themselves. High risk individuals were interested in illicit drugs and had affinities toward the radical left. Sports interests and enjoyment characterized the majority of low risk youngsters but only a minority of high risk ones.

Low risk individuals were rated by their mothers as being less insecure,* more self-confident,* more matter-of-fact, more extroverted,* and more pleased with their own sex role than were other youngsters. High risk children were rated by their mothers as being less cautious and better able to concentrate (a study-related item) than were other individuals. In terms of the mother-child relationship, low risk mothers believed they had struck a good balance between strictness and leniency, but high risk mothers thought they had been too strict. The most difficult child-rearing periods for high risk children and their mothers were adolescence and early adulthood (from seventeen to twenty-one). Psychological problems in the past, just as emotional and behavioral items in the present, were major difficulties for high risk children.

Direct interview. High risk offspring reported arts and

humanities majors, no religious affiliation, and left political learning more often than did low risk individuals. Although most of
the sample said their parents did not want them to use illicit
drugs, high risk individuals said more often than did low risk
youth that drug use was their own choice or that selective use
(marijuana) was all right with their parents. Moderate use of
alcohol was approved by the majority of high risk individuals but
only by a minority of low risk youth. High risk individuals reported that their parents were worried about their alcohol use
more than did low risk youth. These same high risk youth reported a number of symptoms associated with present or incipient
alcoholism. Tobacco dependency (tolerance, inability to stop,
heavy use) also characterized this high risk group. The majority
of high risk youth said they had engaged in sexual activities of
which their parents would disapprove (as was true with a minority
of low risk youngsters), and the majority of high risk youth considered themselves sexually freer than their parents. In contrast,
a majority of the low risk youngsters were in agreement with
their parents on proper sexual conduct. This split extends to
views on masturbation.* The majority of low risk offspring also
believed in punishing young children for naughty words, whereas
the majority of high risk children did not. The majority of low
risk youth think teenagers ought to be grateful to their parents,
whereas the majority of high risk youth did not agree. The majority in both groups held that no child should be permitted to
strike his parents, but fewer in the high risk group than in the
low risk group subscribed to this restraint. More high risk youth
than low or moderate risk youth go to professionals (ministers,
psychiatrists, psychologists) to discuss their problems.

Considerable differences appeared on the value scales. Belief in God and love of parents were given highest priority by low
risk individuals, whereas self-understanding was the highest priority for the majority of high risk youngsters. High risk youth
gave the lowest priority to belief in God, whereas low risk youth
gave the lowest ranking to becoming a real success. Child-rearing
goals also differed. High risk individuals tended to emphasize
providing a happy childhood, whereas low risk youngsters emphasized teaching the child self-control and obedience. Low risk indi-

viduals tended to rank the expanding of creative potentials, helping the child to become a loving person, and preparing the child for a world of change toward the bottom of the scale.

COMMENT

The comparison of low and high risk individuals corroborates the findings of the family study. We found that individual high risk youth have more infant health and feeding problems, more childhood health problems, longer hospitalizations, and more psychosomatic disorders (bedwetting and headaches) than do low risk individuals. High risk individuals receive over-the-counter remedies of every sort and are given tranquilizers and, occasionally, alcohol as infants and young children. During the teen years and early adulthood, drug risk becomes apparent, especially in relation to alcohol problems.

The high risk children suffer from psychological problems during their youth and often cause their mothers to worry about their conduct. The mothers of about one-half of these youth are aware of drug use in their offspring (although not necessarily the extent of use), but drug problems are not specified as the major maternal concern. The worries mothers have about these problem children are varied, and drug use contributes only a small portion. For instance, when mothers learned of marijuana use in their children, fewer than one-half of the mothers displayed distress of any kind. Mothers were not distressed about truancy and police intervention, which reminds us that the mothers themselves had frequent moving (traffic) violations. As individuals, high risk youths are rated as less well adjusted than their peers in many ways. Mother-child relationships appear to be stressful for both high risk mothers and for their children. Occasionally, mothers of high risk individuals apply food deprivations as punishment. Perhaps, this practice leads to ingestion behavior (of which drug use is but one illustration), or an emotional loading in the context of forbidden gratification, anger, and acting out. Moderate children are rated as being moderate on most items, from infant feeding habits to adolescent health.

Parents admit their ignorance about certain conduct areas

of their children. Parents of low risk children tend to presume that their offspring are innocent when it comes to masturbation and teenage trouble making. Parents of high risk children tend to be ignorant of their children's conduct in relation to work and chores (and to drug use as well). Contrary to our own expectation, high risk children spend less time watching television than do low risk children. This is linked to data showing high family control with regard to study hours and the acceptance by high risk parents and children of the importance of achievement through scholarship.

Sex, like drugs and delinquency, is most frequent among high risk children and is, at the same time, often a matter of conflict between parents and children, even though high risk parents are permissive. High risk children have followed the permissive lead of their parents but have gone beyond the limits the parents imposed. The notion that these limits are counterfeit must be entertained; considering a possible denial mechanism in the parents and the implicit license for freedom regarding the pursuit of pleasure, one must ask whether the parents themselves are not of two minds. If so, youngsters are responding to conflicts in their parents' minds and child-rearing intentions. Possibly, some of these children are doing what the parents themselves wanted to do but could not.

The low risk youngsters are, in contrast to high risk children, a secure and healthy group, mostly in agreement with their parents on major issues of politics, religion, and morality. From infancy to maturity, low risk children enjoy relatively nonstressful parent-child relations. Their values, like their parents', are of the no nonsense sort, and they emphasize obedient, affectionate relations with authority (God, parents, and the police), self-control, and little self-indulgence. Low risk individuals apparently are not as ambitious, scholarly, or focused on their own happiness and self-understanding as are the high risk youngsters. Low risk individuals are not as religiously disaffiliated, politically radical, or academically soft (arts and humanities) as are high risk youth.

The differences that discriminate between high and low risk individuals but not between families include matters of infant health, infant eating, and infant allergies. (Low risk children are the healthiest but suffer most allergies.) High risk youngsters take most over-the-counter remedies, have been given tranquilizers by their parents, and began alcohol use early. The traits of security, confidence, and extroversion are more applicable to the low risk group than to the high risk group. Most important, parents of high risk children tend to be most worried about their offspring.

In regard to bathing, high risk boys and girls are given freedom of choice earlier than are low risk children. Regarding masturbation, individual high risk youngsters disagree with their parents' views more often than do other youngsters. On value rankings, low risk youngsters give a very low priority to being free to do what one wants. Moderate risk youngsters indicate sex role conflict least often, although only a few youngsters from any group expressed such views.

Since none of these features discriminate exclusively for individuals, we conclude that the individual data is simply complementary to the whole family data. The individual data affirm the association between high drug risk and infant health and feeding behavior, the teaching of legitimate drug use by parents, the habitual use of legal remedies, and personality traits that suggest maladjustment or diminished self-esteem. In the value area, the high risk youngsters emphasize being free to do what one wants and tend to disagree with their parents on that critical area which we believe has considerably more than just a semantic affiliation with drug abuse—that is, masturbation, or self-"abuse."

At this point, let us posit a genuine trouble variable that has its onset in infancy and that is linked with feeding and health problems and quite possibly with psychosomatic expressions of the mother's own anxiety or some other disturbance in the mother-child relationship. This trouble variable appears to lead to continued parental concern which is increasingly focused on expanding conduct problems and continuing psychosomatic ones. (Although by twenty-one, group differences in risk begin to disappear.) Mother-child relationships are stressful; both mother and child suffer from self-doubt, and from the family materials one has the impression that the whole family is embroiled in disputation and seeks various solutions outside the family, from garden clubs to drugs. Although differences between high and low risk children on the trouble variable are consistent, we must stress that most children in this favored white middle-class sample do not get in serious trouble at any time; the prognosis for social adjustment (if not internal harmony) is probably good, and almost all of these children as well as their families are normal people.

High risk individuals are also identified by self-concern and self-indulgence, expressed through the pursuit of pleasure, the disregard of the rights of others, the disregard of parents' wishes in certain areas, and the deemphasis on self-discipline, obligation, and concern for others. These are relative matters since capabilities for work and achievement are obviously present, and self-discipline in scholarly or political pursuits can be presumed. One correlative (or consequence) of this relative license is instability and anxiety within the youngster; if controls are not developed early, the child may subsequently be plagued by his own impulsiveness and with good reason may begin to doubt that he is his own master. Since self-indulgence is often complicated by the failure to build a strong ego structure, disharmony exists. The individual is then moved to seek pleasure in extreme ways, to blame his distress on external factors such as parents, laws, and schools, and, when distressed, to seek relief through drugs and sex. Thus, escapist drug use is seen among some high risk youngsters and perhaps is most noticeable in regard to alcohol use.

The high risk youngster who is critical of his parents and of institutions for attempting too much control is correct in his target and his theme, but is trapped by his own failure to integrate self-control and confident discipline. All is not lost, for human beings remain teachable and the personality is malleable through the early twenties at least. In short, we infer that controls may still be instilled.

In relation to simple learning, imitation, and modeling, high risk individuals demonstrate the success of child rearing as intentional molding. High risk children absorb their parents' values, reflect their parents' goals, and use drugs as parents teach them to do. For the most part, they are the apples of their parents' eyes—even if there is a worm or two. Some of the conflict behavior is understandable, if one assumes that parents often want two different things at the same time. This especially relates to protesting against authority, seeking pleasure, and developing an ethic of individual expression. When children go beyond certain limits, the guidance system has failed since these parents did not realize that a little discipline goes a short way—not a long way. To a certain extent, then, libertine behavior, self-indulgence, and authority confrontations were unanticipated and undesired by the parents. But since parents are themselves split in their desires and intentions, their children are directed by two minds and are inevitably in conflict within themselves and with their parents' wishes. This theme is an elaboration of the notion of a double bind (Bateson, Jackson, Haley, and Weakland, 1956), of the Freudian concept of conscious versus unconscious impulses, and of Sullivan's (1953) notion of parataxic conduct or incongruity.

IN PRAISE OF MODERATION

Thus far, we have emphasized the high risk correlates such as self-indulgence and the trouble variable, while stressing lawfulness, obedience, and family togetherness as low risk correlates. Our discussion might lead one to the conclusion that low risk individuals are entirely model children. We should make patently clear, however, that such judgments, although supported by both the statistical and clinical data, are merely value judgments. Low risk youngsters may emphasize control and obedience but are not strong on scholarship, self-understanding, or flexibility in a changing world. Some low risk mothers and fathers tend to have adamant beliefs that status quo is right, that racial segregation is desirable, and that those who want social change are menaces. Although low risk youths are reliable, honest, and sensible, some may also be rigid, smug, dogmatic, subservient, uninspired, and uninspiring. Such youngsters may make no mistakes because they venture nothing. And even though they may become solid citizens, our times demand that at least some citizens be capable of innovation, flexibility, skepticism, scholarship, and uncertainty.

In relation to these problems, let us turn to the moderate risk individuals and families. Moderate risk individuals are delinquent in having experimented with mild illicit drugs (marijuana in almost every case), but they have not engaged in regular use of these drugs or in any use of potent substances such as LSD, glue, or heroin. Marijuana experimentation is something that most of the youth in the sample have engaged in, but some individuals stop once their curiosity is satisfied. Drug history profiles, the resulting scores, statistical analyses, and the clinical materials to come, all suggest the existence of two subgroups in the moderate risk classification. One subgroup is in transit from the moderate to the high risk category; the other is a flexible and curious group of youngsters who are like the low risk children but who have zeal and are, in some ways, rather self-reliant.

Since we could not do longitudinal studies on the moderate risk individuals, we have to rely on inference and estimation in regard to eventual drug use outcomes. Nevertheless, moderation appears to be one amenable resolution when uncompromising positions are untenable. In the area of child rearing, the family that gives in somewhat but that maintains a basic firmness is in a position to mediate the risks that are faced by some low risk youngsters—namely, dogmatism, prejudice, and dullness. At the same time, these families can prevent the self-centeredness, extremes of conduct, and basic insecurities that often characterize high risk youngsters. Indeed, it is possible the children of moderate risk families are quite satisfactory models for citizenship and that their parents are doing well in child rearing.

DRUG USE AS A TRACER

In examining individuals and families, the drug risk variable was found to be a most useful discriminator, or tracer, which illuminates a variety of empirical differences and critical issues in child rearing and in community life. Drug use constitutes an avenue of enquiry which allows one to learn much about nondrug matters. Concentrating on drug use without appreciating its origins in family life, in parent-child interactions, in the idiosyncratic development of children, and in drug availability would be erroneous. We have used the term *drug risk* and have demonstrated that such risks do occur, but it would be a mistake to attend only to unhappy drug use outcomes. Most drug use among middle-class and blue collar families seems relatively safe, despite the fact that harmful outcomes do occur and that heavy use does pose particular problems. In the final analysis, however, the associated factors that discriminate high risk from low risk groups are critical issues for developing child-rearing styles and our future communities.

SUMMARY

Individual youngsters thirteen years of age and over were distributed along a drug risk score continuum from low to high. High risk youngsters were compared to low risk ones, and supplemental observations on moderate risk individuals were made. Most of the features that discriminated groups of individuals also discriminated between low and high risk families. Family variables, then, are shown to have the major prediction power for drug risk, and the individual variables that do emerge are complementary to the family ones. These individual variables include infant health and feeding, maternal concern, licit drug use, and values.

Three potential themes or factors are proposed for high risk offspring. One is a trouble variable which begins in infancy and includes early health problems and parental uncertainty. This variable includes behavioral problems at meal times and at school, mild conduct disorders, and a lack of self-confidence. A second theme reflects a philosophy of life which is self-centered and self-indulgent but which does not imply an impaired ability to work or achieve. A third theme is learning both direct conduct and abstract ideas and beliefs from parents. Included here are such things as drug use, antiauthoritarian views, scholarly commitments, and self-centered values.

High
Risk

Special consideration has been given to the moderate risk child. In the moderate risk category, one subgroup is in transit to the high risk classification, whereas the second subgroup is composed of youngsters who are curious and flexible. This second subgroup of moderate risk children has the advantage of adjustment mechanisms and wise parental care. These children lack the

Mod.
Risk

(occasional) dogmatic characteristics of low risk youngsters as well as the (sometimes) neurotic or sociopathic tendencies of high risk youths. Drug use can serve as a tracer to illuminate themes in individual adjustment and family life. The resulting knowledge may provide guidelines for future community as well as family action.

Preface to Minority Families

✤ 6 ✤

Most of the readers interested in our work—educators, counselors, health professionals, scientists, community leaders, and parents—probably lead lives similar to those of the middle- and upper-class families who constituted our major study group. We expect, therefore, that the reader may be on unfamiliar ground as we turn to minority groups such as blacks, Mexican-Americans, and poor white families. For this reason, we shall preface our discussion of minority groups with descriptions of the black community, the Mexican-American family, and the realities of carrying on family research in settings different from those of the social scientists themselves.

THE MILIEU

East of Comfort is the community in which our black families lived. Predominantly black, the community houses seventeen thousand people who live in one of the richest counties in the nation and one of the highest income per capita regions of the world. Some racial conflicts have occurred, especially in the local integrated high school, but no disastrous confrontations between whites and blacks have taken place. The community is not a slum, nor is it a ghetto in the sense of being a run-down bario neighborhood.[1] Unemployment and poverty occur, but employment opportunities and prospects of a reasonable income from nearby electronic and construction companies also exist. East of Comfort receives a great deal of solicitous attention from government and private agencies, but we do not know whether this attention is either welcome or effective. In many families, both parents are employed, and a family income of up to $1,200 a month is not uncommon. However, some minority leaders claim a family income of $750 a month is required to stay above the poverty level —given the high local prices and the relative affluence of neighboring townsfolk. In those homes where a relatively comfortable income is attained, a disproportionate sum of money can be spent for cars, television sets, and home furnishings. Women earn as much as or more than men, since they have opportunities both for service work and for work in industrial plants. Men are at greater risk of unemployment during recession times than are women.

The residential part of the community is divided into three areas, the least attractive being a section with multiple housing units which the residents refer to as the ghetto. (We shall follow their usage in referring to that part of town.) Both of the other two areas have single dwellings, but one is considered rather elite because its residents have formed an improvement association and the homes are attractively maintained.

The drug scene in this black community is dramatic. Marijuana use is common among all ages, and heroin, cocaine, reds, bennies, amphetamines, and LSD are widely distributed. The area supports about twenty-five middleman dealers who get their supplies primarily from a black syndicate and from assorted outside suppliers. Each of these dealers maintains a squad of street salesmen, mostly teenagers sixteen years of age or older. The total

---

[1] For a description of drug conditions in a big city black slum, see Sen. H. Hughes, "Hearings Before the Committee on Labor and Public Welfare, Subcommittee on Alcoholism and Narcotics," Washington, D.C.: Alderson-Monick Reporters, 1971.

number of adult dealers is around one hundred. Peddling drugs is an easy, quick source of money. Peddlers can do well financially; even though they may spend much of their income in maintaining their own habit a good part of their income may be in the form of drugs. As an occupation, dealing is approved by peers, and, except among very straight members of the community ("the Christian people"), drug dealers are looked up to as successful businessmen, who are especially admired for their hip life styles. On the ghetto side, there is a lack of appropriate models (people who have gained a respectable social position through hard work) after whom a young black child could pattern his own behavior. Dealing leads to quick profits and prestige and is one way to compete with contemporaries. Drugs not only bring pleasure but also the possibility of prestige and money to teenagers. In some families, parents peddle drugs with the knowledge and even the help of their children; some, for example, maintain shooting galleries or bag heroin in their homes. Young people are exposed to drug dealing and drug use on all sides, and the fact that dealers are armed contributes to a violent atmosphere which becomes an accepted condition of everyday life. Alcohol is probably the most visible drug problem in East of Comfort, and many ghetto residents are alcoholics.

The area has a high rate of youthful delinquency and crime, and drug behavior among young people differs from drug conduct in white communities in this increased association with delinquency and social disorganization. Furthermore, the very young seem more involved than do the young white children. Teachers have reported seven- and eight-year-old children staggering on the playgrounds and sleeping in class due to the effects of barbiturates. One elementary school has a resting room where the children can sleep off such effects. Some children claim they have unknowingly received drugs in cookies or sandwiches handed out by older children or even by adults. At one time, one schoolyard was mysteriously inundated with marijuana-filled balloons which were picked up and put to immediate use by the young set. Distressing tales involving youthful drug users and dealers abound. One incident, for example, involved a thirteen-year-old dealer who sold bennies, cough syrup, and red devils, and who pulled a switchblade on his teacher when he was discovered distributing them in class. Small children use their spending money for illicit pills and marijuana which are sold on the school playgrounds by young teenagers.

After three years of work in East of Comfort, we estimated that in perhaps one-third of the homes no stable family structure exists; one or both parents use illicit drugs and/or alcohol to excess; no tradition of family strength or values is handed down over generations; discipline is inadequate; no mutual trust exists between parents and children; the father is missing; and the family is mother dominated. Prior to school age, a child is frequently left with neighbors or in a government-sponsored nursery attended by teenagers. Working parents do not customarily use baby sitters. When a child reaches school age, he is on the street and left to his own resources during his leisure hours. Black parents who are nonusing themselves appear more inclined than do whites to turn over their drug-using children to the police. Perhaps, these parents feel unable to handle such situations; or, perhaps, they believe that the police can do a better job than they can of punishing. Perhaps, these black parents have a more punitive and official approach to violations of the law than have middle-class whites (Black and Reiss, 1970).

Our interviewer found greater interest in church attendance and church-related activities among straight black parents than among white middle-class liberals. However, when present, this religiosity does not seem to have the same impact on the white middle-class families as it does on the black families. Even the churches are a problem, for they are too numerous to be well supported and parishioners complain that ministers were more interested in the weekly income than in improving community conditions. Indeed, becoming a minister may fill ego needs rather than religious ones (Jordan, 1969). Some church leaders are untrained, and some are illiterate since some denominations have no standards for ordination. Such ministers tend to be of little help in improving social conditions or in contributing to a stable community. Our initial impression was that church membership among parents did not immunize against illicit drug use among children. Perhaps, the parents lack the strength to combat the influence of a chaotic peer group which makes children antipathetic to any restrictions or constraints. One minister's solution to the problem of his drug-using sons was to move his family back to Mississippi. As he told us, "If the boys get in trouble there, they'll soon change, because in Mississippi they know how to handle the colored race." Hostility toward the law and a fear of the police (including black policemen) are widespread in the community. As one very straight housewife said: "The biggest racist institution in the ghetto is the law enforcement—the pigs. They have no respect for people in the ghetto." The general conviction is that, in any kind of altercation between blacks and whites, the black man will be presumed guilty regardless of the circumstances. Ironically, a strong belief exists that the southern black who migrates north and attains a position of some authority is not capable of acting responsibly toward his own race since he will take out his resentment after having lived a restricted life in the South.

Parents believed one reason for a high drop-out rate is that the cultural contrast between the black community and the adjoining wealthy area is too extreme for their children to cope with emotionally. The black child's attitude becomes one of "What's the use? The odds are too great." On their way to school, black children pass luxurious homes, and in class they mingle with expensively dressed youngsters who own their own cars and have plenty of spending money. Black parents blame such experiences (a sociologist would call it relative deprivation) for feelings of futility, resentment, hostility, sensitiveness, and defeatism in their own children.

The stable parents feel that improved counseling, increased emphasis by school authorities on staying in school, effective drug abuse education, and improved recreational facilities such as playgrounds, youth centers, and athletic clubs could reduce delinquent behavior among their young people. Lacking warm, stable family relationships and exposed as they are to a pervasive drug scene, these children are without wholesome, constructive leisure-time activities. Being culturally and educationally de-

prived, lacking in parental supervision, and having no constructive outside interests, these children understandably drift into the
world of drugs and crime on their own accord.

We cannot confirm the accuracy of these complaints or diag-
noses, although they certainly mirror popular and academic views
of the black community's problems. We can say, however, that
East of Comfort is a town which is sensitive to its troubles.

OUR APPROACH AND DIFFICULTIES

As might be expected, we had our own troubles as we tried
to conduct our family study in East of Comfort. Our original intent was to select families through whole block census work which
would describe families by income and reported drug use in the
children. We would then select ten high risk and ten low risk
families to be subjects for our study. Our census effort produced
data (reported in Chapter Fourteen) but did not allow for family
selection. Much time was wasted trying to find families who met
our criteria (intact families with one child in his twenties or late
teens and with other children at home, some having high and
some having low drug use among the children). Many families
were uncooperative, and our census interviewers failed to complete the poll. We had great difficulty in finding black interviewers (one of our requirements). In looking for interviewers, we
first began with an employment service and were told that our
concern was racist and that drugs were the white man's problem.
Our second effort was with a black ex-convict who, after working
a few weeks, said the East of Comfort scene was too rough for him.
In a third effort, we sought to utilize a local narcotic self-help
group whose sponsors and members, after six months, completed
only a few of several hundred assigned census interviews. Finally,
through community groups, we located a long-time resident, a
teacher's aide, and an active church leader who interviewed all
families, using a young male teacher's aide to interview male
teenagers. Another woman resident who was active with the probation department helped locate families as did a woman church
elder, until she was threatened with violence by some of the families and so withdrew. This process of staffing and family case

finding took over two years; family interviewing itself overlapped that time and took eighteen months.

After the failure of the census procedure, we turned to family case finding (high and low drug risk) through known institutions and agencies (churches, probation department, and NAACP). Our probation department case finder became ill, and institutional leads ran afoul of misinformation and noncooperation (including gun and knife threats). Thus, many of our final families were obtained through neighborhood search and social chain referral by our senior interviewer (christened St. Perry, out of our gratitude for her fortitude and decency). The problem with this approach was that our interviewer knew the Christian families best and had trouble establishing ties with the disorganized high risk ghetto families. As a consequence, our East of Comfort sample did not have any families with drug risk scores as high as those obtained in the white or Mexican-American samples.[2]

Our case finding had a further problem in that we suspected false reporting of drug use among black children. Our interviewer was a good and motherly figure, and appearing to be good in her eyes would be an understandable desire on the part of a child. Our method of verifying family drug scores was first to check the arrest record of each child in the twenty families studied. Our second step was to hire two very able young black men with considerable acquaintance in the drug-peddling world to "nose around." They were given a list of all children's names but were not told anything of the children's self-reports or the family's risk classification. They checked these children to identify those who were active as junior dealers, runners, and customers. They also checked to see the kind of crowd each child associated with. After three months of enquiry, they turned in the lists indicating whether there was street talk of illicit drug use and related activi-

[2] Our groupings are only superficially racial. The Mexican-American group contains people with some Spanish ancestry, although Mexican-Indian ancestry predominated. This ethnic group is defined primarily by language. The black group necessarily has people with some white ancestors, and our white group has some with black ancestors. For our purposes, life style, class, and ethnicity were the important factors.

ties among the children. A final set of checks consisted of reviewing with parents their reports of their children's histories of arrest, hospitalization, or accidents to learn whether drug use had been a correlate. Table 3 summarizes the data for our verification of children's self-reporting.

Table 3

Data Sources and Agreement on Children's Drug Risk
Classification for Black Families

Families	Illicit self-reported drug use	Street talk illicit drug use reported	Serious trouble with authorities verified	Trouble with authorities reported by parents	No reporting of any factor	Classification: low risk	Classification: high risk
1.	X	X					X
2.	X		X				X
3.	X	X	X	X			X
4.	X	X		X			X
5.	X	X	X	X			X
6.	X	X	X	X			X
7.	X	X					X
8.	X	X	X				X
9.	X	X		X			X
10.	X	X		X			X
11.					X	X	
12.					X	X	
13.					X	X	
14.					X	X	
15.					X	X	
16.					X	X	
17.					X	X	
18.					X	X	
19.					X	X	
20.					X	X	

MEXICAN-AMERICAN FAMILIES

Anthropological impressions derived from the work of our interviewer in the region from which high risk families were selected (see also Clark, 1959) suggests a long standing pattern of illicit drug use among Mexican Americans in this area south of us. Glue sniffing may start around the fifth grade (pupils may be as old as twelve or thirteen by this time); marijuana is the next step; then comes alcohol use, and, during late teens, heroin. The age of onset for each drug appears to be decreasing, and drug use is conforming to that of the Anglo culture; barbiturates (reds) are being introduced and the rate of drug dealing by Chicano youngsters is expanding. (Drugs are picked up in Mexico or from acquaintances who move back and forth across the border.) Profits are good even if use of barbiturates or amphetamines is limited. The youngsters say these drugs "eat your brains up," but heroin is not considered physically damaging. Middle-class Chicanos are more likely than are others to experiment with hallucinogens since these drugs are accepted along with other aspects of middle-class Anglo culture.

The ideal family is one that has a stable, responsible, highly respected male at its head. This ideal, however, is not always realized among lower-class Mexican Americans. In Mexico, a corresponding breakdown is occurring, and, for example, the rate of alcoholism there may be increasing. One fairly widespread pattern experienced by the child is an early childhood with an alcoholic father and the eventual separation of the parents, after which the mother finds another husband who is possibly stable but whose assumption of the male role alienates the son from his mother. A strong belief is that stepparents cannot treat their stepchildren well because the children are not really theirs. (This extends to babysitters as well.) Thus, mothers tend to insist upon taking the responsibility for discipline, and the stepfathers do not interfere. At the same time, tradition calls for discipline coming from the male. Individual responses to this fairly common situation vary. The stepfather may be strong enough to assume a dominant, responsible position in the family, or he may watch helplessly as the children drift into delinquency. He may at times erupt into tyrannical behavior because of his relatively helpless position and thus further antagonize the entire family. Mothers with teenage sons frequently resort to the juvenile hall or the police for help, and often mothers request that their children be incarcerated in order to help discipline the child. Some mothers who do not remarry take drugs or use alcohol themselves; others stay unmarried and try to place their children's needs above their own. Among these, perhaps the strongest and most stable women decide to stay home and rely on welfare for their income rather than go out to work.

When considering reasons not only for drug use among Mexican Americans but for their vulnerability to law enforcement, we must realize (1) their ready accessibility to drugs; (2) their visibility (for example, getting arrested for drunken driving while playing guitars in the car); (3) the fact that drugs are the "in" thing (consonant with the "macho" concept of proving one-self as a male); (4) the tendency to call the police (an Anglo institution) when things get out of hand; and (5) a lack of involvement in the society at large and lack of hope for their own futures in that society. Those who have espoused "la Causa," athletics, or higher education are involved and have some reason to live for something beyond the moment. Among families, there are distinctions between the drug-using extremes. In the straight families, a strong emphasis is placed on control over the children and mutual trust; the relationship between the parents is warm and egalitarian. The traditional culture emphasizes control, through the stress on respect. This is a characteristic that tends to break down rapidly under acculturation to American values, where self-assertion of the young is expected. Mutual trust is the ideal, but only a minority of people can be expected to realize this ideal. Nonetheless, fathers who devote time to their families and who discuss the problems of their children in a nonauthoritarian, understanding manner are able to maintain a stable framework for their family. At the other extreme are families where the man finds few satisfactions at home or where the relationship between husband and wife is cold, hostile, or overbearing. A pattern according to which the wife stays home while her husband continues to attend parties or goes drinking with his friends is still prevalent among lower-class Mexican-American families. Young girls, however, are no longer willing to accept this pattern and are becoming aware of their rights according to the law. As a result, many marriages are extremely brittle and of short duration, even though they produce children. A number of children are left without fathers, and many have stepfathers. Second marriages usually last since the men lose the need to express their machismo and since the women become tolerant.

A problem in the relinquishing of traditional adult control so that the young can become freer in the American fashion is that the peer group poses obvious dangers when it is not buffered by parental wisdom. With the onslaught of American ideas upon them, traditional control can only be retained through stern measures (not only must the young girl be chaperoned at a dance, but her father must drive her there and back), which increases the traditional *alma de rebelde*—the rebellious soul supposed to be typical, especially of teenage boys. Unless, that is, there is this quality of warmth and understanding on the part of the parents. For instance, in one straight family, the father takes his daughter and wife shopping on Saturday afternoons. The daughter enjoys this for she is not cooped up, nor exploited, and prefers family activities to having to cope with the teenage groups available to her. Her brother has elected to return to his relatives in Texas, a small town which they believe to be relatively safe from drugs because in the trailer camp where they live there is no place for him to go without being bombarded with the drug scene. The mother observed of the son, "He has to be able to go out, to be with friends"—but, she added by implication, not here where it is too tempting and, indeed, downright unpleasant for a nonuser.

A related problem is the awareness that school (particularly high school) is a place where exposure to drugs is high. Most adults are puzzled as to why the authorities do not crack down on known drug use in school. Many parents indicate that perhaps their children would be better off not going to that particular school at all. Thus, in a culture where the benefits of education are just beginning to be understood, the counterforce of drug exposure in the schools creates an unwanted untimely dilemma. Furthermore, as concerns the lower-class and semirural Mexican Americans, the educational experience itself probably exacerbates the problem. One finds repeated truancies and delinquency, and drugs become a part of the picture because school is almost as unbearable as home. Girls are exploited and the boys feel confined. Jobs for teenagers are believed to help the situation, as would a belief that the system would provide rewards for playing the game. But school is alien and often hostile to these children. In one family, a boy of fourteen was deep in drugs. The youngest son—eight years old—played hooky in 1970 in order to shine shoes at the bus depot. He proudly presented his mother with his earnings, but his truancy and other marked signs of independence were not received kindly by a teacher who was described as prejudiced against Mexican Americans. Perhaps this very bright and independent little boy is a good candidate for drugs, unless, for example, he becomes a militant. The family's lack of social and political involvement, however, makes the latter possibility unlikely.

Another debilitating pattern is that the mother, having left or been left by her husband, begins to rely heavily on her eldest son, who is reinforced by the responsibility and privilege accorded him. His response to this treatment is to act responsibly and maturely, and eventually he is able to handle the discipline of the younger children better than his mother. Most likely, he will be drafted, and the mother is again left to cope by herself. Her younger sons are likely to get into trouble and thus be turned down by the army. The young man who survives will return home with a greatly increased understanding of the world, but the immediate outcome is a weakening of an already precarious family structure and the elimination of leadership and models for the younger brothers. Another consideration is the resentment that many teenage girls feel when their mothers leave the home to work. Daughters may feel that their mothers do not care about them, and frequently the daughters are left to care for the younger children. Thus, girls also view home as a place they wish to escape. Mothers who stay home seem to get on considerably better with their daughters (if not their sons) than do other mothers. The television set is the only source of entertainment or interest, and few parents provide their children with other materials for development. In the straight families, however, outlets are provided in the form of church activities and socials or family participation in athletics and camping.

METHOD

We did not anticipate difficulty in locating Spanish-speaking families of Mexican origin. Two towns, one north of Comfort and one south of Comfort, have Latin neighborhoods; in addition, counties to the south have large Latin populations containing some migrant and some permanent residents. Our plan called for a neighborhood census that would locate high and low drug risk families living near one another. As with black families, this method was intended to control for major socioeconomic variations, school, and drug availability to children. Again the census procedure failed but for different reasons than obtained in East of Comfort.

Our first problem was to find a Spanish-speaking interviewer. Several middle-class South and Central American women did not work out because of their inability to communicate in bario Spanish and because of difficulties (apprehensions or aversions) in establishing a rapport with the interviewees. That interest stemmed from the fact that Spanish-speaking youngsters (predominantly of Mexican origin) have contributed disproportionately to California drug arrest statistics. However, any study that ignores the groups who contribute to real risk misses the point. (See Ball and Chambers, 1970.)

We located a warm-hearted, charming woman, the wife of the pastor of a Protestant Mexican-American congregation. After training she began the census work, but it was soon apparent that our census method would not allow us to complete the work within the three-year time limit of our study. Our interviewer met considerable resistance among families not known to her, and those who did cooperate sometimes took as long as twenty-five hours to do so. As a consequence, we turned to a rather haphazard case finding method. We hired two additional interviewers who were both college students of Mexican origin. An anthropologist who also joined us had been studying Mexican Americans in a county south of Comfort for twenty years. The pastor's wife selected low risk families only. The anthropologist was already acquainted with several hundred families and could readily identify those with high risk children. Those who were willing to cooperate and who met our criteria were selected.

We were forced to acquiesce to two other difficulties. One was the tendency of Mexican Americans to conceal rather than report any intimate family matter that might be viewed as shameful. The other problem was the fact that a family interview might extend over forty hours or even six months as the necessary amenities and indirections were observed. A minor methodological problem also arose. Our plan called for interviewing every child over the age of five. However, families were often very large, and our coding-computer program was not set to process data from over eight children. A systematic rule was set to accommodate these realities.[3] This same rule was applied to East of Comfort and low-income white families.

Interviewing with Mexican-American families presented its own set of problems. Aside from the great amount of time required, the interview form, which made sense for middle-class Anglos, did not mean the same thing to semirural poor Mexican Americans. The notion of a planned baby, for example, is hardly applicable; one might ask instead whether the baby was wanted or accepted after it arrived. Trust was also an issue, as this group tends to distrust outsiders—be they Anglos or middle-class Mexicans. Telling lies is not shameless, but, if one cares about the interviewer, politeness requires evasion. However, a chance to talk and be listened to means more to the poor Mexican American than it does to the busy corporation president, and much material is forthcoming, even if it is irrelevant to the enquiry. Unless a personal relationship is involved, the disordered family may participate simply for the money that was offered and care little about accuracy. Even straight families were sometimes reluctant to discuss intimate matters with anyone. The only areas that caused hesitation in the middle-class university families centered around the drug cabinet, masturbation, and, perhaps, the exercise of authority. In the Mexican-American family, many issues were of a delicate nature—even talking about the family itself in any way. Frankness tends to be a bad thing rather than a good

---

[3] The rule required that (1) the mother's favorite child be included, (2) the mother's problem child be included, (3) the oldest child be included, (4) one child from any five of the following age brackets be included: 24, 22, 20, 18, 16, 14, 12, and 10. If any bracket had two children of the same age, the elder was taken. If the number of children had not yet reached eight, children were taken in order from ages 23, 21, 19, 17, 15, 13, and 11. Again the elder was taken if there were two the same age. If $N = 8$ was still not reached, we began with age 25 and went up until $N = 8$ was achieved. If $N = 8$ was again not reached, we began at age 9 and stepped down.

one. Perhaps, self-deprecating insights contradict basic notions of Latin pride and philosophy.

This is illustrated by one of our interviewers who was recruited during the study of her own family. She spoke of sitting quietly while her father answered questions. The father presented the children as perfect creations, during which time his daughter wondered how this could be so since she herself had never told him about her life outside the home. If communication within the family is so discrete and so colored with propriety, what can the interviewer expect to learn even when thirty hours are spent establishing a rapport? Despite these difficulties, interviewers did learn something, and differences were found between high and low drug risk families.

LOW-INCOME WHITE FAMILIES

Poverty was the major difficulty encountered in our study of low-income white families. Our original criteria for a family of at least four members were: an income that was under eight thousand dollars a year, an intact family structure, one child in his twenties or late teens, and at least one younger child still living at home. Case finding proceeded first through the welfare departments in the two nearest counties, the welfare officer for the nearby school district, medical authorities at county institutions, a neighborhood Office of Economic Opportunity program, a neighborhood drug-help center, the state employment (Human Resources) office, and local Catholic priests. Welfare personnel in one county were most helpful; in the other they would not assist in case finding on the grounds that confidentiality would be violated. The other agencies could not find families to meet our criteria. We therefore modified our stance, abandoned our demand for intact families, raised our minimal income to $8,500 and looked again—still to no avail. Our next step was to do a mailing in white low-income neighborhoods and run the following announcement in the local newspaper.

HELP! We are a group of researchers at Stanford University and need help in locating a small group of white families living in the mid-peninsula. These families should have a mother and father (or step-parents) living at home, one or more children ages 13–22 years, also living in the area if not at home, and a family income of under $8,000 a year. The work we are doing is paid for by the government. We are interested in finding families to study family values and attitudes toward drugs. We are able to pay each family for their participation in the study. If you have a concern about families and the drug problem and your family fits the description (or you know of a family that does) please call.

After six months of this helter-skelter case finding, we obtained twenty-three families. Six families were referred by families we had already seen; seven families came from our newspaper advertisement; four were referred by school nurses; two were obtained through the county welfare department; two came through school welfare officers; two through direct mailings to neighborhoods; and two through personal referrals from other sources.

Two of the families had income of $9,600 a year or more but were clearly very poor. In one case, there were six children, child-support payments from a previous marriage, and a serious chronic illness of one child. The other family had twelve children at home. The median income for all twenty-three families was $7,500. The families themselves and the county agencies dealing with or helping these families would not quarrel with our designation of families as low income. Since the low-income white families were scattered over several towns that varied considerably in appearance, we cannot provide a picture of one specific milieu for this group. We believe their children had the same exposure to drug use as did other children in our studies. These families are the subject matter of Chapter Seven.

SUMMARY

We have described our approach to studying black, Mexican-American, and low-income white families. Difficulties in obtaining each sample were considerable, and we failed to obtain high risk black families and very poor white families. Informal observations on the black community have been offered; but the black families used in our study were respectable Christian families who did not live in the area known as the ghetto. Mexican-American family life is described, and the disorganization and dissatisfactions inherent in that life style are emphasized. Low-income white families were drawn from a variety of sources, so no observations that pertain to all of these families can be made.

Blue Collar
White Families

❧ 7 ❧

In the present chapter, eleven low risk and twelve high risk low-income white families are compared. These families are English speaking and live in the same suburban region as the black, Mexican-American, and middle-class white families in our study. The families to be discussed here come from a conventional blue collar background and have estimated average incomes $7,500 a year. Significant differences occurred among 421 out of 2,071 enquiry and rating areas. As regards the analysis of variance, 807 significant tests indicated that the overall pattern of replies within any enquiry area differed between the low risk and high risk groups more than did the variation within these groups.

MOTHERS

Although both low and high risk mothers disclaimed a political party preference, low risk mothers tended to be liberal Democrats, and high risk mothers tended to be Republicans. These tendencies were reflected in preference for 1968 presidential candidate. Low risk mothers preferred Robert Kennedy, whereas high risk mothers paradoxically preferred the liberal Eugene McCarthy as a candidate. As for nonpolitical interests, the high risk mothers had artistic or creative hobbies, were very interested in civic activities, liked do-it-yourself projects, and enjoyed hunting and fishing, movies, collecting, and travel. Low risk mothers reflected disinterest in many of these outside activities. However, low risk mothers were more interested in their families than were high risk mothers and derived their greatest pleasure from family life. Low risk mothers were more satisfied with their own health than were high risk mothers and reported that, as teenagers, they got along well with their own parents. High risk mothers did not report harmonious relationships with their own parents, but in no other way did low risk and high risk mothers differ in their teenage self-characterizations.

Drug and health histories revealed greater alcohol use, more smoking, and more use of barbiturates and tranquilizers among high risk mothers than among low risk mothers. No illicit drug use was reported by any mother in the sample, except one high risk mother who once took an amphetamine. Prescribed opiate use occurred in the low risk sample, but such use was more sustained in the high risk sample than it was in the low risk sample. (One high risk mother was possibly dependent on such prescribed drugs.) More persistent illnesses and more chronic underweight occurred among high risk mothers than among low risk mothers. On social values and stance, no noteworthy differences occurred.

FATHERS

Differences among fathers were few. High risk fathers tended to be better educated than did low risk fathers. (Some high risk fathers were college educated as compared to high school level education among low risk fathers.) High risk fathers tended to be without religious affiliation, had a political party preference, were Republicans, and preferred Nixon as a 1968 candidate. Many of these high risk fathers were interested in music, shop, and do-it-yourself construction. Low risk fathers were consistently disinterested in such activities or had few hobbies they considered important enough to discuss. Low risk fathers were often family centered and said they derived most of their pleasure from their family. As youths, low risk fathers got along with their own parents better than did high risk fathers. However, high risk fathers reported that others had considered them responsible young people or student leaders more often than did low risk fathers. As adults, fewer low risk fathers than high risk fathers had non-traffic arrest histories or had been in jail.

The drug history profiles indicated no differences between the two sets of fathers in their social or illicit drug use. Except for one low risk father who had nonprescribed stimulants, all fathers denied illicit experience of any kind. In regard to values and social stance, differences were minimal. Low risk fathers tended to see student activities as a threat, and they were less critical of the news media than were high risk fathers.

CHILDREN

Forty-seven low risk and 36 high risk children were described by their mothers. (In two high risk cases, the children were described by their fathers.) Illness during pregnancy and long labor characterized high risk mothers more often than they did low risk mothers. The trend was for low risk parents to name their children after relatives; high risk parents selected names they liked. Having been supplied with an adjective check list, more high risk mothers than low risk mothers described their babies as vigorous protestors, sensitive, finicky (a feeding problem), and frequently sick. High risk mothers tended to worry about their babies during infancy—emotional or behavioral problems being the focus of their concerns. For the high risk families, feeding problems continued to the second year; more of these infants were both breast and bottle fed than were low risk children. Rules on finishing food were more common in the high risk families than they were in low risk families.

Toilet training problems and serious illnesses during childhood (ages two to twelve) and the teen years were reported for high risk children more often than they were for low risk children. Allergies in childhood and during the teen years were specifically noted in the high risk children. Hospitalizations were also more common for high risk than for low risk youngsters. Tension and nervousness (hyperactivity in particular) characterized the high risk youngsters as children and as teenagers. In the year prior to the interview, the high risk group had more doctor visits than did the low risk group, and, in the month prior to the interview, high risk mothers gave their children over-the-counter medication more often than did low risk mothers. High risk children also received tranquilizers. High risk children reportedly suffered from drinking problems and had tried marijuana.

As regards age readiness rules, more high risk mothers than low risk mothers refused to allow their children to baby-sit others, but high risk children started chores earlier than did other children. Low risk children began Sunday School earlier than did high risk children. Few low risk children as compared to other children sucked their thumbs.

School discipline problems were most common in the high risk group. High risk mothers complained about more curfew violations, more theft, more traffic violations, and more drug use among their children than did low risk mothers. Long absences from home characterized the high risk youngsters who were also more opposed to a police career, more interested in drug use, more likely to be on the radical left, more interested in trying new things, and more insistent on having their own way than were the low risk children. High risk children were less likely to meet deadlines, more impulsive, more easily bored, and more in need of excitement than were their peers. Low risk youngsters were considered by their mothers to be less curious and less impulsive than average. In addition, low risk youngsters liked to take medicine less than did their peers.

When reviewing their own roles, more low risk mothers than high risk mothers felt they had struck the right balance between discipline and leniency. Low risk mothers also said they had been sure of themselves most of the time. In discussing the most difficult aspect of child rearing, high risk mothers stressed the psychological problems of some of their children. Low risk mothers believed their children were rational, insightful, efficient, and reasonable.

FAMILY ORGANIZATION

The families differed very little in their discussions of decision making. However, the low risk fathers carried the day when uncertainty or disagreement did occur. Low risk parents agreed that the father was boss more often than did high risk parents. Low risk mothers did not mention problems of responsibility insofar as disciplining the children was concerned. During the week prior to the interview disciplinary events occurred most often in the high risk families. The age readiness list elicited some differences. More low risk children than high risk children were never allowed free choice as to marijuana or LSD use. In all of these families, however, some disagreements existed among parents on age readiness rules. In the low risk group, the mother's opinion on manners, bathing, and career choice was enforced. In the high risk group, the father's opinion carried in the matter of quitting school. High risk families indicated there was a problem child in their midst more often than did low risk families.

On the basic values scale, low risk mothers gave priority to belief in God, love of one's country, and having a high regard for law and order. Low risk mothers gave low priority to maximizing one's own human potential. High risk mothers gave high precedence to understanding oneself, getting along with others, and maximizing one's own human potential. High risk mothers gave low rankings to being a respected citizen. Low risk fathers, like the mothers, gave top priority to belief in God and a high value to loving one's parents. High risk fathers, like the mothers, gave priority to getting along with others. As for goals in child rearing, low risk parents jointly emphasized the importance of teaching the child self-control. Low risk parents felt it was unimportant to avoid frustrating the child. High risk parents, to the contrary, emphasized that they wanted to expand the child's creative potential, and they found no advantage to instilling ideals of the great men of the past. The low risk parents agreed that it mattered whether their children tried marijuana; the high risk parents often agreed that it did not matter. Low risk parents more often agreed than high risk parents that a child who wet his pants should be made to feel ashamed.

WHOLE FAMILY AND HOME OBSERVATIONS

Alcoholic beverages were served more often in the high risk homes than they were in low risk homes. Outsiders had also been invited to this specially arranged evening in the high risk homes. Few other differences were observed, except that low risk fathers seemed to be rigid rule enforcers whereas high risk fathers were often not respectful or trusting in relation to their children during the evening. High risk mothers tended to share feelings and consult with their youngsters—with questionable effects on the children. Low risk mothers enforced rules and sometimes did so rigidly. Low risk children were often rated as shy. Low risk parents were rated as relaxed, warm, and happy more often than were high risk parents. Low risk parents were also rated as physically plump more often than were high risk parents.

In the home observation, no major differences were seen. The television was turned on more often in the low risk homes than it was in the high risk homes. The medicine cabinet check indicated more use of cough syrups in the low risk families than in the other families.

REPORTS OF CHILDREN THIRTEEN AND OVER

More high risk than low risk children were living in a home where one parent was absent. Low risk teenagers often said their fathers were Catholic, although Catholicism was not predominant on direct interview with the parents. Apparently, the parent no longer considered himself a practicing Catholic, but the children still categorized him as such. High risk youth tended to be without religious affiliation, were often independent liberals, and thought their parents were Democrats. (Their ratings often conflicted with the self-reports of parents, which leads one to question how often political issues were discussed within the family.) High risk youngsters said that in their families drinking was often left up to them, but their smoking was disapproved. High risk children also said parents were worried about their drinking.

Table 4 presents data on the prevalence of nonmedical drug experience in the two groups along with data on bad results as a percent of those having used each substance. Table 4

Table 4

Prevalence of Experience with Nonprescription Psychoactive Drugs and of Bad Outcomes among Users for Low and High Risk Blue Collar White Families

Alcohol: Low risk experience 83%   High risk 100%

	Bad Outcomes	
	Low Risk	High Risk
Car accident	4%	16%
Job loss	0	3
Severe discipline	0	3
Jail	0	5
Other accident	0	3
Trouble with friends or relatives	4	13
Physical injury	4	5
Unconsciousness	0	11
Hospitalization	0	3
Chronic trouble thinking	4	8
Loss of self-control	0	18
Sexual difficulty	0	13
Serious study problems	4	0
Worried about overuse	0	3

Tobacco: Low risk experience 54%   High risk 87%

Illicit Amphetamines: Low risk experience 7%   High risk 53%

	Bad Outcomes	
	Low Risk	High Risk
Bad trips	0%	10%
Jail	50% (N = 1 of 2)	0
Trouble with friends or relatives	0	5
Chronic trouble thinking	0	5
Loss of self-control	0	15
Suicide attempt	50% (N = 1 of 2)	0
Hallucinations	0	5
Worried about overuse	0	20

Illicit Sedatives: Low risk experience 14%   High risk 45%

Bad Outcomes	Low Risk	High Risk
Unconsciousness	0%	6%
Serious illness	25% (N = 1 of 4)	0
Hospitalization	25	0
Chronic trouble thinking	0	12

Illicit Tranquilizers: Low risk experience 14%   High risk 29%

Bad Outcomes	Low Risk	High Risk
Serious illness	25% (N = 1 of 4)	0%
Hospitalization	25	0

Marijuana: Low risk experience 21%   High risk 66%

Bad Outcomes	Low Risk	High Risk
Severe discipline	17% (N = 1 of 6)	0%
Chronic trouble thinking	33% (N = 2 of 6)	16
Loss of self-control	17	0
Serious study problems	50	0
Hallucinations	0	8
Worried about overuse	0	8

Hallucinogens: Low risk experience 0%   High risk 40%

Bad Outcomes	Low Risk	High Risk
Severe discipline	0%	7%
Trouble with friends or relatives	0	13
Chronic trouble thinking	0	20
Serious study problems	0	7
Hallucinations (undesired)	0	47
Serious mental disorder	0	13
Worried about overuse	0	7

Opiates: Low risk experience 0%   High risk 29%

Bad Outcomes	Low Risk	High Risk
Chronic trouble thinking	0%	9%
Loss of self-control	0	9
Worried about overuse	0	9

Cocaine: Low risk experience 0%   High risk 18%

Bad Outcomes	Low Risk	High Risk
Trouble with friends or relatives	0%	15% (N = 1 of 7)

Special substances: Low risk experience 4%   High risk 8%

Bad Outcomes	Low Risk	High Risk
Loss of self-control	0%	33% (N = 1 of 3)

shows that in the white blue collar sample the prevalence of illicit drug use and its danger are relatively small when compared to the middle-class white sample and the Mexican-American sample. The blue collar white and black families are similar in this respect. The data also show a much reduced consistency between the classification of risk and the likelihood of bad outcomes. In these blue collar families, bad outcomes were reported by children in families classified as low risk; in three low risk families, one child described bad drug-related experiences. Although these three families had high scores in relation to other low risk families, their low risk classification was nevertheless based on the scores of all children in the family.

The distributions lead us to the conclusion that white blue collar children are similar in respect to their illicit drug use. In this sample, alcohol had the greatest variety of bad outcomes and the highest prevalence of use. Illicit drugs produced the highest number of bad outcomes among users—if we exclude the oddity of the very small samples (for example, one out of two low risk amphetamine users going to jail). The hallucinogens seem to post the greatest dangers for the high risk users as does marijuana for the low risk group. Conceivably the latter phenomenon had to do with problems of conscience and anxiety, as youngsters who were otherwise inexperienced with drugs suffered consequences of guilt, fear, and even self-punishment. Our risk measures still yield consistent findings in terms of the differences between families and the children, but the outcome data in Table 4 demonstrate the necessity of clinical observations to verify the outcome itself, the relationship between the outcome and drug taking, and the roles of nonspecific emotional factors and specific pharmacological ones (Rinkel, 1963; Witkin, Dyk, Faterson, Goodenough, and Karp, 1962).

High drug-using children described their siblings as using more tobacco, alcohol, marijuana, hallucinogens, amphetamines, opiates, and special substances than did low risk children. We did not enquire about sedatives and tranquilizers since these might have been prescription drugs. As regards age readiness rules, high risk boys believed in early free choice of friends, foods, bedtimes, what to wear, church attendance, belief in God, spending their own money, political activities, hair styles, careers, and dating. High risk girls set early ages for free choice of friends, foods, bedtimes, clothes, churchgoing, belief in God, spending one's own money, political activities, hair styles, careers, whom to date, and sexual intercourse.

The high risk children said more often than did low risk children that they had engaged in sexual activities which their parents would disapprove of. As before, the implications are that the parents are very strict or that the children exercise free license with subsequent parent-child conflict. The latter interpretation probably holds. As in the areas of sex and drugs, youngsters do agree with their parents on family dynamics. The high risk children, for example, agreed that there was a problem child in their family. As in the Mexican-American sample, the problem child was most often the second born. The high risk children nominated their mothers as the boss of the family (although both parents is the modal pattern in both samples). High risk youngsters also said that they discussed their problems with their friends rather than with their parents. On the basic values scale, the low risk youngsters gave priority to belief in God, whereas the high risk children emphasized understanding oneself and being free to do what one wants. Low risk children gave a low ranking to understanding oneself and to being free to do what one wants. High risk youngsters gave the lowest rankings to belief in God, getting along with others, having a high regard for law and order, and loving one's parents.

In regard to desirable child-rearing goals, high risk youth emphasized expanding creative potential, preparing the child for a world of change, and giving the child a happy childhood. High risk children believed that turning the child into a respectable citizen was an inconsequential goal. Low risk youth emphasized teaching the child obedience, and they ranked expanding creative potential at the bottom of the scale. As concerns younger children, interviews with sixteen low risk but only two high risk youngsters took place. We shall not analyze the data from this unbalanced material.

COMMENT

The absence of differences between low risk and high risk parents on almost all measures is striking. The dissimilarity of their children on so many measures is also striking. We suspect that the best measure of what the parents really believe or do is, not what they say, but what their children do or say. One must consider the almost "classical" differences between low risk and high risk children on age readiness rules, sex and drug activities, primary social values, and child-rearing goals. Although trends and even significant differences occurred in discussions with the parents, the whole business was buried. One suspects that parents demonstrated a certain moderation in presenting themselves to the interviewer and, therefore, moved toward the norm. Perhaps, these parents have difficulty in verbalizing and say what they think they ought to say rather than what they actually believe.

These white blue collar families resemble the white middle- and upper-class families in regard to the traits and beliefs associated with drug risk. The high risk blue collar mothers tend to be diversified, are less family centered, sometimes use drugs, are likely to rule the household and appear to be internally inconsistent (in politics anyway). Fathers from the white middle-class sample and from the blue collar sample resemble one another in their beliefs and activities. The low risk fathers are family centered and sometimes are authoritative, and occasionally are rigid disciplinarians. As a whole, the low risk family is more conventional, less permissive, more religious, more community oriented, and apparently happier than is the high risk family.

The most important differences occur in the children's descriptions of their parents, the parents' descriptions of their children, and, by extension, in the interactions between parents and children. Infant and child illness, feeding difficulties, toilet-training difficulties, allergies, nervousness, and discipline problems pose important problems in the high risk group but do not occur in the low risk group. High risk mothers see in their childrens traits such as unreliability, impulsiveness, sickliness, boredom, and tendencies toward psychological problems. The same high risk mothers themselves tend to be unhealthy, had poor teen-age parental relations, take prescription drugs, and use social drugs. These mothers are also less confident in their roles and less satisfied with their child-rearing achievements than are low risk mothers. However, low risk mothers are very much like high risk ones in respect to values, education, and conventionality, even though certain differences remain. Beginning with child naming, low risk mothers confidently proceed to produce rela-tively obedient, efficient, religious, pleasure-suppressing, law-abiding, parent-respecting youngsters who are not curious and who avoid delinquency. The high risk family, to the contrary, produces spontaneous youngsters who usually follow the parental lead in the direction of freedom, happiness, self-understanding, the expansion of creative potential, and flexibility. High risk chil-dren tend to be irreligious, politically independent, self-determin-ing, troublesome, and delinquent (which includes illicit drug use). Theft, truancy, human impulsiveness or other troubles are not always to be taken too seriously since the individual often settles down and becomes a responsible adult. Moreover, these individ-uals often rear children who have a very low drug risk.

In this white blue collar sample, both low and high risk life styles have benefits and losses. Low risk parents are without political interests or leisure time activities; they are pleased to produce respectable but not creative children. Are these parents and their children likely to provide the world with inventors, art-ists, or poets? The high risk families pay a high cost in terms of conflict, disappointment, unpredictable and sometimes unac-ceptable conduct, but the pay-offs are individualistic and sponta-neous children, some of whom by virtue of their experiences and troubles could grow up to be profound and understanding adults.

Family centeredness obviously brings rich satisfactions and is associated (in all four of our samples) with reduced drug risk. In the blue collar sample family centeredness may exclude stimu-lating hobbies and interests, and in the Mexican-American group family life is so exclusive that nonrelatives are strangers and community interests are almost nonexistent. In contrast, the high risk family is diffused, and that diffusion of family life opens the child to the outside world. The child's outside interests include illicit drugs on the lawless side but also political action on the lawful one. For the high risk child, peers become very important, while his family retires to the background.

The high risk mother may be accurate in her descriptions of her childrens' many illnesses and psychological infirmities. Possibly, her high drug risk children are born with peculiarities that make them different from their peers. Also, when the high risk mother focuses on health, pregnancy problems, food problems, and drug use in her children and in herself, her bodily concerns may be her way of expressing, not the child's original distress, but her own emotional problems. The low risk Mexican-American mothers had more insight than the high risk ones. Perhaps, in this blue collar sample, these bodily complaints are indicators of a lack of insight. Even though these high risk mothers are child-centered and emphasize words such as self-realization and creativity, they may be intellectualized notions that have no foundation in real emotion, experience, understanding. Such terms may lack saliency for these people who really express themselves otherwise (getting sick, using medicine, focusing on a problem child, etc.). Oddly enough, their children do seem to understand and follow their words. When the child grows up, these parents may be surprised to see that *happiness* or *freedom* means being hospitalized for a bad LSD trip. Until they have such proofs of meaning, however, the parents themselves possibly do not comprehend what they are talking about. To the contrary, *happiness* and *freedom* may also mean a good outcome for both the parents and the child.

SUMMARY

A sample of eleven low risk and twelve high risk blue collar white families were seen. The families were quite similar, with self-reported bad outcomes in a minority of cases. The families were conventional and resembled the black blue collar sample. The differences that did emerge were compatible with previous findings. The high risk families tended to be disharmonious, permissive, and liberal, and the mothers especially tended to use social and prescribed drugs. High risk mothers were dominant, were not confident in their child rearing, and had diverse interests. Both high risk parents were less family centered than were low risk parents. High risk fathers were not religious, were political, and had diverse interests. Both high risk parents were less warm and happy than were low risk parents. The expressed values of the low risk families were clearly transmitted to their children and became the basis for behavior that stresses obedience, respect, love of parents, self-control, and belief in God. High risk children also seemed to acquire their parents' beliefs, but the high risk outcomes were not always as the parents anticipated. Especially in regard to drug use these children learned to imitate their parents, but sometimes they went beyond the limits parents had set. The range of behavior is greater in the high risk children than it is in the low risk children, but this conduct can pose hazards for the high risk childrens' safety. Our descriptions have emphasized the extremes, but all of the families and children described here are probably normal in regard to their general behavior in the community.

The two groups demonstrated differences in bodily and emotional functions from the time of the mother's pregnancy onward. Ill health, nervousness, allergies, and food problems marked the high risk children. Somatic problems and medication use also appeared in high risk mothers. The children of these blue collar families presented with great clarity a picture of their parents' stance toward household and age readiness rules, sex, drug use, basic social values, and child-rearing goals.

Blue Collar
Black Families

❧ 8 ❧

In the present chapter, we present findings based on our interviews with black families. The interview, observation, and rating schedules employed in the major study of middle-class whites were also used here. We compared low risk with high risk families but found that our high risk group was in fact more moderate than high in their drug use reporting. Because the number of families was small and because extremes were not compared, significant differences were not as numerous as those in the middle-class white sample. We shall, therefore, have occasion to speak of trends, when results do not achieve a $P = < .05$ level of statistical significance. Out of the 2,071 areas of enquiry or rating, 269 significant differences occurred. Analysis of variance yielded 313 significant outcomes, indicating that a greater difference exists between high and low groups than exists in the distribution of coded replies within groups.

Two significant differences of questionable importance occurred in the family descriptions. One difference was that high risk parents had been married longer than had low risk ones. The other difference indicated that the first born child of high risk families was often a boy. As for trends that were not statistically significant, we found that more people lived in the high risk household than in the low risk household and that, in the high risk group, one parent was not living at home at the moment of interview (although these were all intact families). Absent children among low risk families were often married or living in their own apartments. Among high risk families, absent children were living far away or were in a reformatory.

Mothers. High risk mothers were less well educated, less involved in religious activities in their own youth, and much less interested in continuing education than were low risk mothers. High risk mothers often found their most pleasurable activities were family centered, whereas low risk mothers found pleasure in their outside work as well as in their families. High risk mothers were less satisfied with their health than were low risk mothers; as children they got along poorly with their parents; and in their teens there was a continued trend for poor parental relations. As teenagers, high risk mothers were themselves considered to be troublemakers. High risk mothers refused to reply on a number of items about teenage conduct, but low risk mothers were communicative. Considering these in combination, we saw trends for low risk mothers to have been student leaders. Low risk mothers were delinquent, heavy drinkers, unmanageable, promiscuous, or revolutionaries less often then were high risk mothers.

High risk mothers frequently had serious current alcohol problems. Sedative use was also considerably greater among high risk mothers than it was among low risk mothers, and a trend appeared for high risk mothers to use tranquilizers. Only one high risk mother admitted to having tried cannabis, and she is a current user. Opiate experience was reported only by high risk mothers, and we inferred this use to be addiction. High risk mothers reported abstinence after using psychoactive drugs more often than did low risk mothers. A trend occurred for high risk mothers to report bad outcomes from psychoactives, but a similar trend did not obtain for low risk mothers. For example, only high risk mothers reported auto accidents from drinking, job loss from alcohol, sedatives, or tranquilizers, discipline problems in adolescence, serious illness and troubles with friends from drinking, thought disorders, loss of self-control, and study problems. High risk mothers often said they suffered from current and persistent illnesses and reported taking medication regularly.

As pertains to values, low risk mothers were more conservative than were high risk mothers. Low risk mothers often saw communists as posing a first rank menace to the community, whereas high risk mothers saw segregationists in that light. Low risk mothers were unlikely to rank hippies or—paradoxically—big businesses as threats to the country, and high risk mothers were unlikely to consider suburbanites or labor unions as threats.

Fathers. Occupational levels among fathers did not differ. Fathers reported having been trained for levels of work which they were not currently pursuing. A trend existed for high risk fathers to have low levels of education, and they often considered themselves to be liberal Democrats. As teenagers, high risk fathers tended to be uninvolved in religious activities and were seldom student leaders. The low risk father, as a teenager, had a devil-may-care attitude and tended toward delinquency, heavy drinking, promiscuity, and revolutionary activities. However, low risk fathers had been arrested less often than had high risk fathers. As regards current interests, the trend was for low risk fathers to be interested in civic and volunteer work, to pursue artistic pastimes, to enjoy movies and parties, and to be sociable. Shop interests characterized the high risk fathers. Low risk fathers derived most pleasure in life from work, whereas high risk fathers claimed that their pleasure came from their families or from recreation.

Reports from our alcoholism list were contradictory; alcohol problems apparently existed in both groups, but we cannot be sure at what rate. Illicit drug experience was rare in either group, and no hard narcotics use (licit or illicit) was described. A trend was that high risk fathers took more medication and had more counseling or psychotherapy experience than did low risk fathers. However, low risk fathers were hospitalized most often. The groups did not differ on their social values.

Children. Thirty-four children in the low risk group and forty-three in the high risk group were described. Premature babies and labor difficulties were most common among low risk mothers. Low risk babies were described as being energetic, happy, contented, and especially skillful more often than were high risk babies. (Most babies in both groups had not been planned.) Breast-fed babies as well as weaning troubles were common in the high risk group. Similarly, troublesome reactions to new foods occurred more often among high risk infants than among low risk infants. Trends showed that high risk infants had more health and feeding problems than had low risk infants; high risk mothers recalled more adjustment problems in the first week of school than did low risk mothers; and most high risk mothers cried at that first parting. Other trends showed that low risk mothers reported more serious illness and more infant nervousness than did high risk mothers; low risk children tended to have allergies as infants, but high risk children had allergies most often as teenagers. Trends also indicated that hospitalizations were most common in the high risk children and that high risk children experienced great nervousness from ages two to thirteen and over. More high risk than low risk mothers admitted to having current anxieties about their children. (These anxieties were not directly linked to drug use concerns.) High risk mothers were uncertain whether their children had tried glue or gasoline sniffing more often than were low risk mothers. High risk mothers did not differ from low risk mothers in estimates of drinking problems. (Only one high risk mother saw drinking problems.) Most mothers thought their offspring had not tried marijuana or hallucinogens.

Children in the low risk families began to have chores earlier than did other children. However, high risk children were expected to share in major responsibilities in the house and yard when they reached sixteen. High risk children spent more time watching television both during school and during vacations than

did low risk children. A history of school troubles, truancy, and
rowdyism was most common among high risk youngsters as was
a trend toward running away and theft. Four high risk children
were identified by their mothers as having a drug use problem,
but no low risk mothers identified such difficulties in their offspring. A trend was for more traffic violations among high risk
children than among other children. Troubles with the police
occurred most often among high risk offspring. Only five children
from among the seventy-seven in the total sample were said to
have high interest in illicit drugs; all five were reported by high
risk mothers.

Low risk children were viewed by mothers as being better
readers than were high risk offspring; high risk children had
been away from home for long periods and were left alone without a sitter at early ages. There was a trend for high risk children
to be described as on the radical left, as having no interest in the
creative arts, and as having either very much or very little interest
in religious experiences. High risk children were also said to be
very interested in trying new things. High risk parents were not
specific in their hopes for their children and showed uncertainty
about their childrens' need for excitement. Low risk parents were
unsure about their children's reactions to medicines but felt that
their children were satisfied in their sex role identifications. High
risk parents often mentioned discipline and health difficulties in
their individual children. In discussing the most pleasurable
aspects of each child, high risk parents mentioned being free, loving, and natural more often than did low risk parents.

FAMILY ORGANIZATION

Our interviewer found that fathers in high risk families
were dominant significantly more often than were fathers in low
risk families. (No reliability data were available with this rater
on black families.) Low risk families shared decisions and duties
such as discipline, children's desires, and the choice of children's
friends more frequently than did high risk families. However,
high risk families felt their children required a great deal of discipline, whereas low risk families felt discipline should be mixed

with freedom of action for their children wherever possible. In the week prior to the interview, a greater number of actual disciplinary events took place in the high risk families than in low risk families.

Low risk families reported earlier ages of free choice for boys' friends, hair styles, and sexual intercourse than did high risk families. Both low risk and high risk families agreed on all other items for boys. For girls, low risk families reported later ages for free choice of political activity than did high risk families. Less parent-child conflict on these items occurred in low risk families than it did in high risk families. The majority of high risk families agreed that there was a good child in their midst—the implication being that some bad children were also present. Families differed on the basic values they wanted their children to learn. On the forced ranking procedure, low risk mothers gave a high ranking to treating all men as equals, whereas high risk mothers valued maximizing one's own human potential. Fathers differed, mostly in that low risk fathers were unable to make choices in a forced ranking. High risk fathers valued maximizing one's own human potential and understanding oneself, whereas low risk fathers did not. No family differences emerged in regard to the police and the law, except that high risk fathers often expressed positive views about police officers as people. Conversations about child-rearing practices revealed that high risk parents felt that children should be made to feel ashamed for wetting their pants and that no child should strike his mother. When asked to set forth advice for new parents, high risk mothers stressed the importance of communication between parents and children more often than did low risk mothers.

FAMILY OBSERVATIONS

The whole family observation took place during and after dinner. In low risk families, daughters helped with serving much more often than they did in high risk families. High risk families did not have a formal dinner hour, presumably due to conflicting schedules and the reluctance of parents to bring various family members together for an evening meal. The trend was for the high risk families to turn on the television during dinner and to serve drinks before dinner. High risk families also tended to use food punishments, urgings, and reprimands for overeating and overdrinking.

Parental interaction with children differed between the families. Low risk fathers disciplined their children through rule enforcement or acted in a respectful or trusting manner. High risk fathers tended to ridicule or belittle their children; they attacked their children verbally and played the hostile game of confusing the child by giving several contradictory messages at once. High risk fathers also often acted indifferently or were overly agreeable to one or more children. Mothers in the high risk families tended to consult a child on some item (with a questionable impact on the child), used humour in a hostile way toward the child, manipulated and competed with the child for attention, punished the child, insulted or criticized the child, sent confusing and contradictory messages to the child, or demonstrated passive aggressive behavior such as pouting or sulking. These high risk mothers also complained about the child to others, acted seductively or indifferently, acted submissively, or occasionally were overly agreeable. During the evening with the interviewer, low risk children were observed to be cowed, obedient, polite, cooperative, and to get along well. The majority of high risk children fit none of these descriptions. Activity levels of family members did not differ, except that in low risk families the second sibling was often quiet. In appearance, low risk fathers were often plump or athletic.

HOME OBSERVATIONS

Only in high risk families did the interviewer rate the atmosphere as extremely negative (forbidding, shoddy, bare). Sloppy or dirty housekeeping characterized high risk homes along with certain peculiarities such as living rooms being used as storerooms and keeping the house cold. High risk families were more likely than were low risk families to have a second car, and the second car was usually a new model. More television sets were seen in the high risk homes than in other homes, and the medicine chest inventory revealed that high risk families took more cough medicine than did low risk families. Fewer prescribed amphetamines and sympathomimetics were on hand in the high risk homes than in low risk homes, but only members of high risk families were currently taking these drugs on prescription. (This corresponds to parents' self-reports on stimulant use.)

REPORTS OF CHILDREN

Interviews were conducted with twenty low risk youngsters and thirty high risk youngsters, aged thirteen or over. More children in the low risk group than in the high risk group were living with both biological parents. (Our requirement for an intact family was that a mother and father be present. We could not require that neither parent be divorced or remarried.) Among high risk children with stepfathers, youngsters tended to be unaware of the stepfather's religious affiliation, and high risk children themselves tended to be without religious affiliation. When discussing their parents' views on drug use, more low risk children than high risk children said their parents disapproved. Only high risk children reported that illicit drug use or tobacco use was left up to the child. High risk children admitted to being worried about their own alcohol use, and signs of alcohol problems were found among these youngsters (blacking out, difficulty in cutting down, escapist use, drinking early in the morning, amnesia after drinking, and having four strong drinks a day for six months or more). These same high risk children reported alcoholism in the father. (Our data on alcohol problems in low and high risk fathers were inconsistent, but children's reports helped us to clarify which group had greatest troubles.)

Tobacco smoking was most common in the histories of high risk youngsters. Illicit amphetamine use, intravenous use, and bad trips occurred among high risk offspring but not among low risk offspring. High risk children also demonstrated illicit use of barbiturates, tranquilizers, marijuana, hallucinogens, and glue sniffing. (Opiate and cocaine use were denied.) However, when looking at prevalence, one finds that the high risk black youngsters are a low-use group in comparison to middle-class whites—as measured either by high school or college studies or by our family data. For example, only one-third of the high risk black youngsters reported any cannabis use, and only one half of these said they were currently regular users. Bad outcomes occurred for six of the twenty-two high risk alcohol users (trouble with friends or family, car accidents, jail, or loss of self-control). No low risk youngster reported any bad outcomes. Bad outcomes from amphetamine use were reported by one of the six users. Among five youngsters admitting sedative use, two reported bad outcomes. Among the two reporting illicit tranquilizer use, one reported a bad outcome, and, among the eight marijuana users, six reported bad outcomes (including two auto accidents). Only one youngster admitted using hallucinogens (morning glory seeds), and he reported going to jail as one of his bad outcomes. Among the seven children who sniffed volatile intoxicants, two reported bad outcomes.

Table 5 shows nonmedical psychoactive drug use and indi-

Table 5

Reported Prevalence of Nonmedical Psychoactive Drug Use and Bad Outcomes among Children over Thirteen in the Black Family Sample[a]

| Drug | Prevalence of Use | | Prevalence of Bad Outcomes Reported by Users | |
	Low Risk Families, per cent	High Risk Families, per cent	Low Risk Families, per cent	High Risk Families, per cent
Alcohol	70	70	0	27
Tobacco	30	48	0	0
Illicit amphetamines	0	19	0	17
Illicit sedatives	0	16	0	40
Illicit tranquilizers	0	6	0	50
Cannabis	0	29	0	75
Hallucinogens	0	3	0	0
Illicit opiates	0	0	0	0
Cocaine	0	0	0	0
Sniffing substances	0	23	0	29

[a] Our list of bad outcomes includes social, family, sexual, and physiological difficulties. All bad results constitute things that go wrong at varying levels of severity and that are attributed (rightly or wrongly) by the drug user to his use of the substance.

cates the proportion of users reporting one or more bad results
from their use. This conception of bad outcomes is the basis for
our use of the term *risk* in connection with the classification of
families according to the scores obtained by their offspring on
drug use and drug risk histories. The data indicate that risks
among these black youths are most often associated with marijuana, followed by tranquilizers, sedatives, sniffing substances,
alcohol, and amphetamines. We asked each youngster about the
drug use habits of his brothers and sisters. Only among high risk
families were any siblings said to use marijuana, amphetamines,
or special substances, which further confirms the self-report data
and verifies the data of Table 4. These youngsters were more
reluctant in describing their siblings' drug use, than they were in
describing their own use. Thus, sibling estimates are considerably
lower than are actual reports from direct interview.

High risk boys were found to be uncertain about the age
readiness rules in their families. The most consistent difference
among groups, however, was that low risk boys indicated an earlier
age for deciding when to study, how to spend their own money,
and how to wear their hair than did high risk boys. More low
risk boys than high risk boys said there was never any free choice
with regard to marijuana and LSD use. Low risk girls reported an
earlier age for making decisions about belief in God, studying,
spending their own money, hair styles, smoking, and sexual intercourse, than did high risk girls. But low risk girls also said there
was never any free choice on using marijuana or LSD. Most children said that their parents considered masturbation to be abnormal. Only among the high risk children was an accepting attitude
toward masturbation attributed to the parents. These youngsters
could not deal with the forced choice procedure of measuring
basic values. In consequence, we could not compare either values
or goals for parents and their children.

Preteen children (fourteen low risk and thirteen high risk)
were asked questions which explicitly dealt with their views on
drug use. Few differences between groups emerged, except that
low risk children noted their own parents' disapproval of alcohol
use more often than did high risk children. In this preteen group,
illicit drug experience was nil. Only high risk preteen children
said that their siblings used illicit substances, but, again, sibling

estimates were lower than self-reports. High risk children agreed with their parents that children who wet their pants should be made ashamed; they also agreed that a problem child was present in their family.

COMMENT

Illicit drug use is generally infrequent in this sample of intact, Protestant, and moderate Democratic families, where the mothers are mostly housewives and the fathers are employed blue collar workers. In comparison to the prevalence of illicit drug use among the total youthful population in the county, drug use among their "high risk" children is actually rather low. (See Blum and associates, 1972a, Chapter 9, for reports of the rampant addiction that characterizes nearby ghetto families.) Thus, it is important to remember that we have drawn our subgroups from very similar backgrounds indeed. The differences which obtain tell us nothing about the real high risk families who live nearby but who could not be persuaded to cooperate. The only advantage accruing from our comparison of these low and the high risk families is that certain differences in parental habits, views, and child-rearing styles are illuminated, which are clearly not due to socioeconomic factors.

In this portion of our study, similarities rather than differences stand out. Moreover, stressing any one difference too heavily may be misleading since that difference might characterize only a minority of families in both samples. It is best to seek themes that embrace a variety of observed differences. Thereby, one moves from quantification to abstraction. Each reader may want to construct his own theory from the data.

One question that comes to mind is whether having a first-born girl constitutes a lucky break. In a neighborhood where boys are the leaders in delinquency and drug use (Ball and Chambers, 1970) having an older girl who could act as a second mother might help reinforce the family against outside influence. As the oldest sibling, she might be able to supervise the brothers and keep the family standards firm.

Factors that are associated with high risk in white middle-class families are frequently associated with low risk in blue collar black families. If we assume this is meaningful rather than a chance variation, interesting issues are raised. Consider, for example, that low risk blue collar black families have the educated mothers who are involved in outside activities; also both parents tend to be less family centered than do the high risk parents in this sample. With regard to readiness rules, low risk families are more liberal than are high risk families in letting the children decide for themselves. Father dominance was found in high risk rather than in low risk families, whereas sharing of responsibilities occurs most often in low risk families. These and other items suggest that in certain ways the low risk blue collar family resembles the middle-class high risk one. Perhaps, these blue collar families have moved toward the general middle-class conception of a democratic family, and this style, when not carried to the permissive extremes of our high risk middle-class parents, is in fact helpful in child-rearing. The implication is that there was a point on the swing of the pendulum away from Victorian authoritarianism toward communication, respect, and sharing, where child rearing found its optimal conditions. But once this point was passed, problems began to occur. Extreme permissiveness, fear of authority, laxity in discipline, and encouragements to do as one wants produced children who could not withstand the temptations of drugs or other dangers in the environment. Perhaps, then, the low risk blue collar black family represents an optimal point on the scale. Indeed, the middle-class black family can be too Victorian (Frazier, 1949). Some freeing from this mold might give the parents leeway and enable them to enlist the child in the joint enterprise of being a family.

At the same time, the high risk blue collar black family does resemble the high risk middle-class white family in many ways. Children sometimes live far from home; the political stance of the parents is liberal; there is little past or present religious involvement on the part of the parents; television is heavily relied upon and intrudes in personal interactions; the parents emphasize free spirit values for their children; parents are permissive in regard to drugs; fathers tend to avoid disciplining the children; and there is much dissent and parent-child conflict. The houses of the high risk blue collar families also reflect increased casualness (if not chaos) and conflict as part of the family style. Perhaps, these are the aspects of permissiveness that carry the pendulum too far in the direction of disorganization or anarchy.

Clearly, permissive values contribute to only some of the differences between families. The group of items related to health, psychosomatic functioning, feeding, and prescribed drug use is also an important set of discriminating features. High risk mothers have more illness, use more drugs, give more drugs, worry more about their children, report that their infants are more allergic and more nervous, and have more food problems than do low risk mothers. Food complaints also occur more often at dinners with high risk families than they do at dinners with low risk families.

Three additional areas are linked to the foregoing comments—the drug use of parents, parents' own childhood histories, and the way parents handle their children. In regard to parental drug use, the trend is for high risk (actually moderate risk) mothers to have bad outcomes from licit and illicit psychoactive drugs, whereas high risk fathers appear (at least in their children's eyes) to have alcohol difficulties. As for the childhood histories of parents, high risk mothers report disturbed or fretful adolescent years and poor parental relationships. This was not the case for high risk fathers; rather, low risk fathers were the ones who reported hell-raising teen years. Perhaps, those individuals who survive and go beyond such years become settled and understanding fathers who can handle their own children and help them avoid the pitfalls.

As concerns handling children, low risk fathers are rule enforcers and respectful, whereas high risk fathers use ridicule, insult, and indifference. High risk mothers are even worse, using mock respect and hostile humor, being sullen themselves, and competing with the child. These parents would also shame a child who wets his pants. The offspring reflect these differences in handling. Low risk children are obedient, polite, cooperative and get along well, but they probably pay the price of having been cowed.

These styles do not necessarily reflect views on authority

since no evidence is available for differing perspectives on the law or the police among these blue collar workers. Neither are these styles expressions of a value system being put into action (although that may be part of it). We wonder whether high risk fathers and mothers are not simply less competent as people than are other parents. The child-handling tools they use indicate anger and inefficiency, if not desperation. Indeed, high risk parents do not know how to advise new parents. Nonetheless, this incompetence cannot be extreme because high risk children seem to love their parents as much as other children love theirs. Moreover, even the high risk children have turned out fairly well to this point. The outcomes, at any rate, were predictable even in infancy when high risk mothers thought their infants were less content, less energetic, and less skilled than were other infants.

Idiosyncratic variables also contribute to individual drug risk—a fact that persistently stares one in the eye. Most likely, a combination of heredity and special forces in the environment does make a difference.

We must conclude with an admission of our own uncertainty. The blue collar black family is different from the white middle-class family in the constellation of factors that lead to moderate illicit drug use and to measurable drug risk. Yet, these two family groups are also similar. Certainly, the disorganized, delinquent high drug risk families (nonfamilies) would be on a different order of being. Hopefully, the themes focused on here do, in fact, constitute factors that are central to how parents affect their children in relation to drug use.

SUMMARY

We identified ten high risk and ten low risk families among the black blue collar families living in the same region as our middle-class white families. We were unable to procure a sample of high drug risk black families; thus, drug use by any of these children is mild when compared to the white sample. Although similarities exist, the black blue collar families differ from the white middle-class families in the constellation of factors that are associated with varying degrees of illicit drug use in their off-spring.

The families in this sample are very much the same—intact, Protestant, Democrats, employed fathers, and respectable. The differences between the low and high risk families appear to be centered on several themes. Low risk families demonstrate a wide diversity of interests, the sharing of power, liberalism in a few value areas, and early trust in children to make their own decisions. Permissiveness in regard to drugs and in association with loss of control and the free spirit ethic is found in the moderate risk group. Low risk families are conservative, religious, exercise quiet discipline, appear to have few family conflicts, and produce children who get along in school, with the police, and who are polite and cooperative.

The high risk mothers report dissatisfaction with their own health, medication use in themselves, and in their children allergies, food aversions, eating problems, and nervousness. These high risk mothers had disturbances during their own adolescent years, but the real teenage hell raisers were low risk fathers. Low risk parents appear more confident, more respectful, and view their offspring in a more positive light than do high risk parents. These high risk parents seem to be simultaneously punitive, hostile, indifferent, seductive, naive, and mocking in relations with their children. These persons are apparently incompetent as parents, and, while we do not posit any necessary differences in affection or interest, these parents seem to be unable to cope with their children for reasons of personal inadequacy. If their children are troublesome, one cannot know whether it is a matter of mismatched temperaments or of a lack of skill in child rearing. The prevalence of drug risk among children (estimated from bad outcomes as a proportion of prevalence of use) is greatest for marijuana, followed by tranquilizers, sedatives, volatile inhalants, alcohol, and amphetamines. Since bad outcomes are reported by more than 50 per cent of the sample who have had experience with marijuana, we conclude that our concept of risk is appropriate in connection with illicit drug use by blue collar youth.

Mexican-American Families

❦ 9 ❧

In the present chapter we compare ten high risk with ten low risk families, all of whom are Spanish-speaking and are of Mexican-Indian or Spanish-Indian background. The low risk families live a few miles south of the area from which our black blue collar families and white middle-class families were drawn. The high risk families live in a rural area about eighty miles away. The families all have an average estimated income of about $6,000 a year; the husbands (with one exception) work at unskilled, often agrarian, labor. The mothers are usually at home, and all families are large. The families resemble one another more than they differ. In 2071 enquiry and rating areas, only 366 significant differences appeared among code categories or between proportions. As regards the analysis of variance, 422 significant differences appeared in the pattern of replies between groups.

Few significant differences occurred between the high risk
and low risk families with regard to size. Differences occurred in
the age and sex distributions of the children and in the average
total number of children at home. (Four was modal for the high
risk families.) These differences, however, offer no meaningful
pattern.

Mothers. The majority of mothers in both groups stayed
in the home; most had five or more children; and most had not
gone beyond grammar school. High risk mothers attended church
more often than did low risk mothers. All high risk mothers had
grandparents who were born in Mexico, and all were politically
moderate by self-description. Low risk mothers were reluctant to
divulge political positions. As concerns their own teen years, low
risk mothers had been involved in church youth activities more
often than had high risk mothers. High risk mothers had begun
working at a later age than had low risk mothers (age fifteen for
high risk mothers as compared to age ten for low risk), and, in
their own eyes, high risk mothers had been considered responsible
young people more often than had low risk mothers. As for their
current interests, low risk mothers enjoyed card playing and reading and disliked movies. A trend among high risk mothers was
for work to be a greater source of pleasure than the family.

Drug histories showed that all mothers tended to avoid
use of the common social or medical drugs. A trend was for high
risk mothers to have tried cigarettes most often, whereas low risk
mothers tried alcohol most often. Barbiturate and tranquilizer
use was also found among the high risk mothers. The high risk
mothers expressed greater dissatisfaction with their health and
reported more persistent illnesses and prescribed medication use
than did low risk mothers. High risk mothers also tended to be
underweight. Low risk mothers, however, had the most frequent
hospitalizations. A strong divergence emerged in views about
remedying distress. Low risk mothers held that counseling and
psychotherapy can help people who have personal problems,

whereas high risk mothers had no faith in such help. Still births and infant deaths were most common among low risk mothers. In connection with social values, low risk mothers considered hippies and black power advocates as threats to the nation, whereas high risk mothers saw communists as threatening.

Fathers. Most fathers in the sample were blue collar workers or laborers who had only grammar school educations (partial or complete). Like their wives, they were Catholic. Although few differences were obtained between fathers, low risk fathers said they were interested in church activities and they had artistic interests more often than did high risk fathers. Low risk fathers disliked gardening, whereas high risk fathers liked gardening or animal husbandry as a hobby. The high risk fathers were sometimes interested in partying, but they were uninterested in card games. Low risk fathers expressed interest in watching sports and in going hunting and fishing; low risk fathers also tended to be interested in adult education and, as opposed to high risk fathers, got their greatest pleasure from their families.

As regards their own childhoods, high risk fathers had difficulty getting along with their parents during their teen years, and they reported having reputations as irresponsible young people. Recent moving violations and a trend toward frequent jail sentences for nontraffic offenses characterized the high risk fathers. Drug histories indicated that only some low risk fathers abstained from alcohol use. The trend was for high risk fathers to engage in tobacco, sedative, and tranquilizer use. Illicit experience with cannabis and the opiates occurred only in the high risk group; illicit amphetamine use occured among both samples, and none of the fathers admitted to having tried hallucinogens.

In connection with social stance, we asked parents to name three great persons of the twentieth century. Two kinds of nominations emerged: conventional figures or persons who held legitimate power or were recognized artistic, social, or religious leaders; and unconventional figures such as revolutionaries, unknowns, or avante garde artists. The low risk fathers nominated conventional figures more often than did high risk fathers. On the forced ranking of groups that pose problems, no significant differences were found.

Children. Histories and description forms were completed for fifty-five low risk offspring and fifty high risk children. For the whole sample, most babies were not planned and, for one-third of the babies, the opposite sex would have been preferred. Labor difficulties (especially long labor) were most frequent among low risk mothers. As regards baby-naming patterns, high risk families named their infants for relatives, whereas low risk families specifically named their child after the mother or father. Low risk mothers described infant allergies in their babies most often and said they combined breast and bottle feeding. High risk mothers used bottle feeding alone. Finicky eating in the teen years was one complaint of high risk mothers, who also punished their children by food deprivation. Although the reported prevalence of childhood illnesses did not differ, the number of accidents and broken bones was greatest in the high risk sample. Low risk mothers (reversing a pattern seen in other family samples) also complained of more allergies in their children than did high risk mothers. Hospitalization was most prevalent for children in the low risk sample. There was a trend for high risk mothers to report nervousness in their children (especially nightmares and insomnia). Low risk mothers complained that their children were too short for their age and described early puberty.

During the month prior to the interview, low risk mothers gave more over-the-counter medicine to their offspring than did high risk mothers. Only high risk mothers had ever given their offspring tranquilizers. High risk mothers also reported glue or gasoline sniffing in their offspring, and half of these mothers said they responded to this practice with indifference. The others were extremely upset. High risk mothers said more often than did low risk mothers that their offspring had tried marijuana, but no mother was extremely upset by this. High risk mothers also reported most hallucinogen use in their children. Low risk children began to do chores around the house at an earlier age than did high risk children. Indeed, only among high risk families did offspring never have to share in the work load. High risk children spent most time watching television both during school terms and during vacations. Low risk mothers more often than high risk mothers did not believe that their children masturbated. Truancy and rowdiness were most prevalent among high risk youngsters. High risk mothers reported that their children were also known for thievery, alcohol problems, and illicit drug use and that, consequently, their children were often in trouble with the police. (Theft and running away were the biggest reasons for police involvement, although some of the mothers' reports were inconsistent on this.)

The high risk mothers tended to indicate reading disabilities in their children. Only low risk mothers noted that their children went to Sunday School even though the parents did not require it. Low risk children were most interested in becoming police officers, whereas high risk children were thought to be strongly opposed to such a career. Interest in illicit drugs occurred in the high risk group, whereas opposition to drug use appeared in the low risk group. According to the mothers, low risk children were interested in the creative arts and in sports and had profound religious experiences. A desire to try new things was prevalent among high risk children. High risk mothers had difficulty in enunciating their hopes for their childrens' futures, whereas low risk mothers spoke of self-fulfillment and becoming a respectable citizen. When comparing their children to others, high risk mothers tend to view their children as less able to meet deadlines, less cautious, more ill, more in need of excitement, and less adequate in their sex roles than are other children. In addition, high risk children were considered only average in reading skills. Low risk mothers emphasized self-confidence and infrequency of boredom in their offspring. Only high risk mothers indicated that they had been too lenient, and they emphasized their own worry, unsureness, and discomfiture in rearing their children. Low risk mothers thought they had been just right on discipline and emphasized that they were relaxed about child rearing and pleased with their children. Low risk mothers reported that there were no difficult stages. In discussions about the greatest pleasure each child has given, the low risk mothers spoke in terms of a natural, humanistic ethic, indicating that their children were natural and free spirited. High risk mothers were uncertain about the pleasures accruing from their children.

FAMILY ORGANIZATION

In the high risk families, the husband had most often decided on the last major purchase; at other times, however, these same families were rather unstructured and said that decision making varied with the task. In child discipline, high risk parents said there was no consistent authority; low risk families tended to agree that disciplinary decisions were shared. High risk parents acknowledged some disagreement between them on disciplining. In discussing how parental disagreements of any kind were handled, low risk parents said they talked them out; high risk families fought or let time pass. When asked specifically about disagreements over child care and child rearing, the high risk parents said they disagreed more frequently than did the low risk parents. During the week prior to the interview, fewer disciplinary incidents occurred in the low risk families than they did in the high risk families. When incidents did occur, low risk mothers said they felt justified in taking the action they did; high risk mothers felt bad about what they had done. The reaction of the children is consonant with this. Low risk children were said to accept discipline, whereas high risk children tended to be defiant.

The age-readiness list was presented to the parents. For boys, low risk parents were less permissive than were high risk parents. Low risk boys were never allowed free choice in regard to belief in God. On drinking rules, free choice varied with the boy. Low risk parents gave boys early choice in their recreation but waited until boys were grown before allowing them to smoke. But high risk parents set marijuana choice at a later age than did low risk parents. For girls, low risk parents never allowed choice of religious beliefs, but they tailored liquor rules to the child. Low risk parents required girls to be mature before allowing cigarettes.

High risk parents agreed that there was a problem child and a good child in the family. (Most often, the second child was the problem, and the first born was the good child.) No differences were found between families on the social values expressed in the problem group scale or in the values parents wanted their children to learn. No differences in respect to the police or the law were noted. For the most part, the families respected the police and the law and sought to convey such attitudes to their offspring. Only among low risk mothers and fathers (in independent agreements) was there a sentiment that children should not be expected to be grateful to their parents. In high risk families there was a sentiment among fathers that children should be punished for using naughty words.

WHOLE FAMILY OBSERVATIONS

One high risk family refused to invite the interviewer to dinner. For the rest of the families, high risk fathers were absent more often than were low risk fathers. Smoking occurred most often in high risk families. Food was urged on diners in the high risk homes but not in the low risk homes; however, only for low risk families did the interviewer describe anyone as actually eating too little or too much. Ratings of parental actions toward the children revealed that low risk fathers shared experiences and feelings, engaged in teaching and guiding behavior, and restricted or curbed undesirable conduct more often than did high risk fathers. High risk fathers often withdrew love or support in the face of some displeasing child. Low risk mothers often joked and were good humored, whereas high risk mothers were commanding or coercing, competing, or nagging and scolding. High risk mothers tended to confuse the child, complained about the child to others, withdrew emotionally, submitted to the child, and unduly blamed herself during exchanges. Children were not described as behaving differently. Mothers, however, were rated differently, the high risk ones being sad and depressed, overactive or manic and the low risk ones being helpful and interested. Parental relationships were rated as pleasant in the low risk families and unpleasant in the high. Irritability between high risk mothers and fathers was particularly noted as was their inability to communicate. Inactivity characterized the high risk fathers.

HOME OBSERVATIONS

Children in low risk families helped with the housekeeping, but in high risk homes, the mother did the housekeeping herself. Few packs of cigarettes were seen in the low risk homes, and these families reported buying few cartons of cigarettes. The high risk houses had most aspirin and cough syrup in the medicine chest but tended to have few vitamins on hand. Low risk families reported giving most laxatives to children, but high risk families had most laxatives on hand. As for prescription drugs at the time of the medicine chest count, most prescriptions were being taken by low risk mothers and fathers. At the end of the family and home observations, all parents were asked what else we might have done in our interviewing and work. Low risk families had fewest suggestions and were, by implication, least critical.

REPORTS OF CHILDREN OVER THIRTEEN

Thirty-four youngsters in their teens or early twenties in each set of families were interviewed. (More low risk children than high risk children were in their midteens, whereas most high risk offspring were over twenty-two.) High risk youngsters reported most often that they were not living with one of their biological parents, and more high risk youngsters than low risk youngsters had grown up in the absence of their biological father. Among low risk children, the absence of political preferences was most marked. Low risk children tended to hold the adamant anti-drug stance of their parents, but those who were already using reported the disapproval of their parents. High risk youngsters most often said their parents approved tobacco use. The drug histories showed that regular alcohol use as well as worries about use were most prevalent among the high risk youngsters. Escapist alcohol use and other drinking problems (amnesia, heavy drinking) were greatest among high risk children. Only among high risk children was the father identified as an alcoholic. Tobacco use was also greatest among high risk youngsters. As regards illicit drugs, high risk children had greatest experience with amphetamines, intravenous use, sedatives, tranquilizers, cannabis, hallucinogens, opiates, cocaine, and special substances. Such use also occurred among low risk youngsters, but the high risk of offspring were highest on frequency, tolerance, and bad trips.

Table 6 sets forth the prevalence of specific bad outcomes from each of the social and illicit psychoactives, along with the proportion of youths over thirteen who reported use and bad out-

Table 6

Nonprescription Drug Use and Bad Outcomes Reported by Youth
in High and Low Risk Mexican-American Families, in Per Cent

Drug: Low Risk (N = 34);   High Risk (N = 34)

Alcohol: Low risk experience, 88%;   High risk, 98%

Bad Outcome of Users	Low Risk	High Risk
Car accident	0	31
Job loss	0	6
Severe discipline	0	19
Felony offense	0	6
Jail	0	16
Trouble with friends or relatives	0	16
Physical injury	0	6
Unconsciousness	0	9
Hospitalization	0	9
Loss of self-control	0	16
Sexual difficulty	0	3
Serious study problems	0	3
Hallucinations	0	3
Worried about overuse	0	3

Tobacco: Low risk experience, 67%;   High risk, 79%

Illicit Amphetamines: Low risk experience, 15%;   High risk, 62%

Bad Outcome of Users	Low Risk	High Risk
Bad trips	0	48
Car accidents	0	5
Job loss	0	5
Severe discipline	0	19
Jail	0	10
Trouble with friends or relatives	0	14
Serious illness	0	14
Hospitalization	0	10
Chronic trouble thinking	0	14
Loss of self-control	0	10
Sexual difficulty	0	5
Serious study problems	0	14
Hallucinations	0	10
Serious mental disorder	0	10
Worried about overuse	0	19

Illicit Sedatives: Low risk experience, 27%;   High risk, 52%

Bad Outcome of Users	Low Risk	High Risk
Severe discipline	0	12
Jail	0	12

Table 6 (cont.)

Nonprescription Drug Use and Bad Outcomes Reported by Youth
in High and Low Risk Mexican-American Families, in Per cent (cont.)

Illicit Sedatives: Low risk experience, 27%; High risk, 52% (cont.)

	Low Risk	High Risk
Trouble with friends or relatives	0	10
Loss of self-control	0	6
Serious study problems	0	6

Illicit Tranquilizers: Low risk experience, 10%; High risk, 32%

Bad Outcome of Users	Low Risk	High Risk
Severe discipline	0	20
Trouble with friends or relatives	0	10
Hospitalization	0	10
Loss of self-control	0	10
Serious study problems	0	10

Cannabis: Low risk experience, 15%; High risk, 80%

Bad Outcome of Users	Low Risk	High Risk
Severe discipline	0	8
Felony	0	8
Trouble with friends or relatives	0	12
Loss of self-control	0	4
Serious study problems	0	4
Hallucinations	0	8
Worried about overuse	0	8

Hallucinogens: Low risk experience, 3%; High risk, 44%

Bad Outcome of Users	Low Risk	High Risk
Car accidents	0	7
Job loss	0	14
Severe discipline	0	7
Felony	0	7
Jail	0	7
Other accidents	0	7
Trouble with friends or relatives	0	14
Physical injury	0	14
Unconsciousness	0	14
Serious illness	0	7
Hospitalization	0	14
Chronic trouble thinking	0	21
Loss of self-control	0	14
Serious study problems	0	21
Suicide attempt	0	7
Undesired hallucinations	0	50
Serious mental disorder	0	14
Worried about overuse	0	43

Opiates: Low risk experience, 0%; High risk, 41%

Bad Outcome of Users	Low Risk	High Risk
Job loss	0	15
Severe discipline	0	8
Felony	0	8
Jail	0	8
Other accidents	0	8
Trouble with friends or relatives	0	15
Physical injury	0	8
Unconsciousness	0	8
Serious illness	0	8
Hospitalization	0	8
Chronic trouble thinking	0	8
Loss of self-control	0	8
Sexual difficulty	0	15
Serious study problems	0	8
Undesired hallucinations	0	8
Serious mental disorder	0	8
Worried about overuse	0	39

Cocaine: Low risk experience, 0%; High risk, 15%

Bad Outcome of Users	Low Risk	High Risk
Job loss	0	20
		(1/5 users)
Severe discipline	0	20
Trouble with friends or relatives	0	20
Serious illness	0	20
Chronic trouble thinking	0	20
Loss of self-control	0	20
Serious study problems	0	20
Undesired hallucinations	0	40
Serious mental disorder	0	20
Worried about overuse	1	20

Special Substances (sniffing): Low risk experience, 12%; High risk, 50%

Bad Outcome of Users	Low Risk	High Risk
Severe discipline	0	12
Felony	0	25
Physical injury	0	12
Sexual difficulty	0	6

comes. One cannot be sure that youngsters correctly diagnosed their difficulties or knew themselves what they had taken. Prevalence (the overall occurrence of outcomes without regard to the number of bad outcomes per using) is in itself only a rough measure of risk. With these qualifications in mind, one can say that unpleasant outcomes, although by no means the rule, do occur. The greatest variety of such outcomes were reported for amphetamines, hallucinogens, opiates, and cocaine. The highest prevalence of any bad outcome occurred with amphetamines (bad trips), hallucinogens and cocaine (hallucinations), alcohol (car accidents), and opiates (dependency worries).

Youngsters' reports about the drug use of their siblings were consistent with direct interview data. High risk youngsters reported more sibling use of tobacco, alcohol, marijuana, hallucinogens, amphetamines, opiates, and special substances than did low risk youngsters. (Sedative and tranquilizer enquiries were not made.) Few differences were found in children's reports of age readiness rules. The trend was for low risk boys to report early ages for free choice on church attendance, belief in God, drinking, hair styles, vocational choice, sexual intercourse, manners, keeping their own room, and respecting the police. (Many low risk children said, however, that respect for the police is never a matter of the child's choice.) Low risk boys reported, a late age for choice or no choice at all for LSD use. The trend was for low risk girls to report early free choice for what to wear, church attendance, belief in God, how to spend their own money, manners, room housekeeping, hair styles, and respect for the police. (Again, respect for police is bimodal since some low risk children said it was not a matter of choice.) High risk children said their parents would disapprove of what they had done sexually (implying either looseness in the children or perceived stern morality in the parents). High risk children also believed that their parents considered masturbation abnormal; however, in this regard, high risk children and their parents disagreed. High risk children and high risk parents tended to agree that there was a problem child in the family (usually the second born).

High risk children are less likely than are low risk children to see the father as boss of the family. (This was also the group most likely to have grown up without their biological fathers.) Low risk youngsters said they talked over their problems with their father or with both parents. High risk youngsters tended to be unable to answer the question. When asked to rank the basic values important to learn, low risk children gave primacy to belief in God, health, strength, and love of one's parents. They gave low priority to love of country or to being a success. Considering goals in child rearing, low risk children gave a rather high priority to giving the child a happy childhood, and a low ranking to instilling the ideals of great men of the past.

YOUNG CHILDREN

Fifteen children twelve years of age or younger were seen in the low risk families, and eleven children were seen in the high risk ones. They were asked, in particular, what families of illicit drug-using children were like. Low risk children emphasized poor family relationships, and the reports of these young children were consistent with their siblings' reports on drug use. High risk children said their brothers and sisters smoked a lot and had tried marijuana, hallucinogens, stimulants, opiates, and sniffing compounds. On age readiness rules, low risk boys said that respect for the police and the use of marijuana or LSD were not matters of choice. The same was true for low risk girls. These low risk children also thought children ought to be punished for saying naughty words, teenagers ought to be grateful to their parents, and children who wet themselves ought to feel ashamed. In the low risk families, parents, young children, and older children agreed there were no problem children in their homes. Again, among high risk children, the trend was to select the second born as the problem child. Young low risk children agreed with the older children that the father ran the household.

COMMENT

Several impressions stand out as we look at the Mexican-American families. For one, a different set of factors is associated with high and low drug risk than one associated with high and low risk in the white middle-class sample or the blue collar black sample. (This will be demonstrated statistically in Chapter Ten.) The distinguishing features in this sample are not socioeconomic since all families are poor. The youngsters differ more markedly than do their parents, whether these differences be in values, conscience, delinquency, or conceptions of the family. A cluster or factor analysis has not been constructed for this data since more families than we were able to sample would be required. We can call attention, however, to themes that run through the families.

The high risk mothers are nearer to their Mexican (peasant) origins and more ritualistic than are low risk mothers. High risk mothers also have a stereotyped view of themselves, show signs of feeling pain and stress, and use drugs more to contain these feelings. We suspect they have had conventional, sheltered upbringings and are less acculturated to the Anglo way and less able to handle the problems in their children than are low risk mothers. They are less insightful or sophisticated than are other mothers, in the sense of understanding their own or other's behavior. Their acceptance of drug use and other delinquent conduct in their young, is probably not an issue of values (as it was in the white middle-class sample) but is a question of fatalism, depression, and surrender. The high risk fathers are more passive, less diversified in their interests, less confident and commanding, less communicative and less acculturated than are low risk fathers. High risk fathers also tend to have drug problems of their own, although these are nothing like the scale of drug use in their offspring.

Low risk families seem to manage child rearing smoothly and have happy relations between parents. Low risk parents allow sharing and free choice in many areas. At the same time, the father is the confident, responsible anchorman with whom people can talk over troubles. In consequence, low risk children have internalized standards and can be allowed to make choices fairly early since the mold is firm and the directions are predictable. Low risk children are cooperative, self-controlled, and discrete in a comparatively well-disciplined environment. Despite the very real problems these low risk mothers face (poverty, lack of education, and sickness), they are sure of themselves and their youngsters and enjoy motherhood. In their reliance on communication and affection, in their sureness about directions and values, in their absolutism vis-à-vis God, law, the police and their own proper role, these low risk Mexican-American families very much resemble the white middle-class low risk families. Unlike the middle-class Anglos (where differences in values are primary determinants of their children's illicit drug use), the Mexican-American families do not hold differing values regarding politics, permissiveness, drugs, or authority. In the Mexican-American families, the determining factor is in the ability of the families to impart the values they hold. In the confident, harmonious family, the teaching is done early and few pathological outcomes are seen. In the high risk family, the teaching job does not get done; the problems are ingrained, and the social, psychological, and medical outcomes disrupt everyone for years. The high risk white middle-class parent gets essentially what he thought he wanted, although a neurotic process may also intrude. The high risk Mexican-American parent, however, does not get what he wanted insofar as his child's beliefs and conduct are concerned.

Neither theory nor data allow us to conclude that the differences in the children are solely due to what happens in the family. Yet the children are different, and the families also are run quite differently. The high risk families have more television, more cigarettes, shorter meals, more conflicts, more school troubles, more delinquency outside the home, more undesired behavior in the home, more food problems, more accidents (probably due to carelessness, curiosity, and seeking excitement), more children with nightmares and nervousness, and less helping around the house than do the low risk families. The high risk families are, in fact, in trouble every day. The facts that two-thirds of the high risk children thirteen years of age and over use amphetamines, that over one-third have had real troubles from drinking, that almost one-quarter fear their own overuse of hallucinogens, and that two-fifths have played with heroin come as no surprise. Such behavior may be expressions of the family plight which is individualized and reverberates within the family creating more problems that cannot be handled by nervous, fatalistic mothers or by passive, bickering, inept, or tyrannical fathers. Nevertheless, California delinquency career data suggest that many of these troubled Mexican-American youths may not only survive but also settle down.

SUMMARY

    Ten Mexican-American high risk families and ten low
risk families were seen. All families were poor and shared similar
cultural values. Those families where drug use among offspring
was low had insightful, confident, flexible, and affectionate
mothers and active, communicative, and authoritative fathers
who had diverse interests. Low risk children had early and strict
standards for conduct which allowed parents to give children freedom in deciding for themselves. Life in low risk families was
family-centered. The high risk families did not succeed in impart-
ing values. High risk mothers were more upset, less acculturated
to Anglo ways, and more ritualistic than were low risk mothers.
High risk mothers also could not rely upon themselves, their
husbands, their children, or their church to be the pillars of
strength in an environment filled with temptation, poverty and
uncertainty. The high risk family was discordant, undirected,
unhappy, attached to television, drugs, or the appeals of excitement in the outside world. The high risk drug use of Mexican-
American children was associated with a history of maternal
distress, child distress, school problems, police problems, and family disorders. Low risk families have bent a little but kept much,
accommodating to Anglo ways without accepting the worst of
those ways and keeping the strength of their own family-centered
tradition. The high risk families have lost both battles: they have
not accommodated in some ways; yet their children have become
loose, and the traditions have become hollow.

Statistical Prediction
of Drug Risk

❧ 10 ❧

The middle class family study is based on a very extensive interview with 102 families. The parts of the interview that concern us here are the first five sections which are answered by the parents and the sixth section which is an observer's assessment of the physiological aspects of the family home. Enquiries in these sections relate to social habits, attitudes, and history and parent-child relationships. The connection between the interview responses and the children's drug use, was analyzed and quantified by an objective score. Families were ranked by the drug usage score of their children and then split into three groups: low drug use (group I), medium drug use (group II), and high drug use (group III). Group I had thirty-three families; group II had twenty-nine families; and group III had thirty-nine families. For individual questions, a statistical analysis was carried out on the group versus response data which served to identify questions whose responses were related to a family's drug use.

171

In the present chapter, we shall describe an overall study of the interview responses in connection with the drug score groups.

Since groups I and III are clearly separated on drug scores, let us examine their responses and ask how items may predict low or high drug use for any given family. In statistical language, we are searching for various combinations of questions that discriminate between groups I and III; the best combination, will be the best predictor. Originally, most questions evoked a qualitative response; we made these quantitative by ordering responses according to ranks (1, 2, . . .). Each question thereby becomes a variable, whose value for any family is the quantitative measure of their response. Each family had a set, or vector, of numbers derived from their responses to each question; the set of questions could be considered a vector variable. The combinations of questions used in constructing group discriminators (predictors) are then linear combinations of the vector variable; and the analysis of these combinations was based on the response averages in each group, the variability of response, and the correlations between responses to different questions.

Our approach to the statistical analysis [1] was determined in large part by the fact that there were over three hundred questions or variables and only thirty-three and thirty-nine families in groups I and III, respectively. (A reliable statistical analysis would require considering only about fifteen questions or variables simultaneously.) Of the 300 questions, we selected 176, omitting those that produced no difference in response between groups I and III and keeping those that seemed interesting and important. We analyzed each of the six interview-schedule sections separately and combined the analyses afterwards.[2] That is, we found a discriminator for each section and then combined the discriminators. The merit of this approach is that different sections or types of questions may be discussed separately. The six sections and the corresponding numbers of questions were: (1) family description (eighteen questions); (2) family study, mother (41) and father (40); (3) child description (thirteen); (4) family

[1] One good basic reference for statistical procedures is Morrison (1967).
[2] With very large amounts of data this would not be an optimal procedure, unless the responses in different sections were uncorrelated.

organization; mother (twelve), father (twelve), and (5) family observation (fifteen); and (6) home observation (eight). Natural subsections occurred in the second and fourth sections. In each case, both mother and father answered a set of questions individually. (In the second section, the mother was asked about abortions and stillbirths, which gave her one extra question.) This gave seven categories from sections 1, 3, 4, 5, and 6 with less than twenty questions or variables but left two large categories from section 2. We therefore split section 2 into the following eight categories: (i) mother's background, (ii) father's background, (iii) mother's present activities, (iv) father's present activities, (v) mother's drug use, (vi) father's drug use, (vii) mother's present attitudes, and (viii) father's present attitudes. These categories all had less than fifteen questions. We were left, then, with the following fifteen categories: 1, 2 (i through viii), 3, 4 (i through iii), 5, and 6. Categories 2(i) through 2(iv) represent background and present attitudes for the mother; 2 (v) through 2(viii) represent background and present attitudes for the father. Category 4 represents family organization in regard to the mother, the father, and both parents.

Let us now outline how we analyzed data for each of the fifteen categories. In groups I and III we have N_I and N_{III} families, where N_I and N_{III} can be less than thirty-three and thirty-nine, if some families did not respond fully to the interview category under analysis. Each family has a vector $\underset{\sim}{x} = (x_1, \ldots, x_q)$ of q responses to q questions. From these we can summarize the data for the category by the two group averages (that is, average response to each question for both groups separately) and the two group covariance matrices. The difference between groups is represented by the differences between average responses to each question. The group covariance matrices measure correlation between responses to different questions and standard errors of response to each question. We expect the two group covariances to be similar, and, after verifying this from the data, the two are combined. We then use the averages and covariances to choose weights $l_1 \ldots l_q$ for each response so that the weighted sum $L = l_1 x_1 + \ldots + l_q x_q$ discriminates best between groups I and III, in the sense of maximizing statistical significance of difference between averages of L in the two groups.[3] The analysis also indicates a number A such that, if L is computed for a given family, we predict group I (low risk) for a numerical value of L less than A, and group III (high risk) otherwise.

It should be stressed that the coefficients l_1 . . . l_q are best for discriminating between the families in the study; we do not have full information about other families. However, the discrimination should not be much less powerful when applied to families with similar backgrounds and similar drug habits. Once the linear discriminant L is computed we get a standardized measure of distance between groups I and III for that set of questions, which we shall call D.[4] The value of D can be tested statistically to see if there is a significant difference between groups I and III on the basis of the particular set or category of questions. It is useful at this point to give the D-values for our fifteen categories in Table 7 since these values measure the estimated effectiveness of the discriminators for each category. The last column shows whether D indicates a significant between-group difference at the 5 per cent level. Note that most categories do not have responses differing significantly from group I to group III. The larger the value of D in the table, the better that category is for discriminating between groups.

We calculated linear discriminant weights for each of the fifteen categories and applied them to the families used in the analysis. Table 8 gives the proportions of misclassifications for families in groups I and III for each questionnaire category. Low misclassification rates are associated with large values of D. One point that must be emphasized is that we should expect higher misclassification rates when one uses these discriminants to predict drug risk in unknown families because we do not have all the information relevant to all families in this study. Hence, the reliability of the preceding analysis is in question. In an attempt to assess reliability, we repeated the discriminant analysis for cate-

---

[3] The method of calculating the weights l_1 . . . l_q is described by Morrison (1967).

[4] D is the squared difference of the two group averages of L divided by the squared standard error of L. The use of D in testing significance of between-group differences is described by Morrison (1967).

gories 1, 3, 4(i), 4(ii), 4 (iii), and 6, using only nineteen families in group I and twenty-six families in group III. The resulting linear discriminants were used to classify the remaining families. Table 9 shows the proportions of misclassifications for each of these six categories. Comparison of this table with Table 8 gives some

Table 7

Between Group Distance Measures for Each of the Fifteen Categories of Responses

Category	Group I Sample Size (N_I)	Group III Sample Size (N_{III})	Number of Responses (q)	Between-Group Distance (D)	Statistically Significant at 5% level
1	33	39	18	2.37	Yes
2 (i)	33	39	8	0.92	No
2 (ii)	33	39	10	1.19	No
2 (iii)	33	39	9	1.26	No
2 (iv)	33	39	13	1.22	No
2 (v)	28	38	8	0.83	No
2 (vi)	28	38	10	1.30	No
2 (vii)	28	38	9	0.66	No
2 (viii)	28	38	13	1.55	No
3	33	39	13	2.02	Yes
4 (i)	29	38	12	1.44	No
4 (ii)	29	38	12	1.17	No
4 (iii)	29	38	15	0.66	No
5	29	31	16	2.03	Yes
6	31	39	8	1.86	No

indication of the false assurance of Table 8. In any event, good discrimination is not forthcoming when using individual categories. Improved performance is attained when we combine the categories to obtain an overall discriminant or classification procedure.

One simple way to combine the information is to look at all the linear discriminants L for each family. As an example, suppose we ignore section 2 for the moment. For the remaining seven categories, we have the corresponding seven linear discriminants $L_1 \ldots L_7$. In each case, we classify a family as group I if L_j is less than some determined number A_j; otherwise, we

Table 8

Proportions of Group I and Group III Families
Misclassified by Linear Discriminant (L)
for Each of the Fifteen Categories

Questionnaire Category	Proportion of Group I Families Misclassified	Proportion of Group III Families Misclassified
1	7/33	1/39
2 (i)	11/33	14/39
2 (ii)	12/33	9/39
2 (iii)	7/33	12/39
2 (iv)	7/33	12/39
2 (v)	13/28	13/38
2 (vi)	7/28	12/38
2 (vii)	14/28	8/38
2 (viii)	5/28	12/38
3	9/33	5/39
4 (i)	7/29	11/38
4 (ii)	8/29	10/38
4 (iii)	10/29	12/38
5	6/29	10/31
6	5/31	14/39

Table 9

Proportions of Misclassifications of Group I
and Group III Families Not Used in
Constructing Linear Discriminants

Questionnaire Category	Proportion of Group I Families Misclassified	Proportion of Group III Families Misclassified
1	2/14	5/13
3	4/14	8/13
4 (i)	2/12	6/13
4 (ii)	4/12	8/13
4 (iii)	8/12	6/13
6	4/13	6/13

classify it as group III. Then, in order to combine the seven classification procedures we could say: if L_j is less than A_j for at least four categories, classify the family as group I; otherwise, classify as group III. We have done this for the families in the study, and

Table 10 compares predicted groups with actual groups. Table 10 is based on the distributions of the number of misclassifications

Table 10

Actual Versus Predicted Groups, Using Seven
Discriminants Simultaneously

| | | Predicted group | |
		I	III
	I	34	4
Actual group			
	III	5	24

shown in Table 11. The improvement from combining the discriminants into a single procedure is due to the simple fact that, if a family is misclassified from one category, it is still likely to

Table 11

Distribution of Number of Misclassifications
Out of Seven Classifications for
Groups I and III

Number of misclassifications	0	1	2	3	4	5	6
Group I families	10	7	8	9	3	1	1
Group III families	6	8	7	3	3	1	0

be correctly classified from some other category. This is statistical justice in evidence! The misclassification rates in the preceding combined procedure are less than 20 per cent, and section 2 of the questionnaire was ignored. In an efficient combination of the fifteen categories, we would then expect to get misclassification rates quite a bit lower than 20 per cent, at least for the families in the study. We have not attempted to combine all fifteen categories into such a classification procedure. A similar joint prediction approach can be used in the situation described prior to Table 8, where predictors for six categories were determined from a subset of the families and then applied to the remaining families. The result is that seven out of twenty-five families are misclassified. This is roughly twice the proportion obtained in Table 9, where predictors were determined from all the families and then applied to those same families.

At this point in the discussion, we should try to appraise our progress and the worth of our complicated analysis. We have already tried to describe how well our linear discriminants classify families, but the responses to individual questions can be examined to see if any small set of them will do as well in predicting drug risk. From the whole questionnaire, we selected thirteen questions whose responses indicate predictive power. The responses have been dichotomized objectively, where necessary, for ease of presentation here. The question topics and possible (dichotomized) responses are: (1) estimated annual family income (less than $25,-000, more than $25,000); (2) mother's present church attendance (no, yes); (3) mother's choice for president in 1968 (Republican or Wallace, Democrat); (4) mother's young involvement in religious activities (no, yes); (5) mother's present frequency of alcohol use (once a week or less, more than once a week); (6) mother's ranking of student activists among twelve groups posing social problems (rank 1 through 4, rank lower than 4); (7) father's present occupation (professional, artistic or creative, other); (8) father's present church attendance (no, yes); (9) father's present frequency of alcohol use (once a week or less, more than once a week); (10) parents' views of their children's interest in becoming a police officer (no child opposed, at least one child opposed); (11) mother's ranking of belief in God in a list of twelve personal values (rank 1 through 4, rank lower than 4); (12) father's ranking of belief in God in a list of twelve personal values (rank 1 through 4, rank lower than 4); and (13) alcohol served before dinner with interviewer present (no, yes).

The frequencies of each response to each question in both groups are given in Table 12. For each two-by-two subtable, the first row corresponds to the first possible response (for example, "no" for question [2]), and the second row corresponds to the second possible response. Columns one and two in the subtables corresponds to group I and group III families, respectively. Thus, for question 2, sixteen out of thirty-three (sixteen plus seventeen) group I mothers and twenty-six out of thirty-nine (twenty-six plus thirteen) group III mothers do not presently attend church. In

Table 12

Response Frequencies for Thirteen Selected Questions
in Groups I and III

(1)	24	18		(2)	16	26		(3)	23	15
	9	21			17	13			10	24

(4)	9	21		(5)	22	14		(6)	16	13
	24	18			11	25			17	26

(7)	11	28		(8)	17	31		(9)	14	9
	17	10			11	7			14	29

(10)	24	13		(11)	19	8		(12)	17	9
	9	26			10	30			11	29

(13)	17	10
	12	22

the linear predictor based on these thirteen questions, the weights attached to each response were approximately constant, except for questions 5, 10, and 1, where responses were weighted roughly three times as much as the others; the distance measure D between groups was 4.0. Application of this linear predictor to the families in the study gave the results in Table 13.

Table 13

Actual Versus Predicted Groups, Using
Thirteen Selected Questions

		Predicted group	
		I	III
Actual group	I	23	5
	III	3	28

We have shown that we can get excellent internal consistency by picking out thirteen variables (questions) that look good. Recall that the best individual category for prediction was section 1, which gave misclassification rates of approximately 20 per cent. (See Table 8.) Also, simultaneous application of discriminants from seven categories gave misclassification rates of approximately 14 per cent. Returning to the linear discriminants L for each of the fifteen categories, we now consider these as fifteen aggregated responses or variables. Using all the data available (that is, responses from all families), we derived an overall linear discriminant which was then used to classify those same families. The results are given in Table 14. Correlations between the cate-

Table 14

Actual Versus Predicted Groups, Using
Discriminant From Fifteen Individual
Category Discriminants

		Predicted group	
		I	III
Actual group	I	25	3
	III	0	31

gory discriminants were quite low (0.2 or less in magnitude). The estimated distance measure D was 13.5. (Compare Table 7.) These last results are, of course, exaggerated by applying the discriminant to data on which it is based. To assess external consistency, we derived a linear discriminant from the first forty-five families and applied it to the remainder. The results are shown in Table 15.

The discriminant does very well for the families on which it is based and misclassifies about 20 per cent of the rest. The overall discriminant will take account of the four group III families misclassified here and therefore should do well as a predictor. One would suspect that, with all the data, a misclassification rate

Table 15

Actual Versus Predicted Groups, Using Discriminant
From Forty-five Families' Values of Fifteen
Category Discriminants[a]

		Predicted group				Predicted group	
		I	III			I	III
Actual group	I	16	1	Actual group	I	11	0
	III	0	21		III	4	6
		(a)				(b)	

[a] (a) = families used in calculating discriminant weights; (b) = families not used in calculating discriminant weights.

of 15 per cent or less should be anticipated for families similar to those in this study. Using all 176 questions, we find that the distance between groups I and III is 13.5, compared with about 4.0 for the thirteen hand-picked questions. These thirteen questions, therefore, contain a disproportionate amount of discriminating power. Their use in a linear discriminant leads to a fairly low misclassification rate, probably around 20 per cent. Misclassifications are approximately halved by simultaneously considering an additional 163 questions.

In order to get two distinct groups for our analysis, we omitted twenty-nine families whose drug scores put them in group II (medium drug use). It is of interest to apply the previously discussed classification scores to this group of twenty-nine families. Using the thirteen-question classification score, we calculated the twenty-nine families' scores and compared them with the objective drug scores. The association does not appear to be strong, although it is in the right direction (high drug score, low discriminant score). The discriminants, or predictors, have also been applied to families with dissimilar backgrounds (ten black families, ten Mexican-American families, and ten lower-class white families) without success. This was due only in part to the economic factor appearing in our discriminants.

MOTHER-FATHER AGREEMENT

Some interesting side results were produced from the fif-teen-category analyses. In breaking up sections 2 and 4, we arrive at categories which include both mother's and father's responses on some sets of questions: mother, 2(i) through 2(iv) and 4(i); father, 2(v) through 2(viii) and 4 (ii). Therefore, we can measure the mother-father correlation on those five sets of questions for group I and III. If for any set of q questions there is total mother-father correlation on every question, the q correlations add up to q. Hence, one crude measure of family agreement is the average of those q correlations. We computed this measure for each of the five sets of questions where mothers' and fathers' responses were available. In each case except one, we obtained values near 0.2 for both groups—the moderate exception being the average correlation of 0.4 between categories 2 (i) and 2(v) in group III. In these latter categories, there is a large difference between groups I and III with regard to the question "At what age did you begin to work at least halftime?" Mother-father correlations of −0.4 and +0.4, respectively, were obtained. Thus, with the possible exception of this one item, mother-father disagreement on questions in section 2 does not appear to be predictive of children's drug risk.

SUMMARY

A discriminant analysis procedure was applied to the family data to determine which, if any, combinations of interview sections could best predict whether a child's drug risk score would be low or high. Using 176 items drawn from all sections, one achieves, on a split-half basis, thirty-seven correct and one incor-rect predictions. After cross-validating, one obtains seventeen cor-rect and four incorrect predictions. Using these same 176 items to predict low or high drug risk from family characteristics in unknown middle-class families, one would expect to predict cor-rectly about 80 per cent of the time. A short-form predictor with thirteen selected interview items was developed and found to be quite accurate. (In predicting back to the data, fifty-one correct and eight incorrect predictions occurred.) Using these thirteen items alone, one would estimate that correct prediction of children's low or high drug risk can be achieved in 75 per cent of unknown middle-class families.

The interview sections describing family characteristics contained the most powerful predictors. Review of the thirteen-item discriminant suggests that factors most strongly associated with children's drug risk have to do with family income, family political preferences, mother's and father's religiosity, mother's and father's alcohol use, mother's acceptance of youthful self-expression and rebelliousness, the hierarchy of family values, and the rejection or acceptance of authority by the child as viewed by the parents. The predictors which work for the middle class do not work when tested in blue collar (white or black) families or Mexican-American families. This suggests that at least some of the factors that are associated with drug risk differ by socioeconomic class and ethnocultural setting.

We believe the analysis has shown that information available within the family and pertaining to parental beliefs and conduct allows rather satisfactory predictions of children's drug risk as defined in this study. Family assessments from discriminants identified here should be useful not only in the immediate task of estimating children's drug use but also in identifying those values and modes of conduct which are associated with complex sociopsychological behavior by the child. The availability of relatively simple and reliable procedures for estimation and analysis leads us to conclude that research on family variables affecting behavior is rewarding.

Hippie Families

❧ 11 ❧

The present study would not be complete without reference to hippies and flower children—an extreme group of families whose conduct centered public attention on the drug scene and preceded widespread youthful interest in illicit psychoactive agents. Since hippies' parents ought to exemplify parental styles, values, and practices conducive to children's drug use, we set out to gather a sample of hippie parents with young children. We anticipated that we would learn most about hippie families if we compared high versus low risk families within the same social class and environment. In this work the "class" was hippie and the environment was the Haight-Ashbury district of San Francisco. At the time we began our work there was concern over the possible teratogenicity of LSD (Dishotsky, Loughman, Mogar, and Lipscomb, 1971; Aurebach and Rugowski, 1967). Consequently, our original definition of risk was based on LSD use by mothers during pregnancy. We wondered whether the mother who used LSD during pregnancy would have offspring with either developmental or psychological damage or deficit. (Developmental damage could not be attributed to LSD use itself because the life style of such mothers might contain many elements which would be pathogenic for the developing fetus. If, however, such damage was not found in a sample of mothers using LSD during pregnancy, one could be somewhat less alarmed than before by the reports of teratogenic effects in animals—R. Auerbach, 1971; Alexander and others, 1967.) Inquiry after psychological damage or deficit was based on the question of whether mothers who took LSD during pregnancy were not less cautious and less adequate personally than were mothers who did not take LSD. The assumption was that LSD abstinence during pregnancy is part of maternal self-care for the child's sake—conduct which would indicate judgment and self-control.

Questions of babies' ages, timing, and knowledge complicated the test of risk. In the first place most flower children of the 1965-on period could not have been expected, by the time our work began in 1968, to have married or had children. Certainly those who had would not have older children, except those few older folk who were members of the beat generation or other marginal groups who transmigrated to the hippie scene and donned that role. As a consequence, our measure of risk had to apply to an infant or young child. Timing complicated the risk question because mothers who were pregnant before the teratogenicity issue became public (Cohen, Marinello, and Black, 1967) had no reason to abstain from hallucinogen use nor can we assume that everyone conceiving after 1967 could have been informed about potential risk. For these initial reasons, we considered our risk variable to be a weak one; we expected to learn most about hippie mothering and about childrearing in general.

Since we were to be working with infants and young children, our curiosity about risk required outcome measures for developmental and psychological damage and deficit. We decided on direct measures of child development and intelligence and on an evaluation by a child psychiatrist. We had also hoped to complete full neurological examinations in a nearby medical center, but that could not be arranged. We settled for psychological testing and gross neurological observations by the psychiatrist. In infancy, development and intellectual tests bear close relationship to neurological status (Paine and Oppé, 1966). Parents were evaluated as well. However, since our emphasis was on the mother and since hippie families may be communal, polypaternal, or unstable, we did not require the presence of a father or his evaluation, except in passing. The evaluation of the mother required a different measure than that used in other family studies. For one thing, our mothers and their children were young and had not had some of the experiences we inquired about in the other studies (for instance, they could not tell us how they handled age readiness rules in childhood or teen years). Furthermore, our hippie families were very casual groups who reacted badly to rigorous forms of enquiry. Their cooperation was not easily obtained even with casual-appearing methods. We also learned that we could not rely on all the replies of mothers. If a question seemed irrelevant or boring, mothers might invent answers or mix fact with fancy. To enlist systematic cooperation, we provided mothers with an infant diary containing horoscopes and psychedelic graphics; they were to use the diary to record the baby's progress and their own reactions. The diary entries were incorporated in the psychiatric evaluation.

It also became evident that finding controls would be difficult and that the LSD risk concept was a poor one. Almost all the hippie mothers whom we met said they had used hallucinogens during pregnancy. Some had conceived while both parents were stoned; some delivered while enjoying LSD as an anesthetic; and some nursed while taking LSD (contending that the nursing infant was turned on that way, which may be the case) (Idanpään-Heikkilä, Schoolar, and Alton, 1970). Some mothers gave the baby LSD. In addition, some mothers could not accurately report what they had been using even if they knew. Some who were chronically intoxicated—for example using LSD weekly, hashish daily, and opium in between with amphetamines "now and then"—could hardly be expected to distinguish what they had taken during the first three months of pregnancy, even if they knew what they had taken yesterday. Even if mothers think they know what they had used, they could be mistaken since street drugs are notoriously mislabeled and adulterated (J. P. Smith in Blum and associates, 1972b). It was unwise to accept as fully accurate retrospective accounts. Other investigators, Stubbs and Jacobson (1968–1969) and Jacobson, Arias-Bernal, Vosbeck, DelRiego, Ahearn, and Magyar (1970), using nonhippie mothers faced similar difficulties. They attempted to surmount them by following expectant mothers from the beginning of prenatal care.

We did find a few mothers who said they had not used hallucinogens during pregnancy (some for fear of teratogenic effects). However, when we learned that some of those same mothers had used cannabis, chipped heroin, and drank considerable amounts of wine each day, we felt rather foolish worrying about the LSD risk alone. Opiates, alcohol, aspirin, tranquilizers, barbiturates, and meperidine used during pregnancy may all effect the neonate (Brazelton, 1970).

Case finding and project continuity were also difficult tasks. Some of our families were vagabonds who disappeared by the time the psychiatrist or psychologist arrived. Several were in flight from the police. One mother was sought by the police as a dealer, and another dealing family had been threatened with death by their supplier. Drugs advanced to them on credit had been stolen. Thus, the definition of a family was not always easy. We did require that the biological mother and her child be central, but it was impossible to require an intact family. About half the time, the biological father was present; sometimes a drop-in or social father was present instead. Sometimes, several women shared in the mothering—a pattern we called polymaternal, or polypaternal if several fathers shared the fathering. Working in such an environment was informal, and our research suffered from these effects of the environment also. In any event, through the utilization of hippie case-finding aides, we found twenty-three families or mother-child constellations in or near the Haight-Ashbury district in San Francisco. (Families were paid for participation.) These persons looked like hippies, considered themselves to be hippies,[1] used psychoactive drugs extensively, and had one or more babies. Nine of these twenty-three families conformed to our original low risk definition.

One of our investigators, the child psychiatrist, became

[1] The self-description variable is difficult because people move in and out of hippiedom not just from year to year but day to day. They may dress outlandishly Wednesday and sedately Thursday, or may agree they went through a hippie period but now are outgrowing it. One mother strongly dissociated herself from the hippie movement, although she acknowledged similar values; another svelte and sophisticated young woman of upper middle-class background did not fit the scene and was, in fact, thoughtfuly planning a very different future.

pregnant during the course of the study. As her pregnancy became visible, it proved a fine entree to households and the discussion of motherhood and infants. Had work proceeded on schedule the pregnancy would not have interfered, but case finding proved slow, appointment scheduling was hazardous, and families sometimes disappeared or suddenly refused to cooperate. Thus, the step from design to project execution proved not only awkward but, for the majority of our families, impossible. After the delivery of "our" baby, the psychiatric work stopped but we did gather three additional "controls," mothers and babies, who were tested by the psychologist.

Psychiatric evaluations consisted of an average of five home visits (ranging from one to nine) and were completed on eighteen families; developmental and mental tests were done on fifteen children from thirteen families; the National Institute of Mental Health Maternal Behavior Profile was completed on thirteen mothers; and the Bayley Infant Behavior Profile was done on seventeen children.[2] (Two mothers had two children each.) Only ten families out of the original twenty-three cooperated long enough to complete both the psychological and psychiatric work-ups. Testing of families was done in a church in the Haight-Ashbury district since our intent had been to provide a controlled environment for testing; most, but not all, mothers were willing to take their babies to the church.

SAMPLE CHARACTERISTICS

The biological mother and her child were present in every family. In 60 per cent the biological father was also a resident in the household. One-third of the families were polypaternal; about one-fifth were polymaternal. The modal education for fathers was one or two years of college, and for mothers was a high school

[2] The psychologist who tested the children did so blind; that is, she did not know which children were controls and which were not and assumed the distribution was half and half. The psychologist administered the Infant Behavior Profile of the Bayley Scale of Mental Development. The Maternal Behavior Profile was developed by Linda Booth Rapaport for use with the Bayley Infant Behavior Profile. It has not been published as yet.

diploma. Sample members ranged in age from nineteen to thirty-one, with the modal age for fathers and mothers in the twenty- to twenty-five-year-old bracket. Reported education is suspect for some sample members (males particularly) perhaps claimed more education than they actually had. Ninety percent of the families reported incomes of less than five thousand dollars a year; almost all of the mothers were on welfare. Fathers characterized themselves as artists or craftsmen. One-fifth of the fathers were employed at the post office (by far the major employer), and the most usual vocational skill for men was drug dealer. Women said they were housewives, nude models, drug dealers, or seamstresses. Only one family declared a religious preference (Jewish) and claimed to attend church (temple) with any regularity. All other families were irreligious and unaffiliated. All mothers in the sample were white (one partly Oriental) as were most fathers; in one polypaternal setting, a black social father was also present. When asked to describe the occupations of their parents, the modal description by mothers suggested lower middle-class origins. Working-class origins ranked second. Biological fathers indicated upper middle-class origins most often.

A review of self-care and nutrition during pregnancy indicated that, of the eighteen mothers whose reporting appeared reliable, one-third followed insufficient diets for pregnant women. Three mothers unquestionably followed dangerous dietary procedures; one of these mothers stated that she ate what she found in garbage cans. Our controls (the mothers who did not use LSD during pregnancy), along with their husbands or lovers, were older and were apparently better educated than were the others. The one religious couple was in this control group.

All family members (mothers, biological fathers, and social fathers) were multiple users of illicit drugs. All used marijuana or hashish chronically and usually daily, and all used hallucinogens, typically on a weekly or monthly basis. Two-thirds were also users of heroin and/or opium, mostly on a less than daily basis but not compulsively as one would expect with persons defined as addicts. Amphetamine use occurred less extensively than other drug use; sedatives and tranquilizers were not popular. About 10 per cent said they abstained from alcohol, but one-half of the sample reported heavy drinking (four or more glasses of hard liquor each day).

DESCRIPTION OF THE MOTHER

The most succinct descriptions of parents were found in the summary ratings made upon completion of the psychiatric observations. For the eighteen mothers for whom evaluations were completed, the most prevalent mood ratings were: responsive, bland, and flat (in that order). For a minority of these mothers the mood ratings were: sad, depressed, indifferent, slowed, apathetic, weepy, excited, elated, and flighty (in that order). Mood ratings in the area of tension and presentation were for the majority: calm, unruffled, confident, quiet, and carefree. For the minority, mood ratings in this area were: careless, sloppy, anxious, courageous, nervous, fearful, and foolhardy. Interpersonal mood ratings for the majority were: affable, polite, friendly, and warm. A minority were said to be affectionate, loving, hostile, neutral, reserved, and aggressive (in that order).

Activity level ratings for the majority of mothers were average, or normal activity and energy level. For the minority of mothers, low activity levels were twice as frequent as were high activity levels. On the ratings of organization of activity, the majority of mothers were characterized as unsystematic. A bimodal distribution emerged since one-half were rated as orderly, and one-half were rated as disorganized. Only a few were rated as well organized, rigid, or tense. In regard to mothers' approaches to situations and problems, the majority were rated as ordinary; a minority were unimaginative and stereotyped. Only a few were rated as imaginative, original, or boring. The controls were found to be at a low level of energy or activity and were disorganized more often than were other mothers, but no other differences were noted. Focusing on minority traits and looking at features occurring only in a minority of the controls we found that only controls were said to be elated, flighty, nervous, and confused.

Since we did not train for rating reliability but depended upon individual psychiatric evaluation, our rating data may be suspect. For this reason we shall discuss recurring themes in the psychiatric evaluation rather than make an item-by-item analysis. Our impression was that the sample consisted mostly of mothers who retained the social graces, who were interpersonally oriented, attentive, and friendly, but whose affect was subdued, if not flattened. Thus, their visible calm can be interpreted not only as part of a cool, easy, or relaxed ethic, but also as an outward expression of their emotional life. In the same way, their unsystematic qualities are partly an expression of their hang loose or carefree values as well as a symptom of reduced capabilities for emotional investment in their surroundings. As a group, they were ordinary in their approach to topics, problems, and life. Our description is incompatible with what a few of them said about themselves. Some said they were innovative, spontaneous, and artistic. The lack of imagination in most mothers probably reflects an (estimated) average intellectual capability adversely affected by blandness, depression, and low energy levels which we attribute to psychopathological features and possibly to chronic drug effects. We must emphasize that such drug effects were not debilitating for the expression of the primary social orientation of these mothers. Most mothers were friendly and responsive.

The minor differences in ratings between controls and others are not very important. In spite of their claimed caution during pregnancy—limited to abstinence from LSD—controls were not in better or worse psychological health than were other mothers. A second description of mothers was obtained by the psychologist who tested the children. She employed the National Institute of Mental Health Maternal Behavior Profile, which limits its focus to mother-infant interaction. The psychologist had been trained in its use, and so we assume consistency for the psychologist evaluator. Thirteen mothers were rated using this instrument. The ones not rated, but completed for psychiatric evaluation, were more mobile and/or less cooperative than were other mothers. The majority of the rated mothers (8/13) accepted the mothering role—that is, they enjoyed mothering, did it competently, and were attentive to and loved the child. An accepting mother was typically described as friendly, passive, in tune with her child, sensitive, and loving, or, from another profile, as attentive, fussy, tense, in tune with her child, warm, spontaneous, and confident. A nonaccepting mother was hostile to the child, irritable, withdrawn, and did not enjoy the mother role, or, in another case, was accepting but not empathetic to the child, was on a peer level with the infant, and was anxious and inattentive to the child's needs.

Two of five control mothers were evaluated as nonaccepting, and three of the eight other mothers were nonaccepting. Neither statistically nor impressionistically can one derive any difference in the two samples. We can infer, therefore, that reported intentional abstinence from hallucinogen use during pregnancy is not related to the adequacy of mothering. We have little confidence, however, in some of our controls' claims of abstinence.

The overall evaluation by the psychiatrist disagrees somewhat with the psychologist's profile ratings of mothers' behavior with their children. To describe the agreement or disagreement of these two measures, we employed a classification system that considered agreement to exist when the maternal profile yielded a nonaccepting global rating and the psychiatrist emphasized depression, flatness, and the like, or when the psychiatrist did not find affect disorder and the profile rating was positive. Using this global procedure, we found only 30 per cent agreement on the ten families seen to completion both by the psychiatrist and the psychologist. When we compared our profile global rating of accepting with a positive psychiatric evaluation emphasizing interpersonal affability and friendliness, agreement between the two methods went up to 70 per cent. When we examined the two methods for the direction of content (positive or negative), we learned that in every case the psychiatrist described both positive and negative features (friendliness and depression or responsiveness and nervousness). The psychologist using the behavior profile tended toward positive wholistic ratings—that is, only five of ten mothers were described both positively and negatively, whereas three were wholly positive and two were wholly negative in terms of the excellence of mother-baby interaction.

These problems in reliability may reflect differing standards of judgment. Conceivably, mothers acted differently with different evaluators. Most likely, the broad behavior base used by the psychiatrist—who also probed quite intensively—revealed more personal and interpersonal limitation or disorders, than did the instrument used by the psychologist. In contrast, the psychologist concentrated on a short behavior sample of one or two visits. Perhaps these mothers, almost all of whom the psychiatrist described as affable and sociable people, were at their best with their infants. Conversely, perhaps those women whom the child tester considered to be inadequate as mothers functioned best in peer relationships. These latter interpretations are suggested by the content of the descriptions, but the styles of evaluation indicate that some portion of the disagreement is due to the differing standards of the two evaluators.

THE MOTHER WITH HER CHILD AND OTHER FAMILY MATTERS

The psychiatrist's descriptions covered a range of parental behavior from dismally pathological to delightfully warm. We shall not engage in intensive clinical analyses. Instead, we shall let the hippie scene speak for itself and present excerpts from descriptions of six of the twenty-two families or mother-child constellations. We have ranked families into three groups from which cases were selected for presentation. The classifications represent an overall impression of the parents based on the range of behavior within the sample. If the mother was the primary figure evaluated, then the rating reflects what she was like; if the father was evaluated, his behavior is also considered. The classification system serves to order the parents from better to worse. Nine of the twenty-two families were ranked as better; seven were ranked as middle; and six were ranked as worse. Among the five controls, we ranked three families as better and two as worse.

"BETTER" MOTHER-CHILD CONSTELLATIONS OR FAMILIES

The following material is a series of excerpts taken from descriptions of hippie families who were ranked as "better" in their overall range of behavior. Carla and David are hallucinogen users. The mother denies having used amphetamines, sedatives, tranquilizers, antidepressants, opiates, cocaine, or special substances (glue, gasoline, paint thinner). She did use LSD during the first, second, and fifth months of pregnancy. She took STP around the second week and took mescaline once during pregnancy—she does not remember when. She is a regular user of hallucinogens at the present time. She takes them once a month or once every three months, and she reports that David does the same. They also smoke marijuana or hashish every day as a family ritual—a pattern which remained the same during her pregnancy.

They are both drug dealers, but surprisingly, they themselves only use hallucinogens and cannabis. The mother says she needs to experiment with different kinds of experiences. Their use is a token by which they remain in their peer group. They say that using LSD "is groovy," and that "all our friends use it."

Carla and David and their new born daughter live in an old Haight Ashbury house with four male friends. Carla and David occupy the first bedroom which has a small annex that has been converted into a kitchen. The bedroom is very small with only a single bed and a chair. There is also a small cradle that David built for the baby. The walls of the room are painted electric blue, which makes the room dark. The room has no windows, and a rug hangs on one of the walls.

Carla and David live an independent life within the household and pay part of the rent. They do not have meals with the other residents, nor do they share in any of the household duties. Carla keeps the door to their room locked and lets people into it in a very discriminating way. She herself unlocks her door and lets me in when I come; she seems to value her privacy. Nevertheless, her relations with the other boarders seem to be friendly and harmonious.

Carla is nineteen years old and looks like an adolescent boy. Her large aquiline nose, her very thick spectacles, her freckles, pimples, nasal voice, and laughter all contribute to her boyish appearance. Nevertheless, when she moves or handles her daughter, she adopts a distinctively feminine attitude that contrasts with the first impression. On the whole, she is an appealing person.

When pleasantries are said about her daughter she readily accepts them with a joyful smile that ends up in a short nasal laugh, very typical of her. She is of average height and weight and her energy level and general appearance show that she is in good health. Her black greasy hair, however, is always sticky and neglected, and her grooming in general is poor. She often wears old blue jeans and a blouse; only for the last interview and for the test did she wear a feminine, short, straight dress.

Her activity is organized, and she always goes directly towards her goal. She is always surprisingly calm even when threatening events occur in her life, as when her common law husband was caught, imprisoned, and sent back to North Dakota to be judged for draft evasion. During such difficult times she is confident that things are going to end up in a happy way. Her vocabulary is adequate and precise, though she sometimes uses hippie slang that reveals her youthfulness. She never tries to explain or find a meaning to her actions. For example when asked why she chose breast feeding, she shrugged her shoulders and said, "I don't know," or "What does it matter?" She finally said, "I like it." When asked about her reasons for taking hallucinogens, she hesitated a long time before she could give an answer.

Toward the interviewer she was always friendly and cordial in an unconventional way. She never offers anything to drink or eat, but once to show her gratitude for the baby book given her as a gift, she offered the interviewer a kilo of marijuana to take home.

She is always responsive and answers all the questions in a direct way without giving details. Nevertheless she enjoys the situation as shown by her complete relaxation. She never offers information on her own but will occasionally give an explanatory answer. She never challenges the project and is always trusting and secure. She never offers endangering information, but neither does she deliberately hide it. For example, when asked about their means of financial support, she said she was on welfare and that David does different types of unskilled work. She did not say that they also dealt in drugs, but she sold some in the presence of the interviewer without any fear.

Carla comes from a low class Italian family, and her father is a blue-collar worker. She always lived with her parents and her siblings (two sisters and six brothers) in California. She is the second child; the youngest child in the family is three years old.

She describes her family as a happy one and her parents as

permissive, accepting people with whom she has a good relationship. They accept her coming to San Francisco and leading the kind of life she has chosen. She plans to visit them with the baby and her husband soon and expects them to give her a happy welcome home.

Carla dropped out of school shortly before finishing high school in 1967 and decided to come to San Francisco with a girl friend to see what was happening in the city. Soon after she arrived, she met David. They decided to live together, and Carla became pregnant very soon. They were happy when they learned that they would be parents, although they did not particularly plan the pregnancy. In her words, "It just happened, and we were happy about it." They are talking of getting legally married now for the baby's sake.

Mother-child interaction. Carla is affectionate and warm toward her baby, Angelina. She holds the baby often, and her movements are never of a confining nature. She is efficient, skillful, fast, and, at the same time, gentle when she changes the baby's diapers. Such experience can be explained by the fact that Carla is one of the oldest daughters in her family and took care of younger siblings and nephews. While she is protective and soothing, she never kissed or hugged the baby, but she did stimulate her daughter with smiles and caresses. Carla seems happy with her daughter in general and speaks with pride of the child's good mood and alertness. Carla says she has helped the baby to a standing position and predicts that the child will crawl at three months. She tells the interviewer with great joy about every new development in her daughter.

Method of child rearing. Carla breastfeeds her baby on a demand schedule, although the baby supposedly worked out a schedule of every three to four hours. She gives the baby one discharge bottle a day, usually at a time that is convenient for the mother. When Angelina was eight weeks old, Carla began feeding her cereal which she accepted after only a few trials.

On a typical day, Angelina wakes up at 7:30 in the morning, nurses, and stays awake for a couple of hours. She is fed some cereal at midmorning and then she sleeps until noon. When she wakes up, her mother gives her milk from the breast or sometimes formula from a bottle. Angelina stays awake for three to four hours; then she is fed and sleeps again. She participates in her family's evening activities and is nursed again at 9 P.M. Then she sleeps through the night with only an occasional night nursing. During the day when the baby is awake, she remains seated in her infant seat while her mother works around the room. Sometimes during the evening, Angelina is taken to the movies. This occurs when her parents have taken hallucinogens. The day that Carla takes mescaline she says the baby is fussy; she attributes this to the fact that Angeline is hungry because Carla does not produce enough milk.

Carla does not have plans for weaning and says that she will nurse her daughter until she gets tired of it. She has no idea about the method she will use for weaning. She gave the baby a pacifier immediately after birth and plans to continue using it as long as needed. Carla does not have any plans for a future and does not know what method she will use to toilet train her child or otherwise educate her.

Carla likes to live in the country where she thinks she will be able to rear her baby in a healthy way. She and the baby and her husband plan to go to North Dakota in the spring to live with David's grandfather on a farm.

Mother's evaluation. No major psychopathology has been encountered in the observation of this young mother. Most of her behavior stems from her adolescent status. She clings to the group with utopic-idealistic philosophy; she wishes to be independent of her family and wants to go to the countryside to work on her husband's family farm. She also strictly follows the precepts of her peer group by taking drugs and needs to experiment with the new things such as the drug experience. Her maternal behavior, however, is generally adequate and mature.

Jane, like Carla, is another hippie mother who was ranked as "better" in her overall pattern of behavior as a parent. The following material is taken from our interviewer's descriptions of Jane and her baby, Carl. Although Jane's house is generally disorderly and dirty, Jane herself is usually neatly dressed. She has long hair, but it is well combed. When outside the house she wears pants or bermuda shorts. She wears a belt around her head as the only sign of hippie attire. She is thirty years old, slender, and of medium frame and height. Her speech is rapid, and her vocabulary is good, although she uses hippie slang. She is somewhat tense. When she talks, she moves her arms as if in an effort to get closer to the other participant. Her voice is of a strong, but neutral tone. She has a frank, outspoken manner of relating. She is also didactic. Although Jane advocates natural methods of child birth and child care, she only breastfed her baby for six weeks.

Mother-child interaction. Contacts between mother and child are characterized by a joyful, playful attitude. Jane allows her child to be at a distance from her, with confidence that nothing will happen to him. This was particularly true in the park where he was at a distance and Jane could not see him. At her house, the child moves freely, crawling from one room to another without being stopped and exchanging smiles or caresses with the adults he approaches. While Jane talks, mother and child do not seem to need many contacts. When Carl wants a cookie he asks for it; Jane quickly understands what he wants and gives it to him. Once, Jane showed the interviewer the colorful posters she had hung in Carl's room to entertain him. Jane responds to Carl's babbling in an adult way. She only holds the baby when she puts him on the table or places him back on the floor, and there is no close body contact. Both mother and child seem to enjoy face-to-face interaction and exchanging smiles.

Method of child rearing. Jane nursed the baby on a self-demand schedule for a month. After an illness, she changed to bottle feeding, and the weaning was abrupt. Carl now has a varied diet and eats table food. Jane has no plan for toilet training nor for sending him to school. She is a licensed grade school teacher, and therefore she plans to teach him herself.

Drug history. Jane took LSD several times during pregnancy. She said Carl had gotten stoned on mescaline when she had put mescaline powder on the table during a party. "There was mescaline all over the place and Carl must have gotten into something, from the floor or the table. He was not coordinating with his shit and had trouble hitting his mouth with his fingers, and threw up in the street when one of the men at the party took him out." Jane feels she is objective when she gets stoned on grass. Carl acts like he is drunk when he has had marijuana.

"MIDDLE" MOTHER-CHILD CONSTELLATIONS OR FAMILIES

Let us now turn to illustrations of hippie families who were ranked as "middle" on the basis of their overall behavior. Mary King and her husband live in an old apartment house in the Haight Ashbury district. Their apartment is on the second floor, and the front staircase is falling apart. Residents in the house use holes in the marble staircase as a garbage disposal, and they say there are rats in the house. The first room is a wide living and dining room, acceptably clean and in order. The apartment has a kitchen, two bedrooms, and a bath, and the children have their own bedroom.

Mother. Mary is a tall, attractive, slender, well-nourished, wholesome looking mother. She is a dark blonde and has a thick mass of long curly hair. She has small features and vivacious brown eyes. Her complexion is mottled and oily. She is clean and dresses in inexpensive trousers and a blouse that needs ironing. Her whole attitude is colored by her carefree, somewhat careless attitude. During the interview Mary was fairly relaxed and calm. Her movements are neither too slow nor too fast. In the apartment, she moves quickly, serving breakfast and getting the children ready to go out. In the park, she sometimes fidgets, but she does not get up; she sits on a bench smoking and watching the children play. She seems to be a healthy woman of average energy.

Mary's vocabulary is adequate, and she appears to be a person of above average intelligence. Her voice is loud and clear. She talks passionately against the American establishment. Her discourse is articulate and logical. When she talks in this manner, she is excited and appears capable of becoming annoyed and hostile. She treats the interviewer as a representative of the Establishment, complaining about injustices that have been committed.

Mary makes a great point of being a womanly female. She is proud of having had a lot of milk so that she could even sell some, although she weaned her children early. She projects a picture of herself as a secure, efficient, strong woman, a person of character, and a former political activist. She answers the questions somewhat defensively. In the areas related to weaning and toilet training, she gives reasons for her methods that sound like excuses. For example, she says she believes in long breast feeding but that her own children were allergic to the fat in her milk.

Evaluation of mother. Despite Mary's presentation of herself as a secure relaxed person, her hostility against the Establishment reveals a great deal of anxiety. She presents herself as a person who is always in control. She does not expect to have problems rearing her children and does not admit to any problems up to the present time.

Mother-child interaction. Mary is efficient although careless. For example, the children are dirty, and her eighteen-month-old daughter has a severe diaper rash which Mary attributes to the baby's oversensitive skin. She excuses herself by saying that she has tried every method she knows to prevent this condition.

She does not encourage physical contact with her children except whatever is strictly necessary for handling them. For example, in the park the children came close to her, but she sat back and talked to them, giving instructions what to do about another child that was bothering them. When they came for money, she gave it to them without any comment. She behaves the same way toward her toddler. While we were sitting near the slide, Candy (eighteen months old) was trying to play on the slide. The child climbed up the steps and slid down on her stomach instead of sitting up. During this, Mary and her cousin were criticizing a straight looking mother who was standing beside the slide helping her toddler; the mother held her child's arms while he climbed up the steps and when he was at the top his mother showed him how to sit down and slide. This brought comments from the two hippie mothers about the climate of tension in which the straight people rear their children. Mary and her cousin said straight people want to impose their way and views on others and, in so doing, restrain and inhibit their own children. The hippie way is not to repress the child's innate capacities.

Mary nursed her children until they were three months old, on a demand schedule. They kept drinking from the bottle until they were two and a half years old. Mary's reason for early weaning from the breast was that all three of her children were allergic to the fat in her milk. She says she was able to sell some of her milk to a milk bank in a hospital. She introduced solid foods at one month after birth.

Mary and her husband believe that children naturally grow up well if parents do not worry too much. They also think that children need directions and that certain limits should be imposed. Children must be taught to love and not to fear others. The boys, for example, went up to a bearded stranger lying on the grass and began playing with him. They climbed all over him and, afterwards, the stranger embraced them. The man and the young woman with him returned both children and introduced themselves to Mary before leaving the park.

Mary says she will not send any of her children to public or private schools. Bill (seven years old) went for six weeks to a kindergarten but failed to adapt, and so Mary decided to teach him herself at home. Although she says she was an active participant in the creation of a local hippie school, she will not send them there because the teachers are too permissive and the children have no chance to learn anything. Bill has learned to write and read and do simple mathematics with his parents as teachers. In Mary's view, teachers in public schools are so repressive that the children learn to hate knowledge and each other. She has come to dislike the neighborhood where she lives because it is too violent. She now has to teach her children to defend themselves against others. Another child in the park was fighting Bill. Both children were about the same age and size, but Bill never hit back. He tried to restrain the other child from hitting him, but the other child eventually had him on the ground. All the time Bill was shouting "No, no," while the other child was hitting him with his fists. Finally his mother came and separated them; all she said was "Be quiet." When Bill was three years old, toilet training was achieved without difficulty. When Bill was able to understand what Mary wanted, she told him to sit on the potty chair. His younger brother is learning from him.

The child. Bill, the firstborn, is seven years old. He is tall and thin, with long blonde hair and a delicate oval face. The boy is average in energy and activity. Although he does not seem to have a need to move constantly, he does not sit still for long periods. In the street, he is able to keep up with the adults; he holds their hands occasionally in an affectionate manner.

Bill possesses self-control, and he is willing to conform to parental philosophy. Particularly impressive is his refusal to hit back at another child. He behaves as a very good, obedient boy, and he is protective toward his smaller brother when they cross the street. Toward others he is affectionate and seeks physical contact. Toward the interviewer he is cooperative and exhibits an extraordinary willingness to please. Once when brought in for testing, Bill was affectionate, embracing and kissing the interviewer. Toward his father, he is friendly and respectful.

His vocabulary is adequate; and he seems more mature than do his agemates. When asked about his experience with LSD, he answered that LSD taught you "what a sloppy thing you really are." Later, he brought in some poetry he had written.

> The sea lark is calling
> While the winter days are falling
> Ping the duck is winging
> While the church bell is still ringing.
>
> Bears are sleeping
> Lizards creeping.
>
> Wet tears fall from the sky
> Why they do, I don't know why
> While a Jude
> Is simply Juding
> In the sun.

Biological father. Martin is a small, thirty-three-year-old man. He wears long straight hair and has a short sparse beard. He smiles a lot and moves a great deal with small movements. His movements are anxious and nervous. He fidgets and can neither stand nor sit still. His moving has a feminine quality, and his activity often has no purpose. He frequently talks in the same nervous manner. Most often he talks about hippie philosophy, and his conversation contains many cliches which make a senseless discourse when put together. He has megalomaniac fantasies of being a leader and a great man; but his sense of reality is probably distorted, and he does not really seem to believe what he is saying. For example, he told friends that he was buying a ghost-town in Arizona to use as a home for hippies and that he would be the boss after moving there. He presents himself as a very busy person engaged in activities that will help the hippie community. When under the effects of drugs, he has paranoic delusions.

He is respectful toward his family and says he admires his wife. He participates in family activities. Toward the children, he is permissive and friendly, and he interacts with them at their own level. Even in his relation to his wife, he is like another child. For example, as soon as we arrived at the park, the children left us to play and he also went away with the dog. When noon came he came back and asked for money for food.

Martin is particularly friendly toward his older son, Bill. He does not have much interaction with the younger children. He is proud of Bill's intelligence and toward him he is permissive and warm, talking with him on an adult level. He likes to go with Bill on walks.

Parent interaction. The parents do not say much to each other. They talk independently to the interviewer. The father always seems to agree with the mother. She acts as the brain of the family, and he verbally expresses his admiration for her. The mother seems to be the authority figure to the children. When the parents separated, two days after the interview, the mother took both the children with her. The father agreed with this decision despite his great love for and comradeship with Bill.

It is interesting to note that the father not only agrees with the mother's statements but sometimes cooperates with her in amplifying her statements, especially in regard to their philosophy of living and their methods of child rearing. Privately, they revealed slightly different reasons for their actions. The mother said she would not have given LSD to Bill if he had not asked for it so vehemently. She thought that children do not need LSD "to be themselves" and that "they are free enough." She felt somewhat guilty and needed to excuse herself by blaming the child. The father, however, thought that he favored his son by giving him the drug and was proud of doing so.

Like Mary and Martin King, the Hobbits were ranked as "middle" on the bases of their overall behavior in our sample of hippie families. The Hobbits use LSD, mescaline, and marijuana frequently. Mother and father had used LSD once a week, but at the present time LSD and mescaline are used according to the availability of the drug. They use mescaline most often because it is a natural drug, and the father is afraid of the effects of LSD. He says that it could diminish his sexual potency, and he thinks that it has already caused urethritis and epididymitis. The Hobbits say that the hallucinogens "are a universal way of understanding things, although they are not the answer to happiness." They use marijuana several times a day, with friends, as a family ritual, or individually. The father says that his awareness increases when he smokes marijuana, and he likes to smoke while he reads a good book. He also says that marijuana often makes him a better driver than usual.

The mother did not use any drugs while pregnant with the first child. When pregnant with the second child, she used mescaline once a month. The baby, Gaudelf, was conceived while under an LSD experience. During the second pregnancy, the mother took diet pills daily. The second child has not been given any drugs directly. The mother wants to wait until he is able to talk. Then, he can be told in advance what he might experience under the effects of drugs.

The first child (Galadril) had an LSD experience when she was eighteen months old. The parents say the intake was accidental; she swallowed a dose of LSD that somebody had left on a table. The father is said to have watched the child doing this and could not prevent it; but he did not tell the mother until she noticed that the child was behaving strangely. Galadril smokes marijuana daily with her parents.

House. The Hobbits live in the Haight-Ashbury district of San Francisco in an old, but well-kept, apartment house. Their apartment is adequate for the family. It consists of a long corridor with a kitchen at one end, a bedroom, a smaller room for Galadril, a living room, and a bathroom. The furniture is old. The apartment is fairly clean and decorated with old posters and photographs of Eowayn (the mother) acting or dancing. Mattresses serve as beds and seats.

Mother. Eowayn is a pretty woman of medium height. At the time of the first interview, she was very advanced in her second pregnancy. Behind her expression of resignation, one can often see a great deal of anger and rebelliousness. She was once dressed in a long skirt and a blouse made of lace. At other times, she wore trousers. Her hair is long, blonde, and straight. Her face is square, her complexion irregular, and she has large brown eyes that seem to express intense suffering. She speaks very slowly and almost in a whisper but with dramatic overtones as if trying to seek understanding and pity from the interviewer. She looks healthy, well nourished, and somewhat overweight. Eowayn presents herself as someone who is resigned to bad luck and frustrated wishes. She sighs frequently and attributes her lot to external events. For example, her husband was not admitted to school because he arrived later than the admission date—this she blamed on the bureaucracy of the college.

She describes herself as being selfish and without patience. She gets upset easily by household routines. For example, she told the interviewer that she was away for two weeks because she felt that things were getting too "uptight." She left the children with her husband. (Actually, her life had been threatened for being unable to pay for drugs that were stolen from her.) She was a topless dancer in a night club in San Francisco when her financial situation demanded it. She does have some courage to be able to continue this life of dealing in dangerous drugs. Eowayn is often discontented. She is always wishing for something else, but does not know what it is she is seeking. She was unconditionally friendly from the start and accepted the interviewer at once as a friend of the house. She is available whenever she can be found, and she is always cooperative even though she might be going through a difficult time. She is warm and responsive and from the beginning wanted the interviewer to participate in family rituals such as marijuana, gathering with friends, and having meals.

Eowayn was born in Washington, D.C. Her father was a

high ranking officer in the army. She describes her parents as very strict and immoral (on political issues). She says she always had problems relating to them. She was married in Paris while her family was stationed there, and Galadril was born there. She and her husband decided to come to San Francisco, and, shortly after, they separated. Eowayn says that their relationship generated a great deal of tension, and they lost their love for each other. She began to work in a theater with a group of friends, and there she met Ent, who was a decorator. They decided to live together in the building which served as a theater. They never married legally. Soon, because the theater was not a success, they left, and Ent began working as a carpenter or at any kind of work he could find. They also dealt in drugs. Soon after the interviewer met the family, Ent went away on a ship to Japan as a laborer. In his absence Eowayn was robbed of drugs, and she did not have the money to pay off the dealer who had consigned them to her. This was when she began working as a topless dancer in a low-rate night club. Part of her job was to have drinks with the customers and to entertain the policemen. The job seemed to excite her despite her indignation for the way she was treated. Ent returned from Japan, but, because of the threat to their lives, they felt too frightened to stay in their apartment. They decided to leave the city and moved to Big Sur.

Eowayn denied having any sad or angry feelings towards Ent for going away. In view of their separation, her expressed happiness was striking. She thought about the "quality hashish" and the toys for the children Ent could bring back and about the fact that "Ent will know the world." The interviewer regarded this as a maniacal denying of depressive feelings. The same type of attitude was apparent after the birth of her child when Eowayn denied her depression, used defensive mechanisms, and was angry with the hospital routines and the nurses. Every time Eowayn has to handle frustration she blames it on somebody else.

After Ent's departure for Japan, Eowayn partially solved her problems by dancing topless. Aspects of her job were in flagrant opposition to her expressed ideology—she had lied to customers and "entertained" policemen in the back of the bar. She detached herself emotionally from the scene and acted as an observer.

Mother-child interaction. Eowayn often harbors feelings of inadequacy especially when Galadril is hard to manage. At the same time she is proud of her child's rebellious, independent personality, thinking that this will be an asset and a real help in life. She likes having a tough daughter, saying that "this way she will have what she wants." These mixed feelings make Eowayn an overpermissive mother and Galadril a difficult child. Eowayn will tell Galadril not to do certain things, but in a tone that is not at all convincing to the child who continues to disobey her mother. In such circumstances Eowayn expresses helpless impatience but never loses her temper and tolerates with resignation her daughter's misbehavior.

Father. Ent is a soft, friendly young man of medium height. He is very thin, and his face is long and pale. He wears a small neatly trimmed beard, and his blonde hair is not extremely long and also is neatly cared for. He looks very young and is very gentle.

He prefers to lie quietly on the mattress on the living room floor. He moves only to prepare a pipe of marijuana which he passes around to the members of his family. He seldom shifts his weight and taps his fingers only once in a while. He complains of a urinary problem (probably VD) produced by the use of LSD. Although he looks healthy, he seems to be hypochondriacal. Although there is not much physical contact between him and Eowayn, he accepts her presence. Ent is playful with Gaudelf. He has much physical contact with his son and is proud of his son's strength and development. Ent is critical of Galadril (his wife's daughter), and he is said to have been punitive in the past. He stopped spanking her when he realized he could not, in fact, correct her behavior that way. Galadril hit back at him, which he took as an indication that she understood his message; he therefore stopped punishing her and preferred to talk to her, which he said proved to be more fruitful.

Toward the interviewer Ent is cordial and cooperative. He participates, with Eowayn, in offering a quite friendly atmosphere. After they had been robbed of the drugs, his mood changed and he became depressed, pessimistic, worried, and fearful. (His wife suddenly became more active.)

Parental relationship. Ent and Eowayn's relationship is pleasant and smooth. They generally agree on topics regarding their philosophies and beliefs and also in their evaluation of the children. The mother predominates in the conversations, and the father tends to agree with her.

Additional circumstances. The interviewer once made a hospital visit to Eowayn, taking along a small gift for the new baby. Eowayn said she was happy that her infant was a big healthy boy, but she was actually discontented, complaining about the hospital routines and the nurses. She complained about the hospital's policy of keeping her baby in the nursery and bringing him to her only for nursing. She blamed the nurses for the fact that the child was not hungry and thought that the nurses gave him water to calm down his hunger.

Another interview was held two weeks after Eowayn returned from the hospital. This interview lasted for three hours, and the mother's interactions with her newborn and with her two-year-old daughter were observed. The interview was unstructured and the theme of the conversation was diverse. Eowayn talked about the reasons for using drugs, about their beliefs in astrology, and about the way she sees her own parents, herself, her children, and her husband. She related these feelings to her fate according to her astrological charts.

Ent talked about his views of the children and about his fears. He said he usually tries to avoid competition in choosing a career. In the theater, he chose the technical aspect because it was less competitive than was the acting area. He is trying to get away from LSD because he thinks that it caused his symptoms of urethritis and may cause sexual impotency.

"POOR" MOTHER-CHILD CONSTELLATIONS OR FAMILIES

Let us now turn to descriptions of families who were ranked as "poor" on the basis of their overall behavior. The first illustrated family was a control because the mother denied using hallucinogens during pregnancy. The mother did use marijuana regularly, and took LSD once while nursing her three-month-old daughter. The mother, Desire, admits to use of cocaine, THC, opium, LSD, glue, and ethylchloride—all only experimentally. The biological father used LSD once a month, heroin once a week (not at the time of interview), methedrine daily, and barbiturates daily (six to seven capsules). The surrogate father uses codeine weekly, glue weekly, and drinks one gallon of wine per day. Diana, the daughter, is said not to have been given hallucinogens or marijuana, but she drinks one quart of wine daily (she is twenty-eight months old).

The biological mother, the surrogate father, and the child first lived together in a very small apartment in the Haight Ashbury District in San Francisco. The apartment consisted of two small rooms. One of the rooms had a mattress on the floor as the only piece of furniture. The other room was Diana's bedroom and had a small mattress on the floor and a box of toys.

The family lived in this apartment for a short period and were then evicted for not paying the rent. They then moved to a second house. During the first interview, the first apartment was clean and relatively in order. But during the following interviews, it became progressively more disorganized. At the time of the third interview, even dog urine and dog feces were on the floor, especially evident in Diana's room.

At the time of the fourth interview, the whole family had moved to another house and were living in a commune with four other adults, three men of nineteen, twenty-five, and thirty-five years and a woman of nineteen. This apartment was also located in Haight-Ashbury and consisted of five rooms, a kitchen, and one bathroom.

Diana had her own room, which was small, dark, and without any colorful arrangement. She slept on a mattress on the floor. Desire and Dave (surrogate father) slept in a separate room. This second apartment was always disordered, and the decor was dull. The floors and furniture were dirty, the beds were not made, and occasionally dog feces were on the floor. People from the streets were constantly coming in and out of the apartment. In addition, music from the record player or radio was often loud.

Biological mother. Desire was well nourished although

fairly plump. Her mass of dull blonde hair always needed brushing and her complexion was blemished and of a greasy type. Nevertheless when she smiled, which was often, she was attractive. She was in her second month of pregnancy when the interviewer met her.

Her speech was adequate, and her voice and movements were moderate. She enjoyed talking about herself and told the story of her life in a romantic way, even when talking of difficult times. During the first interview, she wore a clean, attractive hippie costume and had her face made up. She was nicely groomed and even used a French perfume the day she took Diana for testing. At the subsequent interviews, she became progressively more sloppy. Her hair was messed up and her clothes were dirty. With the progression of her pregnancy, her attractiveness disappeared.

During the second interview, she wore a short duster gown that she left unbuttoned in the front showing her bulging abdomen. During the third interview, she was in bed and excused herself by saying she had the flu. (She did not show symptoms of it.) She wore an old unattractive gown that could have been sexy a very long time ago but which now showed her naked stodgy body. Her hair was messy, and she had a tired expression. As the interview progressed, her face lightened, and she became active. Her variable moods were always superficial. She changed quickly from being tired and depressed to being talkative and active. Her sadness or depression was never deep, and her excitation depended greatly on her romantic exaggerations of her life.

Desire was born in Boston and lived there most of her life. After her second marriage, she came to San Francisco with her daughter Diana, her second husband, and Dave, a friend of both who is now living with her in a common-law marriage. Desire was raised as a Catholic. She says that her mother dominated in her home, despite the fact that she worshipped men. Her mother is a sculptor and a painter. Her father works with large machinery but dreamed of being an adventurer. Desire feels that she was called upon to fulfill her father's dreams. She says her mother admires her for her courage but distrusts her and also criticizes her for "being away from God." Her first husband was an atheist, and her second one was a poet. She blames both divorces on her husbands' atheism and poetry respectively.

Desire, her second husband, and Dave took a whole year in coming to the West Coast. They lived in fifteen different places. When they reached San Francisco, Desire separated from her husband and continued to live with Dave. She and her second husband are still good friends.

Mother-child interaction. Desire has a didactic attitude toward her daughter, wanting her to perform and learn in front of the interviewer. During the second interview, she taught the child words. (Especially in view of the child's poor vocabulary, this is probably not everyday behavior.)

Interestingly, Desire's descriptions of her daughter and the reality are quite different. For example, Desire says that Diana is naturally clean and dainty that the child cannot stand being dirty, and that she is orderly and already toilet trained. None of these statements is true. Although Desire says she does not limit her daughter in any way, she is actually controlling her when she does not allow her to play freely but interferes with her play and at the same time teaches her words. Nevertheless, Desire is, at all times, gentle and speaks to Diana in a soft, calm, sweet manner, which she maintains even when Diana puts up a fuss or when she has a tantrum. When the child has a fit of temper, Desire has a conciliatory attitude and tries to gain her child's goodwill by getting her to accept some other thing.

Description of child. Diana was twenty-four months old when the interviewer first met her. She was born in New Jersey where her biological mother and father lived together until she was one year old. She spent her second year moving about with her parents and a male friend. Her mother explained that she was named after the goddess of love. She was generally dirty and poorly dressed. She had long, thin, messy blonde hair and a dirty face. In the winter time mucus was hanging from her nose. Nevertheless, she looked well nourished, and she was reportedly physically healthy. The shape of her face contributed to her nickname, Mousy. During the first interview, Diana sat with an empty look on her face masturbating in front of her parents. (Her surrogate father was lying naked on the mattress where she had previously urinated.) When she came out of that lethargic state, she acted suspicious for a while and did not answer my greetings, but after a few minutes she came nearer and said "Kitty," and pointed at the cat, as a welcome. The only feature about her which her mother described and which also applied in reality was her sociability. Her mother also reported anxiety signs in Diana; the child used a blanket as a pacifier and awakened in the middle of the night crying and asking to sleep with her parents.

Surrogate father. Dave is a silent introverted man. He is very tall, broad shouldered and he has a long thick curly beard. He was uninterested in the project and neither asked anything about it nor participated in any way. During the first interview he read a book and answered my questions only indirectly through Desire. He is a former serviceman and a former codeine user and is still an alcoholic. He sometimes does some carpentry work and would have liked to study fine arts.

Like Desire, the Bead Lady is another hippie mother who was ranked as "poor" on the basis of her overall behavior. The Bead Lady is a hard core drug user of heroin and methedrine. Her arms are covered with needle punctures. She smokes marijuana and opium daily and uses cocaine, hashish, or THC almost every day. She says that she uses LSD once a week. During pregnancy, she used all of these drugs. When she was sure that she was pregnant, she said she discontinued the use of morphine, heroin, and methedrine but continued to use the other drugs.

House. The Bead Lady lives with a number of youngsters of both sexes, two cats, two dogs, and her infant in a house in the heart of Haight-Ashbury in San Francisco. The dirt and feces covering the floor of her house are a continuation of the dirt and feces on the street. People constantly go in and out of the house, and the radio is on loud, playing rock music. When the Bead Lady led the interviewer into the house, the baby was crying loudly; she went into the bedroom and picked him up. He slept in an old folding laundry cart. This improvised bassinet was always under the bathroom sink. The mother explained that she used the bathroom as a nursery because it was the warmest room in the house. (The baby slept near an unprotected wall heater.) The house has a long hallway with the kitchen at one end. The bathroom and two bedrooms open from the hall. In one bedroom, the mother sleeps with a roommate. The interviewer was not able to enter this room while she was changing her infant. The first interview was held in the kitchen. The interviewer was offered the only available chair which was full of clothes; the other chairs were occupied by the Bead Lady's friends. She took the chair away later on, so she could feed her baby.

The cats and dogs were also running about in the kitchen. One of the cats was reported to be crazy because it had been given LSD. "He never comes down, he's frightened of everything and keeps running all day and all night." Another friend in the kitchen said she had done the same with a rat, and it became homosexual. A dog came close to Kilo (the study infant), and the Bead Lady scared him away saying that she did not want it near her son because it could contaminate him with ringworm. Everything in the house was dirty, and it was difficult to tolerate the odor of the feces spread over the floor of the hallway.

Biological mother. The Bead Lady is a short, plump, half Oriental, young mother. She is called the "Bead Lady" because she strings beads and sells them as necklaces. She is also called "Number 13" because of her bad luck and the "Rat Lady" because of the conditions in which she lived. All those very descriptive nicknames say a great deal about her. The Bead Lady dresses in a pair of blue jeans and an old blouse. Her long straight hair is combed in a fall over her shoulder. She wears one of her necklaces across her forehead. Despite her chubbiness, she gives the appearance of being cute. She has a round large face with small features and oriental eyes. Her skin is white and soft.

Her speech is rapid; her vocabulary is adequate; and she talks a great deal, giving information about herself almost from the start. (Her philosophy of life is based on a bitter and often cynical view of the world.)

She moves quickly, and she can sit still only for short periods. Otherwise she stands as if she were in a hurry. While she talks, she fidgets and gestures with her hands. Her activity is disorganized, and her attitude is careless.

Toward the interviewer she is cynical and hostile. She regards the interviewer as a representative of the Establishment which she obviously hates. Nevertheless, she talks a great deal about herself in a megalomaniac manner; she said, for example, that she was a biology teacher and that she was going to study pharmacy soon. Given her age, attitude, demeanor, and the conditions under which she lives, these are clearly fantasies. In regard to her childhood, she described herself as a precocious sort of genius despite the harsh life she had led moving from foster home to foster home. She averred that she had gone to a school for gifted children. She had a scornful attitude toward the questions asked her. She talks about how she can con the welfare department to get aid. She says that she planned her pregnancy with the purpose of getting welfare and that she lied to the welfare people telling them that the infant's father abandoned her after she got pregnant. She says scornfully that she has promised them that she will return to school and that they will pay for a babysitter. At the end of one interview she begged the interviewer to buy one of her necklaces in the tone of a little child asking for candy. After the interviewer purchased the necklace, she looked at her triumphantly and said, "Now you are also a dirty hippie."

Despite her megalomaniac fantasies, she tries to inspire pity. Mostly that effort fails because it is followed by hostile cynicism. For example, she began to talk about the bad times she had when she was pregnant—sleeping in hallways or in the park without anything to eat. She then said in a hostile tone, "You see I never had problems," and laughed. At one time, the interviewer held the baby and, when he began to cry, wanted to return him to his mother. In response, she said she could not hold him because she had wounds in her arms from the needles. She exposed her punctured arms, saying, "It is painful." Speaking of a crusted spot on the child's head, she said, "Oh, that is only makeup somebody spilled on him. He sleeps under the sink in the bathroom."

Mother-child interaction. Toward her infant, this mother is generally careless. She handles him roughly, and even after she has changed him he remains soiled and smelling of vomit. When she speaks of his precociousness it is hard to believe, looking at the curious looking infant who has the face of an old man. Nevertheless, she is able to quiet him down when he cries by just picking

him up, although she is in no hurry to do so and lets him cry a
good while. She prefers to hold him in a horizontal position, en-
circling him with her arms. Verbal communication was lacking
during the interview despite the mother's insistence that the baby
is precocious and that he already has a personality of his own. She
did not behave as if he could understand her in any way, and he
was mostly treated as a thing. Body contact was seen only at
feeding. Afterward, the mother tried to leave the infant with the
interviewer and refused to take him back. During feeding, the
mother provided no physical intimacy. Her movements were
brief, and her attention was given to the feeding utensils rather
than to the child, as her aim was to achieve a quick intake. While
feeding, the infant had no freedom of movement. She explained
that she was trying to keep him from messing with his food. Her
movements were fast, one spoonful after the other without waiting
until he had swallowed the first. Because she fed him so rapidly,
the food overflowed his mouth and she kept scraping it up from his
cheeks and chin and putting it back in his mouth. There was no
communication between mother and infant; she only talked to
the interviewer or the other people in the kitchen. Although she
concentrated on the process of feeding him, she did not consider
his own rhythm of eating and swallowing. She made comments
about his likes and dislikes, his allergies to certain foods, and his
personality, while concentrating on her task. The feeding lasted
about fifteen minutes, and the baby ate the whole jar of food.
The infant looked at the ceiling and ate passively and unenthusi-
astically, but he did not "blow" or refuse the food at any time.
The feeding was clean.

Mother's history. The Bead Lady is a native San Franciscan,
born to an Oriental woman and a Caucasian man. She says she
was left on a street corner by her mother when she was five years
old. Since then she went from foster home to foster home, never
staying more than a month in each. She says that she went to a
school for gifted children in Los Angeles, that she finished college
and obtained a license to teach biology (all of which seems doubt-
ful). When she was nine years old, she had her first contact with
heroin. (Her foster father was a heroin addict.) Since then, she
has tried every drug on the market. In the Haight-Ashbury, she

starved at first and did not have a place to live. She wanted to get pregnant and be able to get welfare aid. She succeeded in this, but the aid did not come right away. Until she was in her seventh month of pregnancy, she did not have enough to eat and slept in hallways and in the park even when it rained. Nevertheless, she continued to use every kind of drug up to the third month when she said she still did not know if she was pregnant. She then stopped using heroin but continued with the hallucinogens. When the interviewer visited this mother later, she said that the baby had been kidnapped and refused to be interviewed. A friend of hers (another of our study parents) told the interviewer that the baby had been found severely injured and had been taken away. According to the informant, the Bead Lady was facing trial for being an unfit mother.

Mother evaluation. The Bead Lady is a hard core drug user. Her attitude toward others may stem from a need for self-compensation. Her belief that she is actually able to manipulate and, in this way, damage others may be a way of compensating herself and of asserting her own fantasized omnipotence. She manages to conceal conscious guilt feelings and, therefore, depression by acting out the manipulation of others. Example: planning a pregnancy to get welfare, or selling the interviewer the necklace. Her method was to make the interviewer feel the way she felt about herself: "dirty." It was as if she had robbed her of something instead of selling it. That implies that she may be unable to see in herself anything of value and has therefore to resort to more primitive feelings of omnipotence. Her acting out, the manipulation of others, and her history may classify her as a sociopath.

The child. Kilo was an eight-week-old boy. He was an odd infant, thin and wiry, with the face of an old man. His nose was long, his large ears low, and his blue eyes were inexpressive. His head seemed small when compared with his round face, and his sparse hair was of a pale reddish yellow. His body smelled of urine, feces, and vomit. He was quite dirty, and none of his clothes were clean. He looked weak, and he passively maintained the posture in which he was put. He had an empty look and did not focus on anything. Head support was not present; neuromuscular development and muscular tone were poor. His respiration was slow; his skin color was pale, and he had wrinkles around his eyes and mouth. He seldom moved, and that was only when he turned his head. He was unusually insensitive to sounds; he was never startled despite the radio or people shouting. He passively ate whatever his mother fed him, and he did not smile in response.

Method of child rearing. The Bead Lady chose "Kilo" as a second name for her baby because it is a unit by which marijuana is sold. She planned her pregnancy to get welfare and breastfed the baby only for a few days. The reason she gave for such a sudden weaning was that she became sick and had a very high fever. She bottle fed him every four hours, although during some meals she did not give him a bottle since she felt the milk was less important than the solid food. She has not considered methods of toilet training or of weaning from the bottle. She says that she does not plan to give him drugs directly, especially heroin or methedrine. As for LSD or marijuana, the mother said he should be old enough to ask for them himself.

COMMENTS ON CASE HISTORIES

Hopefully, these extracts will allow the reader to compare our classifications of hippie families with his own judgmental criteria. We call special attention to the extensiveness and casualness with which psychoactive drugs are employed. Even in a "better" family, where the mother was warm and enjoyed her maternal role, both parents used LSD and/or mescaline about once a month and used marijuana every day. In a "middle" family, the parents used hallucinogens every other day when the drugs were available and even conceived their child under the effects of LSD. The mother of this child took LSD every day for two weeks during the second trimester of her pregnancy, and, after the infant's birth, she nursed the child while under the effects of the drug. In one "poor" family, the mother dropped speed, smoked opium, and used LSD during her pregnancy. This same mother nursed her child while high on LSD or mescaline and, together with her husband, introduced her one-month-old child to marijuana. This mother was an intelligent woman and member of Mensa but treated her child in an offhand careless manner, suggesting a disregard for the child's comfort or well-being.

The values and attitudes of most of these families, polyparent groups, and mother-child constellations will be communicated to their children. They value peace and freedom, advocate drug use, and hold carefree attitudes toward day-to-day living. Within the group, there is dramatic variation in the degrees of actual control and discipline (as well as care and tenderness) expressed toward the children. At one end are those old-fashioned women whose hippie involvement is akin to the spirit of a Midwestern farm mother denouncing new fangled technology and pollution. At the other end, we have seen some miserable cases of drug dependency, self-delusion, and grotesque examples of infant care. We must posit that drug use serves very different functions depending upon who is using. The solid and sensible mothers relax with marijuana, regarding it as a kind of recreation. The troubled individuals, however, use drugs symptomatically, and what bitter pleasure they derive could hardly be regarded as recreation.

Their choice of recreation is not ours, but we now believe that, among the "better" families, there need be no associations between drug involvement and psychopathology, or between drug use and one's capabilities of mothering.

THE CHILDREN

The behavior of the children is our outcome measure for risk in this study. In addition to an evaluation by the child psychiatrist and an on-the-spot neurological examination of the infants, we employed the Bayley Infant Scales of Motor Development and the Bayley Infant Scales of Mental Development. For the three children over the age of four, the Stanford Binet Intelligence Test was used, and in some cases drawings were used. The Machover-Draw-a-Person and the Bender-Gestalt tests were additional instruments. We also took children's drug histories from their parents. The average age of children in our sample was slightly less than two years. The oldest was Bill (aged seven), who had asked for and been given LSD. The rest of these children could not be expected to initiate drug use on their own, although once taught drug use by their parents they will continue.

We have no measures of drug risk for such children which are independent of psychological testing or psychiatric/neurological evaluation. One may assume (in the absence of direct evidence) that the teaching of illicit drug use to children is unwise; but the data demonstrate that, in some cases, hippie families do expose their babies to the drug use habits which the parents themselves espouse and practice. We cannot be sure of the proportion of families who expose their children to such substances because reporting is vague and ingestion by the child may be accidental. In our sample of interviews, eight out of twenty-five children had had experiences with LSD or cannabis (including fume inhalation) as well as indirect experience through the mother's use during pregnancy or while nursing. One child was given a quart of wine every day and perhaps experienced other drug use. In addition, ten children had indirect LSD experience through the mother. If we consider cannabis, amphetamines, opium, and other substances, all children in our sample have apparently had such indirect exposure. Most parents planned to give hallucinogens or marijuana to their children at some point in the future. No parents were opposed to the idea of their children becoming illicit drug users. Indeed, the chances are quite high that children of such parents will become illicit drug users.

On the Bayley Motor Development instrument a score or quotient of 100 is normal. Scores upward or downward 16 points are within the normal range (one standard deviation). Of the nine infants with whom this test was used, only one scored under 100 (95), but that score was within the normal range. All other children's scores were also in the normal range, except one child whose DMQ was 124. Because that infant was the youngest, the score is not totally reliable and is subject to later change. Scores on the Bayley Mental Development instrument were obtained for the same nine infants. Three of the intelligence test scores were below the hypothetical average of 100 (90, 90, 92)—none, however, was below the normal range. The highest score was 128 (the same one-month-old infant who obtained the high motor score). Again, scores are least reliable at early ages. Another child (aged sixteen and one-half months) obtained a score of 120. The Stanford Binet intelligence quotients are 95, 131, and 143. The two high scores were well above the normal range; the low score was within it. The Bayley Infant Behavior Profile (available on seventeen children) gives descriptive material which we classified as positive or negative scores. A positive score implies normal adaptive functioning or superior performance and adjustment. A negative score indicates a prevalence of maladaptive behaviors. Five of sixteen children received negative scores in our summary measure; eleven received positive scores.

As concerns the psychiatric evaluations, adjective check list ratings are available on twenty-two children. (The instrument was designed for use with mothers, and only as an afterthought was it used with children.) The most frequent evaluation was responsive, followed by calm, friendly, confident, and average activity/energy level. Affect disorders were implied in two offspring; and high levels of tension were indicated in two. The most extensive observations are the clinical work-ups which include the gross neurological examination. We summarized these observations for twenty-three children, using the same positive versus negative classification (plus and minus for uncertain cases). Five negative scores were found. Three uncertain cases occurred, with both positive and negative features. The remaining fifteen children were all normal or superior in performance, neurological status, and psychological adjustment.

In summary, no children were found to be abnormal on the Bayley Motor Development Scales, the Bayley Infant Scales of Mental Development, or the Stanford Binet. The majority of offspring demonstrated normal behavior on the Bayley Infant Behavior Profile; about one-third showed deficit. On the clinical psychiatric evaluations and gross neurological examinations, the majority were found to be normal or superior; one-third had either clear or suspected deficit or malfunction, either neurologically or psychiatrically. Table 16 presents the percentage of agreement among various measures. The percentage agreement is a crude estimate. By excluding the middle group, we may have spuriously

Table 16

Percentage Agreement Among Various Measure in Study of Hippie
Families or Mother-Child Constellations

Measures	Percentage Agreement
Family rank (better, poor) and mother acceptance of mothering role and child (agreement between Maternal Behavior Profile and Psychiatric Evaluation). N = 10[a]	90
Family rank (better, poor) and child's psychiatric evaluation status (plus, minus) N = 14[a]	79
Family Rank and Infant Behavior Profile. N = 10[a]	90
Infant Behavior Profile and Psychiatric/Neurological examination, global ratings. N = 13[a]	93
Bayley Motor Scales and Bayley Mental Scales. (Agreement is when both scores are in the normal range or when both exceed it in the same direction.) N = 9	89

[a] Middle and plus-minus cases were excluded so that both groups may be dichotomous for comparison purposes and so as to avoid comparing a tripartite distribution to a dichotomous one.

enhanced agreement. Nevertheless, the percentages do suggest that the psychiatrist and psychologist can achieve better agreement than that achieved earlier when the psychologist used the Maternal Behavior Profile and the psychiatrist made a clinical/neurological summary rating. This change lends weight to the interpretation that the differences between the results of the adjective check list and the Maternal Profile were due to the diversity of behavior evaluated by the psychiatrist. When maternal conduct and the rather limited parental adequacy measures (better to worse) are put side by side, we see that agreement between independent raters can be achieved.

Correspondence between the psychiatrist's family rank evaluations and her evaluation of the child suggests, but hardly proves, that parental goodness in the hippie sample is associated with results of the psychiatric/neurological measure. In the same way, family rank corresponds closely to the gross summary of the Bayley Infant Behavior Profile, which suggests that parental adequacy is associated with the behavioral outcome in the child when there is no contamination. That is, the Profile measure is independent of the psychiatric evaluation. We also show that the Infant Behavior Profile and psychiatric/neurological examination are in agreement.

The close agreement between the Bayley Motor and Mental Scales is by no means theoretically necessary but is nonetheless expected for infants whose mental and developmental/neurological functions are hardly separated. It is awkward to compare results on those scales with categories that are somewhat crude. For example, if we run family rank against the Bayley Mental Scale and the Stanford Binet, classifying as agreements family ranks of "better" with IQ's of 100 or over, or family ranks of "middle" or "poor" with IQ's under 100, we are doomed to low agreement since intelligence quotients tend to be above average while family distribution was intentionally trimodal. Following that method, one gets an agreement of 60 per cent. The agreement is even worse when one wrestles with the Motor Scale scores since one finds no agreement between family rank and motor development.

SURPRISES

We have indicated that our control measure did not work as expected. The use or nonuse of LSD during pregnancy is a valueless predictor. However, the well-being of the infant—developmentally or psychologically as measured either by the Bayley Infant Behavior Profile or by an overall psychiatric/neurological examination—is associated with the adequacy of the parents, especially the mother. Her adequacy in child care includes personality and the emotions that are invested in child care. We have reason to believe that the same mother can have poor interpersonal relations with her peers and still manage to do a good job with her infant. Indeed, several cases occurred where mothers stated quite clearly that they considered themselves inadequate and inferior as mothers but where the psychiatrist and psychologist both disagreed. The psychiatrist did not discount the importance of the feelings of personal discontent; however, these women were doing a relatively good job of mothering—even if they functioned poorly in other ways and were full of self-doubt.

The other unexpected outcome is of major significance. We had presumed that a sample of young parents heavily involved in the drug life would produce many examples of inadequate parents; we thought that hippie mothers would, in general, be evaluated as incompetent and that this would be directly reflected in developmental, neurological, intellectual, or adjustmental deficiencies in the offspring. Even if the chronic use of cannabis, hallucinogens, and opium were not symptomatic of disorder, one might expect that such use would interfere with child care so as to produce liabilities in the development of the child. These were not the hypotheses which led to the study, but rather, our biases. Our data indicate that about one-third of the offspring show diminished—or at least partly unsatisfactory—functioning. However on motor and developmental scales, no tested child falls below the normal range. One may immediately call attention to serious and pervasive methodological deficiencies—not the least of which is the fact that only a minority of the children contacted were actually tested. For instance, the Bead Lady's child would be expected to show deficit on the Bayley scales, had it been tested. As one would expect the relationship is between infant outcomes and parental conduct, especially mothering. "Poor" families appear to produce deficient children; however, this also means that there are "better" families who produce children who are happy, normal in intelligence, and well developed. Being a hippie mother or using marijuana every day has no inevitable association with being a poor mother or with transmitting any visible risk to the child. We do not know about whatever risks may come along during adolescence. The data in the early chapters may offer some outcome possibilities. Some portion of our findings may be attributed to changing self-definitions among mothers who were moving toward conservative, if not old-fashioned views. In this regard, one notes that neither hippie status nor drug use need be permanent. In a few parents, changes away from drug use seemed to be underway.

In retrospect, we believe we were wrong on several counts. First, we were mistaken in our original hypothesis that risk is related to reported LSD use in pregnancy. Second, we were wrong to expect substantiation of our personal bias. Possibly our error is a result of being too psychopathologically oriented, being straight, and too far over thirty. Admittedly, we had a bad taste in our mouths from aspects of the drug scene intimately observed over the last ten years. Thus, we also erred in a third area, wrongly expecting that the progression from research design to field application would yield a sizeable N—all neatly measured. The investigation suffered in consequence from methodological faults, some of which came from the nature of the sample, some from our own failure to anticipate trouble (none of which was correctable before we had run out of money and had lost one principal investigator to motherhood and South America).

SUMMARY

An investigation of hippie families or mother-child constellations was undertaken. Twenty-three families agreed to cooperate. Psychiatric evaluations of family interaction, maternal and paternal behavior, and young offspring were conducted in eighteen families. Children were also subject to gross neurological examination, and fifteen children were given tests of motor and mental development. Only ten families of the original twenty-three stayed put long enough to allow the completion of all measures. Methodological difficulties associated with maintaining the cooperation of these families are pervasive, and the findings of this investigation must be considered with caution. Our initial concept of risk sought to divide the sample into mothers who had taken LSD during pregnancy and those who had not. We expected not only different developmental outcomes in infants but also associated correlates of personal or maternal adequacy. This concept proved difficult to test. Our information indicates that the use of LSD during pregnancy is related neither to the mother's capacities for mothering nor to the child's health and mental status. The major weakness in our risk test was methodological; we could not be sure maternal reports of particular drug use were reliable. Also, focusing our attention on abstinence from LSD alone was an experimental weakness in that our design did not reflect real-life situations.

We found that psychiatric and psychological evaluations of parental or mother adequacy were in agreement. Such psychiatric evaluations also tended to correspond with the psychiatric and psychological status of infants and children. This correspondence did not extend to test results. Although about one-third of the children had some diminished or maladaptive functioning, all children in the sample were normal on motor and mental development. On the basis of a global classification of evaluation materials, mothers or families were classified into better, middle, or poor parents. Since drug use, especially cannabis and hallucinogens, is extensive in all the families, it is evident that drug use per se does not prevent adequate mothering, nor does it necessarily lead to developmental, mental, or adjustmental difficulties in the offspring. It is noted that neither hippie status nor drug use need be permanent, and some mothers were undergoing changes in a conventional direction. There is some reason to believe that young women can do well in their child-rearing task, even if otherwise suffering from some personality problem. It is also evident that some of the mothers (from one- to two-thirds) were suffering from personal malfunctions which were expressed in child care and associated with problem behavior in the offspring. The expectation that hippie families exemplify the transmission of drug use to their offspring by direct exposure and by teaching of values is supported.

Intensive Clinical
Study

❧ 12 ❧

When something goes wrong
with a youngster, the sophisticated observer will not blame him,
but his family. So it is with young people's drug use, but we should
ask whether families can and actually do play a role. If they can
exert such an influence, we should try to discover what they should
aim for and what they should avoid. A large sector of the older
generation deplores drug use in the younger; but drug use in
young people is so widespread that we must ask ourselves whether
we are faced with a novel symptom of growth that is consonant
with the times, or whether there really is cause for alarm. The
clinician will be likely to worry more about the child who lags
behind than about the child who goes along with the herd; he
may even wonder whether the child who abstains from drugs
might not be such a lagger. One of the first questions the clinician
will ask is: "If certain ways of child rearing can indeed prevent
drug use, what, if any, is the price attached to a youngster's
obedience to parental teachings?" What might the family and the
youngster have to give up in order to achieve abstinence? Looking

at it from another angle, a clinician will consider the fact that drug use of all kinds, licit and illicit, is a fact of American life among parents as well as among children. Some say drug use has reached epidemic proportions. It is public health practice to inoculate the susceptible population in an epidemic. But in this so-called drug epidemic, where is the vaccine? The optimistic clinician might consider that drug experimentation among the young is itself such a vaccine, analogous to a mild case which acts to immunize the person against severe illness. The pessimist fears such experimentation, worrying that the youngster will contract the disease for good and succumb. Possibly both attitudes are right. In any event, it is of the utmost importance to discover what factors protect one young experimenter and what factors render another one vulnerable.

The epidemiologist thinks in terms of his patients' micro- and macroenvironment, of disease vectors, and of primary and secondary disease hosts. In order to understand at least one part of the spread of drug use among the young, we have limited our study to factors in the microenvironment of the family since these factors are different for each youngster. The macroenvironment— school, peer groups, climate, socioeconomic standing, the national and world scene—are the same for all of the families in our study by virtue of the experimental design. Our assumption was that the interaction among family members would provide clues about the primary hosts and vectors. This assumption was based on the previous finding (Blum, 1969) that an older sibling can be the means whereby a younger sibling has access to drugs. The older child frequently initiates the younger. We had also learned that the degree of prescribed and unprescribed drug use among parents is positively correlated with children's illicit drug use. Such a correlation pointed to the possibility that the parent is in some way part of the child's drug-use syndrome. We conceived of the family (both the siblings and the parents) as the primary host. This hunch did not tell us what form the drug-generating syndrome might take in the parent, how it is transmitted, or what other forms it could assume in the new host, the youngster. We were also unable to guess under what conditions the youngster would be susceptible or resistant.

We had additional reasons to focus on family interactions. In our previous investigation of students' value systems (religious beliefs, esthetic interests, and political convictions), we discovered that we could partly predict drug-use patterns. We also found that a student's value system was not invented by him independently; rather, his values are taken over from his parents. We had been surprised to discover in the latter-day revolutionary a chip off the old liberal-radical block. As several students told us, "We are only practicing what our parents gave lip service to." To anticipate, these are the very words used by a mother in our intensive video tape experiment to describe her child-rearing practices in relation to her own mother's precepts. In all our studies we have found— and other investigators report similar results (Lipset, 1971)—that the reformer is not necessarily substituting revolt against the political system for rebellion against his father. On the contrary, it is likely that the revolutionary is carrying on a family tradition. A prominent example of such an occurrence is Bettina Aptheker, a student radical leader who comes from a solid radical background.

We had other reasons to suspect that parents are more important in forming their children's outlooks and subsequent behavior than they often realize. During one of our first drug studies (Blum & associates, 1964), we had conceived of the pioneering LSD user as akin to religious converts. We went about looking for converts, trying to learn about the phenomenon of conversion. We did not find any. It appeared that, unlike the Middle Ages, the present day offers little opportunity for profound shifts in religious belief. We saw a strong persistence in beliefs from one generation to the next, whether the belief consisted of atheism, agnosticism, indifference, or religious conviction. A child might change labels; a son from an agnostic Jewish family might, for example, join the Unitarian church, following his father in leaving the question of God in abeyance. Or a child from a Catholic family might become an Episcopalian, allowing him to continue to worship the Virgin. In both cases, the shift would be insignificant insofar as the basic credo is concerned. The change involves a social move only from membership in a minority to one in the (Protestant) majority. Throughout our previous investigations, there have been insistent reminders that parental attitudes are not easily disregarded or rejected. A number of factors indicated that parental attitudes toward drugs in general had an effect on children's drug use. The child is not indifferent to his parent's assumption that medicines are basically good and are not to be feared (as attested by the fullness of the family medicine chest). The child is also aware when parents are dubious about the value of medicines and concerned about the potential side effects (as attested by a medicine cabinet empty of pharmaceuticals). Clearly, families pass on certain values very successfully; yet, the extent to which this is intentional remains unclear. For example, if a parent is permissive, believing that his daughter should make decisions for herself, and if the parent also believes that sexual activities are in themselves not bad, should he be surprised and chagrined if this same teenage daughter comes home pregnant? The same analogy holds for drugs. A parent with no interest in illicit drugs might well wonder why his adolescent child is on various trips; he may wonder whether he should step in, even though he believes that he should not frustrate the child's curiosity. We surmised that the modern parent who does not follow the precepts of child-rearing which have evolved from the wisdom and experiences of past generations, has no way of foreseeing how the child will interpret and apply the principles he has absorbed. Such a parent cannot predict whether the value system he has taught the child will protect the child from danger or whether it will induce him to take risks with drugs, sex, or political innovation. The cherished values of freedom, curiosity, and pleasure are interlocked in the teenage experiments with drugs, sex, and radicalism. Is it not inevitable that these values will lead to quite unpredictable results, unless they are imbedded from early childhood on and within a context which limits and circumscribes their application? It is this context which we investigated. Yet both limits and proscriptions are part of the old-fashioned methods of child rearing. These methods have served us relatively well in the past. Have they become irrelevant? Will they lead the child to another form of disaster as he grows up to become an anachronism? Again the context of the family atmosphere, the quality of family interactions, or family dynamics appeared to be the appropriate subject for enquiry.

In formulating the initial hypotheses, we drew on previous studies, clinical experience, and psychodynamic theory. Our first assumption was that the families themselves could tell us in words and deeds what and how they have taught their children and to what end. They could tell us what methods were effective and what factors were ineffective in getting the message across. From their experience of "growing up together," as one of the fathers put it, we believed that parents and children could recommend or discourage certain courses of action. Our second assumption was that reliable clinical observations could be made by psychologists and psychiatrists on family interactions. We felt that these observations would yield further information which family members had not been willing or able to give spontaneously but which was nevertheless important for an understanding of the family dynamics. Such an understanding would allow us to specify the factors that had produced the outcomes. We were concerned with two sets of outcomes in each family. One was the drug-risk score leading to the drug-risk rank of the family. The other was the excellence of the family interaction in terms of promoting the social and emotional growth of all of its members.

We wanted to learn what relationship existed between the family's drug-risk rank and the excellency of family interaction. We expected a correlation, but not on a one-to-one basis. In the intensive clinical observations, we set out to look for differences between families whose children were drug users with a high risk of getting into serious trouble and families whose children were low risk users. We expected positive attitudes toward authority, tradition, discipline, self-control and firm standards in the low-risk families. We predicted negative attitudes or indifference in the high-risk group. High-risk families would be more interested in innovation, more permissive, more indecisive (or possibly more flexible), and more helpless vis-à-vis their children than would low risk families. The emphasis in high risk families would be on impulse gratification rather than on impulse control. Pleasure, not abstinence, was the expected theme. In line with respect for authority and tradition, we expected our low-risk families to obey laws, to maintain close ties with their fathers, and to attempt to model themselves on their fathers. As a consequence, a strong differentiation between parent-child roles would emerge as well as a strong sex role differentiation, where the mother plays the traditional feminine-nurturant role and the father assumes the emotional and financial leadership. In the high risk families we expected the opposite: the children and parents in an egalitarian relationship instead of a hierarchical one. Ties to the parental father would be weak or nonexisting; or, if a tie existed, it would be of a derogatory nature. As a consequence of the rejection of the parental father, there would be sex role diffusion in the parents; the mother would dominate in family affairs, and the father would defer.

Our last postulate was that the value system would be different in the two sets of families. We expected low-risk families to embrace religion, faith, traditional principles, patriotism, and altruism (civic and personal virtues and responsibilities). We expected the high-risk families to embrace notions of freedom, experimentation, curiosity, skepticism, and science, with a stress on personal growth and pleasure. We foresaw that the result for the future-oriented high-risk parent would be doubt and self-distrust, whereas the low-risk parent would profit from the certainty and self-assurance of traditions. In summary, our hypotheses stated that in the areas of authority, pleasure, sex roles, and values, major differences exist between the high- and low-risk families and that the latter are more secure than are the former. Our hypotheses stated nothing with regard to the excellency of family interaction.

Our hypotheses are closely linked with concepts that other investigators have pursued for some time. Some of our expectations also derived from the results of the formal pretest and rating study of middle-class families. Thus, our clinical enterprise and the interview and rating studies described previously began with the same set of concepts, but each approach set out on a different path.

We believed that the family has an important role to play in transmitting and shaping drug ethics and drug use patterns from one generation to the next. The family is an enduring entity which continues in a distinct way for many generations. We were convinced that it would not be sufficient to learn what the specific teachings of parents about particular drugs had been. To comprehend the family, that is, the essence of their beliefs and style, required identifying something more pervasive and underlying. We would have to search for belief and value systems that are intergenerational and that influence a variety of behaviors— drug use, truancy, self-discipline, and so on. We would have to discover special ways in which one family worked as a unit, how its individual members interacted, and how their own personalities mediated the transmission or reception of styles and values. Such enquiry is subsumed under the term *family dynamics* and asks how the whole mix is translated by the child into his particular kind of drug behavior.

One of the two approaches to learning about this complex transformation is to question the participants in the process; the other approach is to observe the process itself. We wished to use both approaches; therefore, we conducted discussions and observations in a controlled setting, filmed on video tape. Our thought was that if we put our questions and hunches directly to the families, they would be able to tell us much, not only by their words but also by their deeds. We wanted to give the families an opportunity to instruct us in a realistic setting. We wanted to avoid contrived and superficial elements in order to generate a spontaneous discussion of important topics bearing on child rearing and drug use. We had to have a way of stimulating and guiding families without biasing them so that they would "tell us what we wanted to hear."

We also wanted to collect information which would provide us with insights and which would allow others to decide whether they agreed with our interpretations and conclusions. We also wanted a mechanism which would allow an intensive study. This meant looking again and again at the material to be sure our observations and conclusions could be replicated. These considerations helped us choose our procedures and apparatus. We decided to video tape all of our family discussions. Discussions would be held in the same place with the same people present and the same themes under consideration. Video tape allows repeated study and can be studied by anyone who had not been present during the filming.

The 101 white middle-class families, which we already had studied in the interview-and-rating, constituted the pool from which we selected families for intensive observation. The voluminous data we had on them were to contribute to the clinical work which was to go beyond interview and surface-behavior rating to inference and psychodynamic characterizations. The families had already been given a drug-risk rank. The task was to secure further cooperation from a few of them. (Our intensive study method was restricted by time and money and did not allow all of our original families to be seen again by clinicians.)

We had intended to see the five highest and five lowest scoring families in the total sample. Expecting some to refuse or drop out before filming, we contacted twenty-four families. Among the high-risk families, two refused and three were unable to participate. Among the low-risk families, three refused, and four claimed inability to participate. This gave us a sample of seven high-risk and five low-risk families. As an afterthought, we decided also to see one moderate-risk family for comparative purposes and so we invited one family whose score was at the exact median. This family accepted, giving us a total sample of thirteen. The staff managed the selection process, and the interviewer who had originally seen the family preferred the invitation to participate in this second phase. Thus, clinicians remained ignorant of the drug-risk scores and, beyond knowing that there were at least five each from the high- and low-risk groups and one moderate family, they did not know from which end of the distribution the remaining two families had been drawn. Before beginning the video tape experiment, we wanted a chance to test equipment and procedures. Three families from the Caucasian blue-collar sample were paid to be subjects for a pretest, the results of which were used to ready us for work with the middle-class sample.

All parents and children in the experimental families were invited to a group discussion on how families could prepare children for the opportunities and the dangers that are met in life. The families were informed that the purpose of these discussions was to assist us in the writing of this book. The families were promised anonymity and confidentiality. All materials were handled by code numbers, and an alias was assigned so that only the two staff psychologists knew the families' true names. Families were advised never to use their true names during filming. Two staff psychologists, one male and one female, directed the film sessions. To minimize their influence on the discussion, their activity was circumscribed. Before filming, they explained the purpose of the events and introduced the five standard topics for discussion. The psychologists kept track of time and facilitated transitions from one topic to the next. The burden of the questioning and probing fell to three discussion leaders who constituted the rest of the film staff. The discussion leaders were to challenge family members to take a stand on the issues of authority, tradition, pleasure, the here-and-now, and religious values. The discussion leaders, or role representatives as we called them, had been chosen on the basis of how their special life styles related to the issue areas. All role representatives were genuine since we wanted authenticity.

Tradition and secular authority were represented by a narcotics officer (a sergeant). Sacred authority and transcendental religious values were represented by an Episcopalian minister. Both appeared at the film sessions in their official regalia; the officer carried his handcuffs and gun as he did ordinarily. These were visible. The minister was dressed in cloth and collar. The here-and-now, pleasure, sex, drugs, freedom, and individualism were represented by a hippie girl. We had two such girls in the course of the filming, one of whom called herself a "neohippie." The other preferred to be "she": a changeable, unpredictable creature of the moment. One day, she dressed in a transparent blouse without brassiere, had long wild hair, bare feet, and unshaven legs. The next day, she wore a prim jacket borrowed from the female psychologist, and put her hair in a bun. At one session she espoused love, at the next, violence. Throughout, one could count on her to resist being pigeonholed in a consistent point of view.

We had attempted to find a young, pretty, hippie girl with sex appeal. We succeeded only in part, for we had to compromise when it proved impossible to combine the ephemeral quality of the out-and-out hippie with the demands for faithful attendance at every film session. We had to content ourselves with a role representative who believed in hippie values but did not live them to the fullest. Even so, one of the girls quit in the middle of the project and had to be replaced; the second girl preferred to provoke the staff instead of the families. Notwithstanding these difficulties, the families accepted and reacted to the hippie according to our intention—as spokeswoman for freedom, drug use, sex, pleasure, and the right of the individual to decide upon his own conduct regardless of the law.

The filming occasion was organized as follows: arrival of the family, introduction by pseudonym to the film staff, and a short get-acquainted period over coffee and cake to set an informal tone. Family members were also invited to inspect the video tape equipment while it was idling. They could see each other in the finder.

The filming started when one of the psychologists asked the family members to introduce themselves and to state who in their family had not been able to come and why. The psychologist then emphasized our wish to benefit from the families' good and bad experiences and from their recommendations for preventing drug abuse. The families were told why the two psychologists would try not to give their own opinions; instead, experts in three life styles would stimulate and challenge the families. No unanimity among family views was necessary; on the contrary, much would be learned from disagreement. We told the families our hope was that as many different opinions would be voiced as possible; polite language was not necessary. Our hippie girl was usually the first to demonstrate that in practice.

Each discussion leader was introduced and asked to make a five minute position statement covering two major points of his philosophy. The narcotics officer expressed his genuinely emphatic stand against illegal drug use, his conviction in favor of obedience to law and parental authority, and his belief in firm parental discipline. The hippie girl spoke of her basic belief in freedom and love:

Some people want guns, they want to fight a revolution; but
the revolution starts with the individual. In order to be free you
have to throw off *all* authority; you can't be *free* until you are
rid of all fear, fear of the past, wants of the future. [You have to]
live totally in the present; sometimes that is very frightening.
If something in the past was true, it stays true through the ages,
the true is there, and you need no one to tell you about it.
Traditions, religions, and nationalities separate people because
all of these make one person right and the other one wrong.
You have to be *free* to love, that's basic. You have to get rid of
all the garbage first to be *free* to *love* people—not romantic love,
and Christian love is not it either. That's hate, because Christians
want to save the world. They want everyone to be the same
because Christians love themselves. Love is a great compassion
for humanity and understanding enough not to let humanity die.
Fun, enjoyment, pleasure are important. LSD and the other mind-
expanding drugs are good. They are *fun,* and they help you to
see yourself, see the things that are usually hidden. Sex is one of
the most important things. Children are curious, they are curious
about the trees, about their bodies. If they want to explore they
should not be stopped: curiosity should be left. I don't know any
virgin over fourteen. The natural tendencies in women are the
same as in men. I don't believe in marriage, or that people are
monogamous—men or women. But *enjoyment* must be there, at
least physical enjoyment. It is by being *free* himself that the
parent teaches the kid to *enjoy*. If a parent is everything I have
stated, not afraid, has thrown out all the garbage, then he'd be
such a beautiful person himself that it would automatically elimi-
nate violence and hatred. Then he can't do evil or teach the kids
evil. The worst parents can do to their children is to make them
obey *their* rules without question because that teaches the child
to depend on someone else's say-so and the world will stay in the
same mess the parents have left it in.

It was an appealing, seductive statement. Although she
varied her opinions at each session, her gift of words and, when
she was in the mood, her appeal remained the same, and our intent
to involve the families in her discourse was served.

Our replacement "hippie" (when the first left us) stuck to
a script she had worked out. It too dealt with rejection of authority,
with doing what one wants about drugs and sex, and with experi-
encing new emotions and relationships regardless of convention
and propriety. She talked about not interfering in others' affairs

("he has his bag, and I have mine") and about the need for parents to teach their children how to enjoy and experience everything. She regarded school as boring and stifling. She believed each person has a right to "ecstatic learning experiences; to learn in new, untried, and unapproved ways, through mind-expanding drugs. The worst parents can do is to make their children obey them, to keep them from trying out for themselves, and from inventing their own lives." Young and attractive, our second hippie had no trouble evoking family reactions to her views.

The minister offered his views last. He talked of eternal values, the hazard of using drugs to achieve valid spiritual insight, and the importance of religion and ideals for family life and for the survival of society. After his five-minute position statement, the second staff psychologist turned the meeting over to the families and discussion leaders for a fifty-minute brainstorming session on the issues that should be included in a guide for parents. They discussed what solutions should be considered for problems faced by most parents and what observations the families had made on how children should be reared. After the initial free-for-all a coffee-and-cake break was scheduled—only part of which was filmed. The filming resumed with a five-minute period during which only the families were to give their final recommendations. All families were allowed as much time as needed.

The discussion leaders then asked the families questions about the generation gap. How had the parents' own fathers handled educational and child-rearing issues in their time? The children also commented about the grandfathers. To facilitate recollection, the families brought pictures of their parents which they looked at while talking about them. Another fifteen minutes were devoted to an enquiry about resemblances between the children and other family members. The final area for discussion was the staff itself who left the room to afford the family at least a semblance of privacy. The mother in each family was to decide whom among the three male staff members (psychologist, minister, or narcotics officer) she would choose as (a) father for her children and (b) as husband or lover (or both). The father of each family had a similar choice between the two female staff members (the psychologist and the hippie girl). The children were not offered any choices but were invited to comment. As soon as the parents had made their decisions, the film staff returned for leave taking. What time was left was spent in talking over the families' reactions to the meeting and their suggestions for improvement. The total film time was two hours.

In sum, the meeting was structured to permit observations of a variety of verbal and nonverbal behavior elicited by the role representatives, the refreshments, and the tasks. The period of free discussion told us how each family member thought and felt about matters such as respect, obedience to the law, belief in God, reference and spiritual values, attachment to the past, and enjoyment of the moment. We noted their opinions on how these values are related to child rearing and on which values are most important. On the nonverbal level, the various phases of the meeting allowed us to study how family members approached unfamiliar tasks, ranging from the relatively unstructured brainstorming session to the specific task of giving recommendations. We noted how they responded to the conventional request of recalling their own parents' conduct and to the unconventional request of choosing love objects and father figures from among the staff. The coffee break afforded us an opportunity to learn about the family's ingestion patterns—an area related to drug intake.

Film analysis allowed us to identify the leaders and followers, defenders, conciliators, and troublemakers in a family. Some families proceeded directly and efficiently to the tasks set for them; others never managed to cope effectively with all of the situations. Some parents turned to their children for help and guidance; some spoke for their children, and some gave their children precedence but reserved the last word for themselves. A comparison of reactions to the role representatives and a family member's own stated point of view allowed us to infer discrepancies or harmony between his intellectual and emotional convictions or, in other cases, harmony between belief and behavior.

For example, did a family who professed great respect for law and order listen carefully to the narcotics officer? Or did the children in such a family whisper and laugh discreetly while the parents stifled a yawn? What about a family who appeared in far out dress and hairstyles? Did the children cry "right on" every time the hippie made an outrageous pronouncement? Did mother or father look down their noses, taking exception to her remarks? Did the same parent give explicit consent to vulgarity, promiscuity, or profligacy but silently renege by some gesture and other indicator of repudiation?

A family's recommendations allowed us to compare what had been emphasized and what had actually emerged during the film sessions—that is, recommendations and behavior were amenable to a discrepancy and congruency analysis. If a family recommended love and consideration, did its members demonstrate these qualities as well? If one member should fall from grace during the session, was he corrected? If so, was this done with tact and concern for his feelings? When discussing the grandfathers' methods and possible failings, did the speaker relay the impression of thoughtfulness and acceptance? How did the recommendations compare to the parental fathers' styles of child rearing and to his grandchildren's approach to sex and drugs? The technique of having parents recollect their own fathers' methods of discipline had been devised to assess the continuity of value systems. Erickson's (1950) brilliant analysis of the influence of the father imago (imagined and real characteristics which are consolidated into a dynamic memory) on his daughter's choice of husband and her subsequent ways of rearing her sons suggested this technique. By also having fathers tell about their own fathers, we learned about the great impact that the child's paternal grandfather has on the second generation family.

The task of identifying family resemblances provided relief from the emotionally loaded tasks. This task was designed to assess the role a given child had been assigned or had chosen for himself. We deemed it significant if one child was said to resemble cousin so-and-so, who has a serious drug problem and is a troublemaker, or if another child indicated that he was like his father whom he admired for his ability to follow through in a self-discipline manner. Whereas recollection of the paternal father tapped the model for the parents, the resemblance of the child tapped the models for the children. This technique was not always successful, but it did produce some results. For example, a family who prized the individuality of each child strongly refused to discover resemblances precisely because they did not want to cast any child into a preformed mold.

The love choice and the father choice were intended to be the denouement—the final clue as to how parents resolved the question of choosing a mate or lover. From the family's point of view, the shoe was put on the other foot; they now had a chance to evaluate the staff instead of being prodded and quizzed, startled and observed. The forced choice gave the parents a number of alternatives: they could refuse to comply, either spontaneously or under jealous pressure from their mate or their children. They could comply merely as a matter of form, in which case they made a pretend choice and not a real one. One way to accomplish this was to delegate the task to the children who had been explicitly instructed only to make comments. The children could then either refuse to choose, make the choice for their parents, encourage their parents, or indicate that they did not think much of their parents' decision making abilities. Finally, real choices could be made. This could be done wholeheartedly or with various degrees of ambivalence or rationalization. The basis for the real choice was also interesting. Status was one deciding factor, as when a prestige-oriented mother chose the person with an academic degree (the psychologist). Personal appeal could be another reason, or transference might play a role, as when one small girl chose a pipe smoker since her father also smoked a pipe. An avoidance of sexuality may have motivated some mothers to chose the minister "because he would think of higher things than sex alone." Sexual attraction was another basis for choice, as when the very masculine and dominant narcotics officer was chosen for a lover or when the father of a family chose the hippie girl because she was "very attractive." When a middle-aged man picks a pretty young girl for a "wife," he can do so in a spirit of adventure or happy sexuality, or he can do so with misgivings about deciding in favor of pleasure when the older woman (staff psychologist) would seemingly have been the reasonable choice. Indeed, many wives were eager to convince their husbands to change their minds. The films made it quite evident whether a husband would pretend or really give up pleasure for the sake of peace or decorum or whether he would stick to his guns.

The father and mother choice helped us infer what qualities

the parents were looking for in a father or mother. Did they look for qualities such as insight into human behavior and feelings? Did they prefer someone who could take a strong stand on right and wrong? Did they prefer one who was dedicated to eternal truths? Or should the mother of one's children be happy, free, and easy? The love choice was intended to make the conflicts between duty and pleasure or between convention and individualism very immediate and real. The technique accomplished this goal and led to other unexpected benefits for the clinicians.

RELIABILITY OF OBSERVATION

We wondered whether it would be possible for separate viewers of the film to agree on delimited areas of well-defined behavior, elements of family interaction, and gestures expressive of mood and feeling. The video tapes of family discussions were shown to one of the staff psychologists who had directed the film sessions and to two staff interviewers who had conducted the interview and rating study of the middle-class families. With one exception, one of these two interviewers had also been the original interviewer of each family that agreed to cooperate in the intensive video tape enterprise. We were, therefore, able to test the agreement of the interviewer with herself, seeing the family in two ways. We first saw the family through the interview and rating study which averaged eight hours. Then—usually about one year later—we saw the same family on tape discussing matters related to child rearing and drug use. Comparisons were limited to conduct and query areas common to both sets of occasions. Because the three raters were looking at the video tapes anew and were rating conduct during those sessions independently, we had a chance to determine interrater reliability. We also did a repeat reliability test for the raters on the film material, presenting the film to three raters on two occasions to test agreement beween the first and second showing.

To allow for maximum error, raters were required to indicate whether a certain behavior (discipline, humor, ridicule, or the like) was present or absent. If a certain behavior was present, the raters were to note its impact—that is, whether the child responded to that parental action. Such ratings required detailed qualification. The rater had to decide whether there was general agreement, some agreement, some disagreement, or complete disagreement. Thus, the reliability measure includes judgments of the presence or absence of particular traits or behaviors. For certain items, there were subsequent evaluations on a scale of one to three, or one to five. On each such item, raters could disagree in two ways. They could disagree on presence or on the subsequent position on the scale. Because this method allows the rater to indicate the absence of a behavior, the total number of items to be compared differs. We used an average per cent agreement method centering on twenty enquiry areas with thirty-two items in each area. We arbitrarily considered agreement as scaled ratings one place removed and disagreement as two scale points or more removed. The maximum number of entries by any one rater was 2,933 and the minimum was 2,709 for interrater comparisons on the video material. From the original family ratings and video tape ratings 1,241 items were rated for consistency. As regards the latter procedure, error is maximized by the fact that the filmed sessions were held in a very different setting with different people and different topics than those of the original home interviews. Our reliability test results on the video tape viewing are shown in Table 17.

Table 17

Results from Reliability Tests of Video Tape Viewing in Intensive Clinical Study

First Viewing	% Agreement
Rater 1 with rater 2	86
Rater 1 with rater 3	85
Rater 2 with rater 3	88
First Viewing Compared *with Second Viewing*	
Rater 1	92
Rater 2	95
Rater 3	92
Original Family Interview *with Video Tape Ratings*	
Both interviewers combined	83

We consider these results satisfactory and conclude that families and interviewers acted consistently from the time of the original interview at home to the video filming one year later. We conclude that the two trained interviewers and the psychologist were in good agreement when independently rating aspects such as ego strength; energy level; interpersonal affection or hostility; moods; children's actions; appearance; domination; attitudes toward the interviewer; verbal and nonverbal participation; eye contact; family consensus on education, discipline, religion, and law and order; and family perseverance on tasks. We also conclude that raters were individually consistent on two viewing occasions.

The demonstration of the reliability of judgments allows us to infer that we were looking at real behavior. We then proceeded to compare independent clinical evaluations of the psychodynamics of family interactions. This step occurs at a further level of inference and abstraction, embraces broader behaviors, and includes theoretical constructions. The task of the clinicians was independently to review all information available on the experimental families. With one (accidental) exception, clinicians did not have access to the drug risk sources and relative ranks obtained by the families until after evaluations had been made and ratings and rankings compared. This does not mean, however, that the clinicians were totally unaware of the children's drug use or nonuse. For one, parents and children sometimes alluded to it during the film sessions, although we made a deliberate effort not to ask any questions on this topic. For another, the interviews from the middle-class study contained a detailed drug history on each child. We deliberately gave the clinicians access to all information, including the interview materials, because we had decided against blind clinical evaluations, hoping to maximize their knowledge and insight. We wanted the conditions of evaluation to approximate those of a real diagnostic and therapeutic situation.

The clinicians did not know the total drug scores since these were worked out by a rather complex calculation which comprised all of the children in a given family. Nor could the clinicians guess the rank of each experimental family within the middle-class sample. The clinicians did have some rather imprecise

notions of the existence or nonexistence of drug use in the
families, but they had no way of comparing one family with
another. Thus, clinical ratings and rankings were without regard to
drug use except for indirect consideration. The evaluation schedule outlined the method by which each clinician approached the
family material and wrote up his impressions. That procedure
called for each clinician to make statements on vulnerability to
stress and likely outcomes for the children. This section (called
general risks) required the clinicians to estimate the likelihood of
children's future participation in delinquency, school problems,
character malformation, and psychosomatic or psychological illness. Drug dependency potentials also required a statement. In
another section of the evaluation schedule, clinicians were required
to consider the functions of drug use. Avoidance, experimentation,
symbolic employment, and overuse were all to be conceived in
terms of the constellation of forces in the family and the personality and motives of each child. Emphasis was not on drug behavior
but on drug functions and the likelihood that forces in the child's
life would be expressed through some employment of psychoactive
substances.

CLINICAL EVALUATION

Clinical evaluations were made by two professionals—one
a psychoanalytically trained psychiatrist experienced in treating
drug users and their families. The film materials from the video
tape experiment and the individual interview material collected
on each family in the middle-class study were the psychiatrist's
sources of data. The other clinician was a psychoanalytically
trained psychologist, one of the two who had directed the filming
but had not participated in the first round of ratings. The psychologist had a strong hand in the previous drug studies and in
formulating the hypotheses for the intensive video tape observations. Each clinician wrote a separate description for each of the
families. For ease of comparison, they followed an outline which
specified the topics to be covered in the evaluation. The clinicians
did not have to limit themselves to the outline and could add to it
if a family provided novel or unexpected insights.

Each clinician then rated the excellence of family interactions. This was done independently. After each of their ratings were converted to ranks, we could compare how each clinician had judged the relative standing of the families with respect to the excellence of interaction. This procedure was followed for each clinical evaluation that led to the rankings. Topics covered by each clinician were compared for communalities and discrepancies, as was the overall interpretation of family dynamics. The two clinicians were in close enough agreement both on psychodynamics and on ratings of excellence to lead us to the conclusion that two clinicians of the same theoretical persuasion, with experience in the field of drug use, and using the same material can produce reliable descriptions of complex interactions and can rank overall impressions congruently.

We next attempted to resolve differences over detail and to reconcile thinking about those families where rankings of excellence were discrepant. The pooled judgment method was used, with intensive discussions and a pooled reviewing of data. To match the original ranking procedures, families were placed in one of three groups: excellent to good interaction, moderate or average interaction, and troubled or pathological interaction. By this time, family drug-score ranks were known to the clinicians; thus, the test was simply one of learning whether excellence ratings corresponded to drug risk categories. The final clinical task was a pattern analysis to discover ways in which families from the three categories differed. Since there is a relationship between excellence of interaction and family drug risk scores, the pattern analysis served to propose features in family interaction psychodynamics which are associated with varying drug risk for children.

SUMMARY

A diagnostic film technique was employed to make available information about individual family dynamics and interaction. The setting was a realistic and spontaneous situation which was experimentally controlled at the same time. The aim of the method was to produce descriptions of family patterns that were associated with kinds of drug risk among children. Fundamental to the choice of methods was an interest in parental and grand-parental belief and value systems, family organization, and family dynamics. All of these areas positively or negatively affect children's emotional and social growth. The film method consisted of discussions in which high-risk, low-risk, and moderate-risk middle-class white families discussed child rearing and children's drug use, making recommendations to parents for appropriate action. These two hour sessions sought a spontaneous exchange keyed to certain issues and eliciting family feelings and interactions. Three genuine role representatives were included in the sessions to ensure emotional loading. One role representative was an Episcopalian minister, one was a narcotics agent, and one was a young pretty hippie girl. Each dressed appropriately to his role and undertook to examine important issues. A sequence of tasks and activities took place, and the reactions of the families constituted the information for clinical evaluation. Reliability of rating was achieved (1) among three raters independently viewing the films for surface behavior, (2) for these same raters' agreement with themselves on a first and second viewing, and (3) for the family interviewer who had done the original interview and, one year later, the rating study on the same family.

Two clinicians, both psychoanalytically oriented and experienced with drug-using families, independently evaluated the film material according to an evaluation schedule. They had access to all the data from the original interviews, but they were unaware of the drug-use scores of the children and the subsequent family ranking on drug risk. In addition to required topics for evaluation, each clinician independently ranked the families for excellence of interaction. Clinicians were in agreement on their dynamic conceptions and on their rankings as to excellence of interaction. The clinicians reviewed the materials again to iron out discrepancies on details and to make a final ranking. Three categories of excellence (good, average, and troubled or pathological) were used for the final ranking. A family portrait was written for each family which set forth major patterns of interaction and dynamics. Postexperimental sessions averaging eighty hours per family were required for final reviewing and evaluating.

Family Dynamics

❧ 13 ❧

In the present chapter, findings from the intensive study are presented, and patterns which distinguish excellence are analyzed. Before proceeding to the clinical descriptions, however, we shall first report results that bear on the agreement between the two clinicians. Independently, the two clinicians developed portraits of the film families after analyzing previously specified interactions and personality traits. The clinicians independently rated quality of interaction between family members on the basis of these portraits and then ranked each family in order of excellence of the observed and inferred dynamics. The ranks were from one to thirteen, with the lowest score signifying the most excellent family interactions and thirteen the most psychopathological.

Comparison of the rank order of the thirteen families yielded a coefficient of correlation $r = .82$, significant at the .05 level. Clinician agreement was considerable and significant. To maximize clinical acumen and to benefit from each other's views, clinicians then discussed each of the families in detail. A few changes in ranks were made as a result. Before presenting the resulting pooled ranks, we must mention how and why clinicians differed in minor ways in their independent rankings of family interaction.

247

The clinicians were unanimous in the placement of four families. A one-point rank difference occurred in four other families, and two-point differences occurred in another three families. For one family, there was a three-point rank difference, and six-point rank differences occurred on the remaining two families. Analysis of the individual family portraits revealed that none of the differences arose from evaluations of family dynamics or personality traits. In all those families where rank differences occurred, discrepancies hinged on the degree of pathology.

Let us take the Sullivan family as an example of the clinicians' disagreement. One clinician ranked the family one point above the most pathological score. The other clinician gave the family an average rank. Despite a six-point difference in placement with regard to excellency of interaction, the clinicians agreed on all the dynamic features. Opinions were at variance on the severity of Mrs. Sullivan's disturbance. One clinician believed that Mrs. Sullivan was in greater emotional difficulty and had a more pathogenic effect on her children than did the other. The latter clinician described her as merely confused, timid, and without firm convictions. The clinician assumed that she had lacked proper upbringing and schooling and, therefore, had little equipment with which to judge and decide. She applied childish and inadequate techniques to situations which demanded mature handling. The clinician saw her as a frustrated and ineffective person. The other clinician also saw her as ineffective and incapable of coping with her children, but this clinician believed that Mrs. Sullivan was more than frustrated. She had given many indications that she was suffering from inchoate rage. Her indirect way of speaking and inability to express her feelings or to take a stand on any issue were believed to be due to her efforts to control all emotion, lest she explode.

Both clinicians agreed that Mrs. Sullivan was not feminine. One believed that Mrs. Sullivan actively disliked being a woman, that her lack of pleasure and pride in being a wife and mother contributed to her low self-esteem, her inability to take a stand, and her low level of maternal skills. The one clinician considered Mrs. Sullivan an unfortunate model for her daughter—one who had already demonstrated difficulties in sexual adjustment. The other emphasized that Mrs. Sullivan was sexually neuter by accident, not by design. This clinician conceded that this would nevertheless have pathogenic effects on the children. Both clinicians agreed that Mrs. Sullivan would have wished her impact to be different—certainly a factor in ranking this family above the most pathogenic.

The clinicians also disagreed somewhat in evaluating the degree of structure in the Sullivan family. Whereas one characterized the family as disorganized, the other thought of it as chaotic. The latter noted that it was often impossible to hear what was being said because all members spoke at once; the other observed that eventually the family would cede the floor to one of its members. This clinician pointed out that the children contributed to family unity since the eldest had taken over as the parent, lecturing, criticizing, and directing the real parents as though the parents were wayward children. The other clinician agreed to this description but felt that such behavior was undesirable, underlining Mrs. Sullivan's immaturity and Mr. Sullivan's incompetence. Both clinicians were in accord that the Sullivans, while unable to offer their children an optimal or even average home atmosphere, had at least no malevolent intentions toward the children. They neither exploited the children nor did they abuse them. Final pooling of evaluations placed this family into the troubled and pathological category. A two-point rank difference between clinicians could not be resolved. One clinician gave the Sullivans a rank of ten, putting it in the troubled category. The other clinician gave the family a rank of twelve, putting it into the pathological category.

In considering the thirteen families, we found five classifications according to which the families were ordered. These were: superior, good, average, troubled, and pathological. Thus, as our thirteen ranks were reviewed, there was a movement toward condensing our classification system. We jointly reevaluated and reranked all families. The final scores from one to thirteen as presented in Table 15 represents an order which reflects both the agreement and disagreement of the two clinicians. A comparison of these ranks yields a rank order coefficient, $\rho = .97$, significant at the .01 level. The differences in point scores proved to be easily reconciled with further condensation of the classifications into three groups: superior and good were combined into group I; average became group II; and troubled and pathological were combined into group III. Table 18 shows ranking of the individual

Table 18

Distribution of Pooled Ranks and Final Group Placement
of the Thirteen Experimental Families

Group	Classification	Pooled Rank	N
	Superior	1	
		2	
I			4
	Good	3.5	
		3.5	
	Average	5	
		6.5	
II		6.5	4
		8	
	Troubled	9	
		10–11 [a]	
III			5
	Pathological	10–12 [a]	
		11–12 [a]	
		13	
	Total		13

[a] Scores were the unresolved differences between the clinicians on the ordering of the thirteen families prior to placing them in the condensed three-group classification.

families and how the five operating concepts and the three final groups correspond. The irreconcilable score differences did not affect our subsequent presentation and pattern analysis since the families that were disagreed upon all fell into group III.

EXCELLENCE OF FAMILY INTERACTION

Our pattern analysis indicates that families can often protect their children from dangerous experimentation with drugs. The pattern analysis began by comparing the families' drug-risk and drug-rank scores with the clinical classifications obtained in the intensive study. Table 19 summarizes the results of this com-

Table 19

Excellence of Family Interaction Compared with
Drug-Risk Score and Drug-Risk Rank

Rank and Group Assigned in the Intensive Sample (N = 13)			Scores and Ranks Obtained in the Middle-Class Sample (N = 101)		
Pooled Clinical Evaluations Group					
Group I	Group II	Group III	Drug-Risk Score	Drug-Risk Rank	Quintile [a]
Super Good	Average Troubled	Pathological			
1			30	19.5	lowest
2			58	54	third
	3.5		20	6.5	lowest
	3.5		25	10.5	lowest
	5		130	89.5	highest
	6.5		140	93.5	highest
	6.5		27	13.5	lowest
	8		1	1	lowest
		9	108	82.5	highest
	10	11	108	82.5	highest
	10	12	120	86.5	highest
	11	12	150	95.5	highest
		13	110	84	highest

[a] All families but one had been drawn from the extreme drug-use groups. One had been drawn from the median drug-use score level.

parison. None of the children in the four families rated superior and good belonged in the high drug-risk category. The children in one of the superior families have never used any illicit drugs at all, but they have had an occasional drink of wine and some have smoked cigarettes from time to time. The same pattern prevails in both of the families rated good: no illicit drug use, occasional or no drinking, and no smoking. In the second family judged to be superior, there had been licit and illicit drug use, albeit benign and temporary, which gave the family a moderate drug-risk score of fifty-eight and a midrank position among all of the 101 middle-class families. In that family some of the children had tried marijuana; one gave it up, and another—an adopted child—worries about bad effects from his continuing amphetamine use. This family occasionally drinks wine, and a few of the children sometimes smoke cigarettes. In this family, some of the children have experimented, but none has gotten into difficulty. All of the five families rated as troubled and as pathological are in the upper fifth of the distribution (high risk group) with regard to the children's drug use.

In those families where interaction was diagnosed as disturbed, the children reflected parental problems through risky drug behavior as well as in other ways. This was not the case in the families where interaction was considered optimal for child development. Shall we conclude that zero drug use indicates parents are doing the best possible job of raising their children or, conversely, that drug use is a sign of trouble within the family? Because drug experimentation occurred in one of the superior families, we cannot infer that drug use alone is a sign of trouble; nor can we conclude that the children from superior or good families will never try illicit drugs in the future. We can predict that in all probability such experiments will not be damaging; indeed, experimentation (including drug use) can contribute to the overall growth of the child.

The four families rated average provided further clarification. Two of these families had children whose drug use placed them in the high risk group—both scores, in fact, were higher than those of the most pathological family. The rest of the average families had children whose drug use placed them in the lowest risk group. In one of these families there was zero illicit drug use; as for other drugs, one child had once tried a glass of wine. This was the lowest ranked family in the entire middle-class sample of 101 families. Both this family and another average family were lower in drug use than were the two families rated as superior. We see, then, that to be a superior family is not to be free from illicit drug experimentation, but rather, to be free from a high risk of dangerous drug outcome. To be average means that drug use is distributed widely over the risk continuum. To be troubled and pathological signifies high drug risk.

IMPORTANCE OF PARENTS

Many observers have come to believe that parents are losing their hold over their children to outside influences—especially to children's peers. Bronfenbrenner (1970) has reviewed impressive evidence of peer group dominion, whether it be manipulated by and for adult's purposes as in the Soviet Union, or whether it constitutes antiadult norms. Although we have no quarrel with these findings, we feel that studies which view behavior at a given moment in time will differ in their findings from studies that look to the origins of life styles. No one doubts that school performance can be influenced by class mates or that peers can instigate aggression or cheating in the child. Social influence is a fact of life, and the power of peers is sometimes taken to be the only influence in the life of the child. Yet, as our work shows, drug risk is best predicted by family factors; other factors hardly enter in. When looking intensively at families, we can see how this comes to pass.

All children in our study demonstrated how important their parents' love is to them. Some stated this explicitly; some showed it through resentment and misbehavior when they felt abandoned by their parents; and some merely implied it through the high price they were paying to maintain their parents' regard. Clearly, their parents were the dominant force in their lives—whether the child was seriously disturbed or ebulliently well adjusted. As far as the youngsters were concerned, what their parents had to teach them was far more important and effective than anything school teachers, officials, and law enforcement and health experts might tell them. These youngsters stated or implied that they do care about father and mother. One young person from a pathological family, explaining why he had returned home after running away, said to his parents: "You loved me, the police didn't." Another child told how he had taken to drugs and sporting long hair because his parents had left him for a long period in a boarding school. After their return, he gave up both long hair and drugs. His was an average family, though his previous drug use was only second to that of the highest drug user in the intensive study.

Another youngster recommended that one should never alienate one's parents "because whatever you have done, you can always come back; they'll always take you back no matter how dumb you have been." Whether his was a hope, a fear, or a belief is hard to distinguish. He continued: "You've got only one set of folks, don't blow it—that's the line I follow—don't cut off the connection with your family." His love for them was implied, not directly stated. The speaker had the highest drug risk score in the intensive study. He was a member of a pathological family. Contrast his statement with one similar in words, yet quite different in implication, by a child from a superior family: "There is no ultimatum, I have a home anytime; I respect their [the parents] opinions, I don't want to blow their trust." His sibling added: "If you know that your parents care for you, you have a responsibility not to hurt their feelings." Interestingly, the father of these same children gave an identical reason for his obedience to his own father's wishes. In other words, the pattern had repeated itself.

In regard to drug and sex education, the youngster with the highest risk score said: "School could have told me anything, and it wouldn't have impressed me. You are my parents. School is a standardized authority; at home we are told why; at school we were told the rules." We infer from this statement that the child wished to emphasize the emotional teaching of home and to minimize the merely intellectual teaching of school. A child in another pathological family complained that he and his parents were not open enough with each other. He added thoughtfully: "Maybe it's not worth it. It's not that I don't care." He looked sad and embarrassed and repeated the fact that indeed he cared very much.

One child from a good family explained that he emulated his father: "I think he presents an adequate example of what I want to be or the way I want to be. I don't respect him because he says 'don't do this' and hits me; I respect him because he's able to say 'don't do this' and can show me that I don't have to. For example, he quit smoking and because of that I can say my father

did it; he showed me the way, set an example. The same, he loves
my mother, so I plan to love my wife; and he loves his children,
so I plan to love my kids." In one of the four average families,
a child spoke directly about the importance of parents: "I don't
want to hurt them [father and mother]; I respect their views, but
I am the last born, very independent. [When I leave home] I will
make up my own mind, that's the way it's going to have to be."
In response to a question about taking drugs, this same youngster
said: "Kids should live by their (parents) rules; that's the least
thing I can do as long as I am supported by them, as long as I live
at home; of course I don't want to hurt them." In the other average
families and in some of the troubled and pathological families, the
children's behavior implied the importance of parents as models.
A condescending youngster from a troubled family was quite
critical of his mother, grandmother, and adults in general. But he
was not so very different from his own parents. Indeed, he was
described by his family and by himself in very much the same
terms! His mother had been the first to denigrate his grandmother,
and the child merely followed in her footsteps. The mother had
rather discreetly let it be known that she found one of the filming
staff beneath her in status. Her child crudely relayed the same
kind of derogative opinion. Another child from a good family
commented on the difference of opinion between the hippie and
the police officer: "There seems to be no middle ground; the
attempt here is to understand each other, so I'll ask you [the
hippie] and you sergeant, are you all saying the same thing?"
The mother laughed and said: "That's what I was thinking."
When dissent occurred the child tried to make peace between the
opponents. She had become even more conciliatory than was her
mother who was considered the mediator in the family. Thus,
here again, a child had followed a parent's example.

　　In the good, average, and troubled families, the children
affirmed that they complied with parents' wishes and followed
parents' examples. Compliance, obedience, and identification could
also be observed in the other families, but to a different degree and
in a different manner. Average and good parents calmly assumed
that their beliefs would be adopted by their children. In these
families, we often heard a parent insist or tender an ultimatum.

One father told his child to change his hippie attire "or else"; the child complied. Several mothers in the average group described promiscuity in derogatory terms; their children hastened to assure their mother that none was intended. The children were striving to adhere to the mother's ideals. The profound influence of parents on their children (not necessarily beneficial) was especially well illustrated in an average family. Here autonomy was praised, but conformity was demanded. The child attempted to obey the two mutually exclusive demands. His success in this is testimony of the strength of parental authority; but the price he paid for maintaining his good standing was intellectual confusion. He compromised and so lost the basis for inner conviction which he would need in time of stress. To live up to the standards set by his parents he had to convince himself that he had not accepted his puritanical heritage out of obedience but out of independent judgment; at the same time, he was dimly aware of his fealty. He believed that he was "free on command," but his ensuing confusion was a portent of weak personal integration.

The average and good parents assumed that their wishes for their children were also shared by their offspring. Pathological, troubled, and superior parents made no such assumption; the pathological parent counted himself for little in his children's eyes; the troubled parent was genuinely modest. The superior parent ascribed his delightful family life and his competent and attractive children to "90 per cent luck." The average and good parents expected to be important to their children. The pathological, troubled, and the superior parents were surprised to learn how much their children valued what they had to offer. Our conclusion is that parents need not worry whether their children hear them—for they hear well. The problem, then, is in the message, since it is sure to be received.

FAMILY UNITY

We had expected that pathological and troubled families would be less of a unit than were the average families, and that average families would be less united than were good and superior families. This expectation was met unequivocally as far as the extended family of grandparents, cousins, uncles, and aunts was concerned. Only in a superior family had a child actually spent months with the grandparents (who lived next door) because there was temporarily not enough room at home. In only the superior families, the good families, and also some average families, was a deliberate effort made to cultivate the extended family. Sibling relationships were also most meaningful in the expected direction. Group III families tended to lack cohesiveness more than did the other groups. However, this trend was attenuated since the majority of the families were united.[1]

Indifference to one another—"doing one's own thing" without much concern for others—was found only in four families (one average family and three troubled or pathological families). The rest of the families were united by strong bonds of affection and dependency. In one pathological and one average family an additional ingredient appeared: the mother had an overriding desire to dominate. (One mother tended to needle and provoke; the other wanted to exact conformity.) In another average family, the mother panicked at any hint of discord or dissatisfaction. She asserted that no dissension existed. The children understood her need, corroborated, and reassured her at every turn. The major difference between the three groups was the degree to which they had fun together—not in the strength of the bond. Happiness and pleasure within the family circle were characteristic for superior and good families. Pain and humiliation were inflicted in troubled and pathological families. This painful relationship, however, did little to minimize family cohesion and family impact. We can understand the latter in psychodynamic terms (a sado-masochistic bond), but we had not expected it to be demonstrated.

The intensity in the relationship between mother and child in the most pathological family was equal to the intensity of relationship between father and child in a superior family where the interaction was growth promoting. In one case, the mother

---

[1] Quite possibly the high incidence of family cohesion is, in part, the result of sample selection. The requirement was that the whole family participate in both the middle-class and the intensive studies; consequently, there was a decided bias in the direction of intact and, presumably, relatively united families.

was deeply involved in her child's sexual adventures, promoting them and enjoying voyeuristic satisfaction. In the other case, the father deliberately refrained from exerting his paternal power and prestige; he encouraged his child to develop independence instead of obedience. In both cases, the bond, selfish in one instance, selfless in the other, served to conduct emotions from parent to child. Whether for better or worse, the emotions had become motivating forces in the child's life.

TENUOUS FAMILY TIES

One may legitimately question whether family unity is to be applauded and encouraged. Clearly, there is no cause for enthusiasm if the unity characterizes the criminalizing family. Nor can one extol the virtues of a family that is held together by exploitative or sado-masochistic bonds. Perhaps a lesser parental involvement in the children's lives would be best. We believe that children in loosely knit high drug risk families (groups II and III) have a better chance for emotional growth than do children in closely knit high risk families because they are likely to seek and find parent substitutes. The prognosis for the children from the relatively closely knit but most pathological family presents a case in point. Despite the fact that their drug risk scores were less than were the scores of the other two pathological families and the two average families, we considered these children to be the most endangered in the sample.

Four high risk families were loosely knit; they had brought a total of seven children to the film sessions. Two children were still too young to have any drug or sexual problems, though one child was accident prone. The remaining five children had all used drugs, and four of them had been in a variety of difficulties. The fifth child had managed to overcome his addiction. Aside from family pressure, he had found a sensible and sympathetic relative with whom he had achieved a fine understanding. The parents from two of the families with problem children were almost oblivious to one another during the film session. Neither wife nor child listened to the father's speeches—which were overly intellectual in one case and tangential to the topic in the other.

The two mothers were both insecure and inept in their maternal role, and both were unwomanly. One tried to make up for this by forced giggles, tense laughter, and the display of legs; the other had apparently despaired of her attractiveness and femininity; she made no efforts in this direction. The children had passed through many difficult times and were not yet out of danger. Nevertheless, with the exception of one child, their futures seemed brighter than did those of the children from those troubled or pathological families which were more united.

One child who had been heavily involved in drugs found a friendly adult who was able to help the child come to terms with his disappointment in his parents. He accepted the limitations of his home and appeared to be at peace with himself and his world; he was well on his way to an adulthood which would be more satisfactory than that of his parents. Another child had become a drug user while attempting to find someone outside his family to whom he could attach himself. The relationship did not last, but neither did the drug use. One wonders whether this child will be able to maintain close bonds. One child from an average family was a very heavy drug user but found a delightful mate. At the time of the film session, he was in excellent shape and likely to have a much more pleasurable family relationship than the one he had experienced before at home. The fourth child from the troubled pathological group was comfortable with his age mates and had followed their example in drug use and truancy. This child was still searching for a base but appeared to have little hope of finding a way out. Nonetheless, if the child were to find a mature individual who would take an interest in helping him out of his morass, he would have a good chance for emotional growth. This child gave every sign of readiness to attach himself to a positive model since he was still looking beyond his family and delinquent peers for a constructive leader.

UNITY OR DIVERSITY

Our sample contained nine cohesive families—four in group I (superior and good), three in group II (average), and two in group III (troubled and pathological). These nine families brought a total of twenty children to two film sessions. Children in the superior families had achieved honesty, independence of thought, originality, the strength to voice and follow convictions, and self-confidence in the face of parents, peers, or any other authority, without resorting to aggression. These families were tolerant of differences; they were able to keep conflicts in harmonious equilibrium within the family circle; and they were willing to accept strangers (members of the film staff) just as they were. Superior families did not require conformity and had encouraged their children to develop individual differences in thought and style of life.

We observed the same lack of aggression, the same friendly firmness, and self-assurance in the good families. Here, however, the children's views did not differ substantially from those of their parents; these children were much more inclined than were others to follow in their parents' footsteps. At the same time, children in the good families were searching for honest answers with as much dedication as were children in the superior families. But children from good families were not as original as were children from superior families. Within each good family, the speakers tended to be interchangeable, parents and children conforming to the same pattern. Good families were as persuasive and as eager to include the stranger as were superior families; the difference was that the good family made efforts to assimilate the stranger, to fit him into the family mold.

In the other two groups, conformity to a common style occurred even more often than it did in group I. However, whereas the child in the good family often managed to persuade his parents, the average parent and sometimes the troubled and pathological parent insisted that the child adopt his outlook. If the child did not adhere strictly to parental values, an average father might threaten or give the child an ultimatum. Groups II and III differed in that average families were decidedly conventional in their conformity, whereas troubled and pathological parents took pains to show a liberal or radical stance and forced their children into the same mold. The childrens' responses were as predictable and as stereotyped as those in the average families, even though the responses were unconventional. None of the children in these families had arrived at an independent view.

In the two superior families, parents as well as children had critical things to say about the church and about the police. Their statements, however, contained no undertones of hostility toward the minister and the narcotics officer present at the film sessions. A difference in view was recognized and accepted. One of the children inadvertently mentioned a taboo word, saying, "I've met some real pigs and some good ones." He earned an immediate, albeit gentle, reprimand from his mother. "When we talk at home we don't refer to police and riot squads as pigs. It's a nasty word and lacks imagination." She addressed herself to the whole group in apology to the police officer present. The father seemed to feel that his child was in a somewhat exposed position. He took up the cudgel, stating his disappointment with police methods during peace marches. An older child joined in calmly, saying, "The police are against us [peace marchers]"; and a younger one added: "I've been on three or four peace marches. If you see policemen laying about [in wait] anywhere, you look at them warily and walk on, hoping for the best." Everyone laughed at the picture he had evoked, including the police officer. The older child, in support of the others, elaborated on the scene with much verve and charm: "If I am walking by a row of policemen and one looks even reasonably friendly, I smile at them, and generally they will smile back; but most of them look very fierce." (Here the speaker used dramatic gestures and facial expressions.) "Like you are going to do something evil; and I am not a crook, I think policemen are expecting something criminal." The speaker was uncommonly attractive; the tone was firm, explanatory, yet jolly; and there was no hint of personal criticism. As a result, the police officer did not feel personally attacked; he had been included in the family, despite some very real differences of opinion.

The same matter-of-fact, nonhostile approach was evident in the parents' reactions' to their child's use of the word *pig*. There was comment and standards were set, but the child was not excluded from the family circle. Other members rallied around to assure their support, with the father in the lead. He had been described as the one who "soothes the wounds of each"; the one who "breaks up the 'crab-in' with a love-session," (referring to her own crabbiness). "Dad is there binding us all together." Father, quick to sense hurt, this time self-inflicted, responded by praising his wife's contribution: "Mama makes the kids do their work. Mama really makes the kids come through." There was constant back and forth between emphasis on tolerance for differences and efforts to cement the family. Both were successful. Although all family members considered themselves deeply religious, not all belonged to the same church. This was also observed in the other superior family where the children said that the mother regularly attended services of a denomination not subscribed to by the rest of the family but had made no effort to convince them to join her. Individuality was fostered in these families, and attempts to define oneself independently from parents and siblings were praised. One of these mothers became very uncomfortable when asked to describe resemblances among family members. She did not want to burden the children with a model: "I don't see any of the youngsters as me. I see each as an individual." The father of the same family explained: "Everyone is very, very different from the other and from us."

The other superior family, also rewarded their children with praise and admiration when acted independently from their parents or from one another. One child asserted with a great deal of good humor: "I happen to think that grades are not important (for me); I think they are important for him [pointing to a sibling]. We can hurt each others' feelings; all the facts come out, [and] then we can come to an understanding and still hold a difference of opinion." While both parents listened with great pride and affection, the child added, "We know that part of them [the parents] has rubbed off on us; but we have our own opinion." Another child corrected his mother who had said that she taught her children "*my* ideas of right and wrong." Quietly voicing his dissent: "But that is a mistake." Mother admitted "Oh, I get very angry," but obviously this did not deter her or her children from voicing their convictions. The father admitted to pride when his children showed "the gumption to fight back."

Members of the superior families were able to be quite frank with one another without destroying their relationship. They achieved this frankness by showing genuine admiration for one another. One child stated that his mother was "very highstrung, very vocal." He followed this remark by saying, "Mother will first make a very strong statement and then taper off. She has a very major voice in the house." Or another would admit: "Father is dominant." Such a description was then modulated ". . . when it comes to a major decision (dominance) means that when something goes wrong he's the first to say, 'oh, oh, something is going wrong.' . . ."

Gentle humor pervaded the atmosphere. In this the fathers set the tone: when there was tension in the air, a father would generally make a diversionary joke. Sometimes a son used the same technique to get a family member off the hook. In one family, the father was called the "comedy relief" as he often cheered up a family member with a joke. His child, who also played this role when necessary, told us that in his family "someone can always think of something that is funny when somebody is in a real tight spot." There was a great deal of laughter and goodnatured teasing in both superior families. Home truths could be told in this way, the sting removed.

If we had done a laughter count in the good families, we might have found an even greater incidence than in the superior families. But our impression was that the laughter in the good families had a slightly defensive quality; it was a little less spontaneous than it was in the superior families. In the good families, tension and potential strife had to be dispersed more often and more vigorously than in the superior families. In the superior families, laughter and teasing made it possible to be more outspoken and served as a transition at difficult moments. In the good families laughter interrupted and covered up the difficult moments and in the expression of troubling emotion. In the average families, laughter and wit were used to avoid difficulties altogether; in the troubled families there was little to laugh about. In two of the pathological families laughter was observed, but, in one case, it was phoney and served to hide anxiety, embarrassment, or regrets. In the other pathological family, there was a touch of cruelty in the laughter; it did not express affection but derision.

Genuine laughter shared, humor, affectionate teasing, matter of fact comments which lacked the sting of personalized criticism, all these made it safe to express one's true feelings, made it possible for superior families to tolerate divergence without disruption.

The discussion leaders asked families to make recommendations of what not to do in rearing a child. One mother from an average family worried about what her children might reveal. She turned to them and said in a tone which was anxious, pleading, and, at the same time, threatening: "Are you secure? Would you prefer to belong to another family?" In view of the mother's concern, what child would deny his security and affirm a desire to be elsewhere? Sensing the mother's need for reassurance, the child calmed her fears: "No, I know someone who would like to belong to ours." The mother's maneuvers throughout the film session were consistent; she suppressed every hint of strife. From all appearances, this was the most cohesive of all families in the sample. No child disagreed with the mother on any subject. One, on being asked what he thought of a statement of his mother's, quickly replied: "Oh, I agree." But when he had to explain what he meant, he admitted that he had not understood the subject of discussion. But so as not to fall out of line, he had gone along with her. No doubt, such children were obedient; none had ever come close to an illicit drug, and the family had the lowest drug risk rank in the whole middle-class sample. At the same time, the mother was concerned, and rightly so, about the tenseness and insecurity of her oldest child. The clinicians were concerned because this child appeared too unemotional and too set in his ways at an early age. He was the most overconforming child in the sample. The child had a subtle wit, but it was tinged with sarcasm. The father made the most jokes of all; yet he was basically a sad person who wore a clown's mask over a tragic face.

In one pathological family, a child had been provoking his mother with the fact of his drug use. He skillfully mimicked an exaggerated state of intoxication and said mockingly: "I'm crazy

. . . my eyes are dazed." When the mother reminded him that his grades had gone down, an older child came to his rescue, turning to the mother and exclaiming, "bullshit." The mother told him to "shut up," and when someone else wanted to talk the mother would interrupt with "Goddammit!" One of the children described how he and his mother conduct their fights: "I'd get kicked and try to kick everybody." The father got his digs in as well. Turning to the older child he meaningfully recommended: "You should never start with the first child, you should start with the second." The mother, to make sure the point had been noted, patted the child so addressed on the knee and, with a sweet smile, added: "We really don't want to *tear* you out [of the family], dear!" The child shook his head helplessly. Another child reminded his father not to be "ridiculous" and described his mother as a "cheater." In this pathological family, only hostile feelings were openly acknowledged; no one could let down his guard. It is no wonder the children had adopted a variety of countermeasures to protect themselves. Unfortunately, they were too busy defending themselves to develop individuality. Their unusual behavior could be understood in terms of developmental deviations imposed by parental pathology.

Another pathological family illustrates how a child is forced to conform to parental needs, however much this may deflect his own needs to be truthful with himself. The mother of this family described with forceful gestures how "terribly upset we get with each other." Laughing derisively, her child explained: "You hassled me so much, so I lied." Another child disdainfully counseled the mother, asking, "Why don't you reason with him, instead of screaming?" One child summed up why it was not possible to speak truthfully: "If a child says something to his parents and he [the parent] immediately takes it as a personal reflection of his personal failure and goes around sulking and feeling sorry for himself, you won't say anything because it's honesty that hurts. And it is not necessarily a reflection on your [the parent's] failure if a child says something about what you [a parent] are doing that you don't like. It isn't saying that you are a lousy parent." The mother, trying to understand, replied that a parent should not put the child in a position of lying, but another child commented that sometimes that is exactly what parents do. In this family, several of the children returned to the theme of lying. One mentioned that he had too much respect for a distant family member to be able to tell him the truth about drugs or sex. Neither father or mother could tolerate reality and so prevented their children from confiding in them. This attitude could be compared to the calm assertion made by one superior mother: "There is not much they can do that would really shock us." Her child felt that he was "a good person" and believed that self-esteem gives one freedom and confidence. The children in the pathological family, however, had neither self-esteem nor self-confidence and certainly lacked the freedom to be themselves. As we have seen, diversity and individuality can be achieved within strongly united families. It comes about when parents deliberately foster self-expression in an atmosphere where children feel sure they will not be hurt themselves nor hurt those around them when they speak their mind. In families where unity takes the form of total unanimity, however, self-expression is stifled and conformity rewarded.

The four loosely knit families showed little interest in their members. Of their seven offspring attending the film sessions, two children were clearly differentiated individuals. They gave views that were at variance with those of their parents, and, as adults, they were likely to lead more satisfactory lives than their parents. One possible exception was a very young child from a united but pathological family. Expressing himself with a great deal of strength and independence he stated: "I am going to be me." The clinicians were not at all sanguine that he would be able to maintain this stance when he reached the critical age of puberty —the time when deleterious family influences would be brought to bear more forcibly. One parent had already predicted with much assurance that the child "is going to be very much like me." The parent listed a variety of downfalls that were in store for the child. Unquestionably, children in loosely knit and disinterested average or troubled and pathological families can achieve an independence which children in cohesive families of the same type cannot. It is our impression, however, that the independence of the average and troubled/pathological children is of a different order than that found among superior families. The ebullient, charming, and confident child who is independent will have more verve than will the bland, depressed, or aloof child who has also managed to gain independence. We confess that ratings here were made more difficult by the appealing character of the former in contrast to the less attractive natures of the latter.

LOVE

Pathological and troubled families have been seen to adopt certain measures to protect themselves. Average families and, to some extent, good families also institute protective measures to ensure that external influences will not affect family unity. We saw that freedom to be oneself and to express one's innermost feeling without fear was most prevalent in the superior families. Battles there were, but neither blood was drawn nor victims felled. Conflicts were aired, but, at all times, it was in a context of love, expressed through tender words and touch. Love was also stressed in the good families but not in any other groups. In group III, when the subject of love came up at all, it was only obliquely. We are not surprised, for such admissions make one vulnerable, and sarcasm is a great deal safer. "Did that give you a nice feeling about sex dear, when father goosed the girls?" was one of the more kindly remarks.

The families in groups II and III stressed the need for education and information to help parents deal with their children's interest in sex and drugs. Parents and children in group I, however, showed no desire for special courses. In other words, they did not pin their hope on facts; concern for each other was the most important theme in growing up together. Indeed, these parents taught us a great deal. A father in group I said that love and understanding and a sense of direction are the main ingredients in raising children. He and the mother did not once criticize their children—who did nothing to offend anyway. Throughout, these parents had only words of praise. The mother stated, "We have a lot of love . . . respect." She looked with admiration at her husband while he spoke; he, in turn, was extraordinarily sensitive to her. This family made every effort to be tolerant. They stated: "We should not judge people. God made us all, so we should not

judge absolutely. . . . Parents should praise children at many
points. Later on they will be better able to withstand criticism. If
a child is getting love and understanding at home, he does not
have to get acceptance in his peer group."

In a superior family one child and one parent listened so
closely to what was being said that their lips moved with those of
the speaker; everyone was leaning toward each other. One child
clapped the other on the back in approval, and a great many
endearments were used. The mother's solution to a problem
was "to start loving each other, that starts out with each individual, honey; that means forgiving each other the mistakes."
Her eyes twinkled, she smiled, both convinced and convincing.
One of her children expanded the mother's thought on love,
describing it as "making another happy." In a clear unhesitating
voice, the mother added: "We have very hot discussions. The generation gap is there. But when we go to bed even though we
hadn't solved it, we had our ideas and they had theirs. . . . We
loved and kissed; we agreed to disagree and still respect each other
for that." She smile at the children questioningly. The father said
that there was no secret or no magic formula: "Understanding,
love, and a lot of fairness and faith and belief in God are essential." During this discussion all had been looking back and forth
at each other, eager, assenting, jolly; mother's gestures were particularly outgoing and embracing; there was a happy sparkle in
the children's eyes.

One father commented: "The reason we do something is
out of love and respect; we don't want to do something that will
hurt. The family is a close knit affair . . . all love each other." One
child: "We had fights, but no harm done." Another: "I always felt
secure because mother and father had a good relationship."

Another father: "One of the ways you can show love is to
be actually a father and a mother to your children . . . we are
their parents. "Love is not being permissive and kind at all times.
The strongest love you can have for your children is the love
where you take time to be tough; and once in a while even use
your foot to give them a good swift kick on the bottom, [but]
everything is tempered by love. . . . To take the trouble to give
them a mental spanking, to get angry. It's easier to let someone
else raise them—the schools; the schools don't care. . . . It takes

a lot of trouble to get upset *before* something happens that's bad; you have to love a lot [to do that]." In another family where love and care were evident a child stated that the key is a strong interdependence among [the family] members. "Every person has a lot to do with what every [other] person does in the family. . . . We're interested in [pointing to the youngest] being happy and we're interested primarily in them [our parents] being happy. . . . Now, how to develop that? It takes years and years. Also it takes a strong interest in what we want our children, or in our case, what we want our parents to be like (he turns to his parents). We'd just as soon have them [our parents] accept our values as they would like us to accept theirs, and I'm sure they would like to have us like them. But they do want us to be happy and express our freedom . . . [and] start developing our own values, guidelines, and rules [which] we want to live by." Looking at his mother, the child added: "She's always made a point of saying 'you are good kids, but, even if you weren't, we are your parents and we still love you.' The prevailing attitude is that they care." Indeed, one of the most moving episodes during this film session was when mother confessed her love for her husband smiling at him with shining eyes, "He was just right for me."

STICKING TO YOUR GUNS

We heard one parent say that a child who was loved and understood at home would not have to seek peer acceptance. This belief was affirmed among the good and superior families. Two of the average families cited peer pressure as a reason for disapproved behavior, including illicit drug use. Some of the troubled and pathological families shared this conviction. Children from groups II and III are the spokesmen on the issue.

One, "I tried marijuana when I was away at school [when my] parents were far away."

A second, "I'm against drugs for young kids. The problem is that a lot of people get hard drugs before they even realize it. It's peer pressure." One mother remarked: "You are admitting that peer pressure is very important to you!" The child replied: "Yes, Mother, I think it's terrible."

In comparison, a child from group I stated that it was "a

personal thing whether or not you smoke pot." Another child in this group pointed out that he had "freedom, and the ability to stick to his own opinion." Quoting father, the child elaborates, "you are a self-identity, have your own ideas."

A child who had described himself as a mimic—and one would presume that as such he would be particularly vulnerable to peer pressure, indicated that our fears were unfounded: "I always look forward to coming home and the loving relationship (there); even though I have good relationships with all my friends, it's the attention of those at home I like to have." None of these children had been swayed by their age mates. Indeed, one father in this group had offered to smoke marijuana with his child if trying it out was that important to his youngster. The child understood what it would cost his father and desisted. A totally different outcome occurred in one troubled family where the father, in order to keep up with his children, had begun to smoke marijuana.

It was instructive to compare the reaction of children in the different groups to the blandishments offered by the hippie discussion leader who was advocating drug use in seductive terms. In group I the children were bored, disagreed, or made attempts (one nearly successful!) to convert the hippie to a straight point of view. Children from three families in group II (including those who had used drugs) reacted much like those in group I, with the exception that no one tried to convert the hippie. In the remaining group II family, a specially straightlaced one, we could observe three children and one father coming under the hippie's sway, eager to be converted themselves. In group III, the children were already on the hippie's side; many had used drugs and considered themselves liberated. One had passed through this stage. The other allied himself with the hippie in an attack on his mother. His eyes glistening, he accused her of what the hippie had taught him she was guilty of: "avoiding emotional contact with her children."

For the most part, the hippie's attempts at persuasion failed. We presume that the children in group I, bolstered by parental love and self-esteem, were incorruptible. Some from this group had already experimented with drugs and had drawn their own conclusions. In group II, outside influence had little chance against the overwhelming ammunition parents had brought to bear in one "hermit family," as mother described it. The other three average families were not immune. Two of the families reported that one of their children had been lured into drug use by associates at school. In group III, the older children had already become involved in drug use. One child was anticipating peer-led adventures; the other was "scared" but was also looking forward with some pleasure to a variety of sexual and drug experiments that his parents—not his peers—were expecting from him.

Our conclusion is that special circumstances are required for peer pressures to become effective. This judgment is in line with the findings of Coleman (1966), another investigator who showed that the child draws sustenance from whatever sources are available—home or school. We believe that if parents provide for the child's emotional needs, the child will not become dependent on someone else. But, when emotional sustenance is not forthcoming in the home, the child looks to others and exposes himself to potential risk. We agree with the parents in group I that families can and do protect the child from noxious influences. Parents do this by encouraging the child to express his ideas and to judge for himself. Above all, parents need to express their approval and love so that the child has enough confidence to develop "intestinal fortitude" (as one father put it), to remain steadfastly on his chosen course.

Superior parents do more. By personal example and specific lessons, they teach their child tolerance for his shortcomings and charity for others. They create so joyous an atmosphere at home that the child learns to expect good from the outside world as well. Their child has no wish to discover within himself the rewards of paradise. "I am satisfied with my real-world oriented self" one of them told the minister in answer to a query about why he did not wish to try mind-altering drugs. Another explained on what grounds he had given up illicit drug use: "What turns me off of pot is that it interfered with sensitivity to others. You can't really respond to others' sadness when you are on pot." Rather than peer pressure, the family ethic of concern for others won out.

LEADERSHIP

Faith and doubt. The capacity for leadership varied strikingly between group I and group III families. Group I children were persuasive and independent of peers. They appeared to be leaders themselves, and their parents were also leaders. Parents in group I families were confident leaders. The parents in group III were mired in self-doubt and, in consequence, deferred to their children as authorities on major matters such as sexual activities and drug use. Whereas group III parents sought advice from their children, group I parents gave advice. Group III parents could not cope, whereas group I parents responded with strength. Some group III parents attempted to hide anxiety behind intellectualized conversation. Some giggled inappropriately and avoided important topics. Their flight from genuine, positive emotion and sincere interaction prevented these troubled and pathological parents from being personalities in their own right. In other words, one could not be sure how they felt or whether they were saying what they meant. Their insecurity led them into pseudopositions, and, for the most part, the positions they adopted on major topics of child education, family life, and pleasure were conventionally unconventional. Their intellectual skepticism was a front for self-doubt. Moreover, their self-doubt was spread to their children who used the same mechanism to evade issues and avoid genuine commitments.

In group I, all the parents had strong faiths founded in their religion. But their capacity for sureness went beyond the realm of the religious to encompass other aspects of life such as child rearing. Confidence in right and respect for rights appeared related concepts. Consequently, these parents respected the personalities and beliefs of others. Their children were not allowed to step on their own parents nor to disregard the rights and feelings of those outside the family. When a child interrupted his mother, the father merely lifted an eyebrow in surprise and the child was silent. In contrast, group III parents and children did not respect themselves and, therefore, infringed upon one another's rights. Parents and children were in competition with one another.

Mutual influence. In two cases, older children in group III displayed leadership qualities and maturity greater than that of their parents. Little attention was paid to these children, however. In group II, one child had been able to exercise his leadership potential, for his fond parents were willing to negotiate their stance rather than lose the child entirely. These parents changed their overly strict attitudes in the direction of moderation. In group I, everyone displayed a capacity for leadership or for influencing others. Family members cared about what was important to each other and were willing to adjust to it. Everyone had an opportunity to have his say. In these families, parents were quite explicit about maintaining their leadership, but their flexibility allowed for appropriate leadership on the part of their children. One parent proudly pointed to his child's clever ways of getting around him, commenting that the child's cleverness was just the sort they enjoyed using to maneuver the kids and, that by dint of learning such technique for persuasion, he was "learning to get along with people."

Group I parents were strong, and both fathers and mothers spoke with authority. One mother declared, "I am tenacious and added, "we are all strong." That was the case, for the whole family was easily self confident and courteously assertive.

Maternal leadership and leaderless families. In those families (group II and III) where the mother was dominant, one saw a corollary in their close personal relationships. These mothers, in that portion of the experiment which required them to choose a "husband" and/or "lover" from among the film staff, in each case rejected the male—the police sergeant—who, physically and socially, was symbolic of an aggressive, dominant, and virile masculine role. Conversely, some of the children in these families clearly indicated that they wanted a strong man around the house and counseled the mother to choose the policeman instead of the gentle minister or the quiet, understanding, pipe-smoking psychologist. These same mothers also tried to dictate to their husbands who they should choose as a "wife" from the film task, advising them to select the older professional woman and to avoid the young, sexy hippie to whom they were obviously attracted. In contrast, mothers in superior and good families usually encouraged their husbands to get "two for the price of one" and make both women their choices. Some advised their husbands to "take the pretty and more durable one"; that is, these mothers sanctioned the obviously preferred masculine choice of the young and sexy girl.

In short, these mothers were not threatened when their husbands acted like men.

The leaderless families of groups II and III demonstrated a contrast to those where mother was dominant. The parents of these families turned to their children for advice on whom they should choose. Some children refused to take such a responsibility. One was disdainful, saying to his father, "If you don't know by now who you want for a mistress . . ." implying either the inadequacy or dishonesty of papa.

Paternal leadership. Dominant or authoritative fathers were found in the superior and good families. In one average family, there was an authoritative father; but he was away from home for long periods, and his son had taken over as the interim leader. In one troubled family, the father might have appeared to be dominant, but actually he felt himself to be weak and defeated. Inspection of his behavior revealed that he was simultaneously domineering and uncertain, that is, not authoritative. His leadership was false since he catered to his children, supplying them with the slogans of rebellion and following them in their use of obscenity and illicit drugs.

Superior fathers both encouraged and protected their whole family. When there was a good opportunity, the father would urge the youngest child to speak and father—along with older siblings who had learned that style—listened respectfully. However, should the occasion become uncomfortable, as for example, when conversation led the child over his head, papa would come to the rescue. On any occasion when a family member was threatened, father would again intervene. The father's readiness to protect was such a powerful model that one saw his children intervening to shield one another and to rescue outsiders as well. This behavior could be contrasted to the actions of the domineering, yet weak, father in a troubled family who led his family in an attack on the police officer and authority in general. His children followed, barking joyfully at his heels. Consider the problem of that father, having taught hatred of authority, were he ever to try to assume it genuinely himself.

Benevolent dictatorship. How does one make power palatable or leadership acceptable? In the group I families, this was done by equating leadership with protection from danger. Parental leadership must be followed if security is to be assured. Perhaps, at another level, one can say that the price of protection given is authority acknowledged.

A second approach is to instill the notion that immediate authority is but an intermediate step to still higher powers. The father acts within the hierarchical framework of the laws of God and man. Among other things, this allows the father to admit fallibility as well as to ground his strength on sources that are greater than himself. As one father said, "There is only one Jesus Christ; the rest of us make mistakes."

A third source of powerful authority comes from the notion of the family as a living entity, continuing over generations. In group I families, family tradition serves as the reason and the appeal for children to do as their parents have done. There is a kind of historical equality in this. The child becomes the father who becomes the grandfather who becomes the ancestral ideal. It is a process in which all family members have a place and an obligation. A fourth mechanism for making power palatable is to exercise it discretely, with humor, affection, and flexibility. This kind of authority is also exercised in the superior and good families. Further it is not unyielding power, children early learn that they are to share in it, meagerly at first but as they grow to deserve it, it is increasingly theirs; although as long as they live in their parental house—or their life time—it is never as great as the parents. Indeed even after the parental death it lives on and assumes the hallowed aspect of tradition and honor to the lovingly remembered dead.

IMPORTANCE OF GRANDFATHERS

Our evidence shows that the family is, indeed, a continuing entity. In the group I families, the strength, love, and sometimes glory of father is presented as a reflection of the father before him. This is also true for the mother's father. In only one case did a group I father describe his own father in other than glowing ways; in this instance, the grandfather was an understanding, loving, and generous man, but he was also an alcoholic and "a beast" when drunk. The result was that the whole family had come to understand that people are complex and may be simultaneously good and evil. When loved ones stumble and fall, forgiveness is required. This family, more than any other, taught its children forgiveness of others and of oneself. The father had also come close to alcoholism but, like the grandfather, had given it up. What his child is learning from the missteps in admired models is self-discipline and abstinence.

In the troubled and pathological families, there were more deaths of grandfathers when fathers were small than in the other groups. Fathers from such backgrounds tended to be chronically depressed, and they had married dominating women. Consider the fathers in this group who were alcoholic, self-indulgent and overindulgent of their children. Consider also all those who were psychotic, or grandfathers who were divorced after much distress when the son was young. Or consider those who were autocrats, or the reverse, weak and afraid they had failed. What had they bequeathed to their children?

In general, fathers in group III were distant, overly intellectual, took on mother's functions, were bland, emotionally impotent, strangers in their own family, ineffectual, weak, gentle, afraid of women, shallow and boring. Their sons (the grandchildren) were also bland, weak, immature, sexually undifferentiated, preschizophrenics, or psychopathic. The maternal grandfathers had been just as cold or distant as were the mothers' own husbands. The distance was sometimes a result of divorce. Often this coldness was reflected in the mother's inability to recall anything about her own father. Though the grandfather cannot be construed as the cause of the grandchildren's behavior, our impression is that the grandfather is a critical element in the family mix, and, when he is missing, ill, or not a good father, that is a liability. If other liabilities are also present, then we have troubled or pathological family outcomes.

Respect for authority was a theme common to the three generations in the superior, good, and in one of the average families. Authority was related to adherence to the laws of God and man and to the rules laid down by one's parents. In these families, grandfathers had been strict and lawabiding men. When laws were unjust, these grandfathers had set out to change them, providing their children and grandchildren examples of political activism within the rules defined by society.

This was not the case in group II and group III families. Here, the grandfathers were models of dodging or disobeying the law. As one father said of himself and his father, "Bending the law is a way of life." The grandson had done likewise, and was a heavy drug user. These parents, unlike those in group I, referred to various misdemeanors such as brewing bathtub gin during prohibition, driving without a license, speeding, foiling the police, and hunting on posted land, with a smile of hidden satisfaction that could hardly escape their children's notice. Some of them stated that in view of their own behavior at the same age (or that of their parents), they did not feel in any position to dictate to their children. Thus, we see that the generations in groups II and III are linked by the belief that if laws are not convenient, they are circumvented. The general attitude which justified this stance was that one's own personal moral judgment is what counts in the end. As with many other aspects of belief and behavior, a major difference between the group I families and most other families is the stress on shared community values as against the stress on idiosyncratic values. This difference in emphasis was transmitted from grandparent to parent to child.

FEMININITY

In all group I families, mothers were womanly—not girlish or matronly, but attractive, warm, firm, and well groomed. They all loved their husbands and stressed the importance of physical contact and sexual love. They did not wait for their children to ask questions about sex but encouraged enquiry and responded with frankness. Their children did not, as one father put it, wonder whether girls were merely "soft boys." They knew they were not. They all had also married very masculine men who were warm, gentle, and dominant. One woman, for example, was an easy-going person who had passionate and lively daughters. Another mother was an outgoing and profoundly nurturant person whose daughter was the same. The sons of these mothers were open, good-natured, effective, and masculine.

One group II woman was athletic, well groomed, and lovely. She made deliberate efforts to be a good wife and mother—deliberate because she was not born to the role. She had married a masculine, warm, gentle man whom she dominated. Two of the average family mothers acted like adolescents; one giggled, whereas the other was serious and obedient. Both of these mothers pretended naiveté, displaying girlish charm rather than mature womanhood. Both had married masculine men, but one husband had selected his wife because the relationship could not be a close one. He made sure of this by having outside affairs which also did not require closeness. These women rejected their sex and maternal roles; one said: "I can't stand pesky kids. I get so sick of them. I hated to be left with them all day when they were small." The other commented: "I'm not a hugger, not physically demonstrative. It's a personality defect. I'm glad I have no daughters because I wouldn't have the patience to teach them to sew or cook." The fourth mother in group II was masculine, and her parents had wanted a boy. She did not pretend to feminine charm. In the experimental choice task, she chose the minister as a lover because "he would put sex above the purely physical."

Three of the five mothers in the group III families posed as young girls. One wore a mini-skirt, was a rifle champion, and denied that women should be accorded special protection. She could not understand why her adolescent daughter was afraid to walk on dark city streets at night. Two other mothers, knowing that they were both very pretty, used soft smiles, an attractive manner, and studied attentiveness to divert one's attention from their lack of involvement with those presumably close to them. Both of these mothers were snobbish, and they tried to make up for their lack of warmth by social grace and activity. Both worked hard to appear maternal and were practiced, if bored, listeners to their husbands. But their hearts were not in their homes, and some of the children suspected as much. Both had married weak and sad men. The fourth mother was at a pre-Tomboy stage of emotional development. To this mother, torturing boys in small ways was more pleasurable than succoring them. Her influence on the men in her family was malignant. The fifth woman was not feminine and, knowing it, had given up trying.

POLITENESS OF THE HEART

It sometimes seems as though manners and etiquette count for little. The emphasis in confrontation groups on being "open" and on avoiding "hypocrisy" often puts a premium on insult and publicizing the vulnerability of others—"Tell it like it is" may mean a field day for unbridled aggression. Even if the aggression is bridled, the sentiment can emerge sideways, snorting, to accomplish the same end, "putting down" another. In contrast there is that politeness of the heart which marries formal courtesy to a genuine concern for how the other person feels. It allows people to live together and contribute to the joyfulness of the other's good company. In group I families, politeness of the heart was evident. People in these families were well mannered, and they cared for those forms of polite exchange which allowed strangers as well as friends to join into honest dialogues. These families exercised that self-discipline which disallowed unkindness or destructive frankness and were, inside themselves, warm and happy so that there were no volcanic fumaroles struggling to erupt to the surface. One group II family also displayed this quality of politeness of the heart. In the remaining group II families, however, there was only a drilled politeness which arose from a sense of social obligation not out of sensitivity and love. In the troubled and pathological families, manners ranged from simple disinterest in others to contrived rudeness (proving how liberated one was) to a field day for social mayhem. This did not mean that parents and children were unaware of the social graces; indeed, they were capable of courtesy and followed some of its forms but never with the heart.

COMMENT AND SUMMARY

This chapter opened with questions about the role of the family in transmitting or immunizing against drug risk. Questions were asked about the relationship between family excellence and children's drug use. We learned that illicit use may occur in excellent families, although it is not likely to do so. If drug use does occur, it does not lead to serious outcomes. No excellent (superior or good) family was in the high risk category. All troubled and pathological families, however, were in the high risk classification. We concluded that the features found in the excellent families do immunize against drug risk and that features found in the least excellent middle-class families do predispose their youngsters to engage in drug-taking behavior.

However, illicit drug use per se was not our concern. Indeed we propose that from the standpoint of child health and development that need be no one's major concern. One asks instead, how drugs are used, what drugs are used, what condition the user is in, what his family environment is, and what the outcome of that drug use is. Illicit use can simply be a stage through which a child passes; it can even be a constructive event insofar as in trying something well-touted but finding it wanting the child becomes more convinced of his own values and judgments.

We learned much about child-rearing from the thirteen families in the intensive study. Love was the most important factor stressed by superior and good families (group I). These families spoke of the need for the physical expression of affection and for concern and interest in one another. Group I parents also described their devotion to their own parents. Another important element in these families was their forgiveness for failings. This extended to such serious downfalls as alcoholism in a parent. When children made errors, attempts were made to correct them, but disapproval was centered on the mistake, not on the child. The children, in turn, felt that their parents were good persons and believed that they themselves were also good. They stated that they derived self-confidence from their feeling of worth, which helped them to decide what they really wanted—regardless of peer pressure. If they tried marijuana, it was because they wanted to—not because they were afraid of being excluded by peers.

Confidence and charity allowed children and parents in the superior group to have wide variations of self-expression within the family circle without endangering its stability. The parents were unflappable: as a consequence, the children believed that they could lean on their parents in case of need and that nothing they did would lead to really serious upsets. These children were free to experiment with a number of different lifestyles before settling down to a happy medium. The same confidence and charity allowed the parents to be themselves. They were comfortable in their roles, and felt no fear of their children, nor did they worry lest the children did not love them. They made no effort to ingratiate themselves with their children by playing the role of a pal, nor did they presume any superior judgment in their children or become overly permissive. They told their children in no uncertain terms, that they were not "their children's friends; they were their parents." These parents assumed leadership as a part of their parental responsibilities, and were in control. When there was trouble in the air, the parents sensed it and prevented it. The children knew that if they were about to make a serious mistake, or wish to engage in really dangerous experiments, the parents would be there to protect them from ultimate folly. Although the leadership was strong, it was by no means autocratic, and children were permitted a great deal of leeway.

Superior and good parents (particularly the former), were not afraid of mistakes; they did not fear emotions; tender feelings as well as anger and disappointment had a place in their lives. These parents did not fear themselves, nor did they fear to engage in battle. They did not fear harm would be done to them; they were quite sure they would not be destructive to their opposition. The families were able to ride out the storms together and emerge in renewed harmony, retaining their opinions and their feelings of personal integrity intact.

These parents not only loved their own parents, but they also respected their authority. Just as they might have disagreed with their own parents, so they allowed disagreement in their children. At all times, however, there was respect for parental authority. It had stood them in good stead when they themselves became parents, for they quite naturally expected their children's respect—and got it. They did not feel the need to reject authority in general and did not demean themselves in front of their chil-

dren as some of the troubled and pathological parents were com-
pelled to do out of hatred and rebellion against their own fathers.

Above all, in the homes of the superior and good families
and in some of the average families, there was great joy and happiness within the family circle itself. Family members had fun
with one another. In all of these families, there was much laughter.
Each member knew good things would happen when they got
together with the rest; they looked forward to being with each
other. Attention was focussed on others in optimistic anticipation.
At the same time, this attentiveness to one another's wishes made
them sensitive and ready to help others.

The support which superior and good families lent to one
another allowed them to turn outwards and to include strangers.
They accorded the stranger the same courtesy, freedom of expression, kindliness, and readiness to be friends and have fun as they
did to each other. In consequence, the stranger, more often than
not, would accept their point of view, instead of converting them
to his. Conversion to the hippie view had occurred in one of the
average families and also in one pathological and one troubled
family. The conviction that the world and the people in it are
good made the superior and good families very attractive to those
who came in contact with them; it gave them an aura of leadership
to which others wished to conform. Thus, they were more often
persuaders than they were persuaded.

Tolerance for individual difference and deliberate teaching of respect for the values of others were not the only means by
which these families absorbed the stresses of life. These families
also teased one another considerably. The teasing was done and
accepted in good humor; at the same time, it served to open up
a grievance, a failing, or a conflict in the most benign manner
possible. A joke would often illuminate a controversial point
without inflicting hurt. None of the families in groups II and III
had this capacity to lighten the atmosphere with innocent laughter. The wit of group II and III families was barbed, adding to
family tension as each wondered who would be the next target.

Clarity of communication was another method employed
to reduce strife in the good and superior families and also in two
of the average families. Each person made his stand known, pre-

sented an explicit opinion on a given issue, and showed his feelings unequivocally. This was particularly pronounced in the parents, but the children were almost as vocal. They also knew that they could afford to be honest and outspoken in the nonpunitive environment of their family. This was certainly not the case in the other groups where the family members were far less sure of themselves and of the benign nature of their world. They resorted to clichés, lies, vagueness, double messages, poses, and evasions. The ambiguity created uncertainty in their lifestyle. A child might flounder in one direction, drug involvement, for example, which though there had not been an explicit taboo, nevertheless brought down the roof upon him.

Love, charity, tolerance, respect, self-confidence, trust, humor, clear communication, and an ability to create a joyous atmosphere are some of the ingredients that lead to excellent parenthood.

CONFIRMATION IN DEPTH

When we compare the clinical findings derived from this intensive study with the ratings, observations, self-reports, and interviews earlier reported (Chapter Four) for the larger sample of middle-class families, we see a confirmation of earlier findings. The clinical work brings understanding to bear on some of the psychodynamics which underlie the statistical differences of Chapter Four.

By way of illustration, that which emerged from the large-scale observations as traditionalism and respect for God and country among low-risk families is seen in the clinical study as part of a profound transgenerational pride in family—a primary affection and respect for family authority, which goes back to grandfather and the ancestors. What was reported in the larger study as greater satisfaction and lesser strife in the low-risk families came to be understood as part of a pattern of joyful and affectionate being together aided by tolerant and humorous ways for handling conflict. In contrast, in the larger study, high-risk families were found to be permissive and quarrelsome. In the clinical study, it became evident that these characteristics reflected neurosis and psychopathology, insecurity and selfishness. In the same way, the homogeneity of views among low-risk parents and children in the broader study was traced to clarity of communication and the loving, authoritative, and family-centeredness of child-rearing revealed by the clinical study. What was demonstrated statistically in the broader study as self-centeredness expressed in the pursuit of self-realization and pleasure among high-risk youngsters can be linked, now that clinical insights are available, to precisely the same attitudes in the parents, the same emphasis on personal goals rather than civic and social ones, the same preoccupation with a transient self, rather than permanent traditional values. Further, the vulnerability of high-risk youngsters to peer influences which carry them far in the exercise of liberty can be traced psychodynamically to the absence of the family as the center of emotional gravity from which all the most significant influences issue. In contrast, the warmth of low-risk families attracts and converts strangers, bringing children from other families under the sway of self confident parents and children. It is also the case that the heterogeneity, discord, antagonism, and rebellion which was evident in high-risk youngsters seen in the large-scale study can be tied clinically to the relative absence of love, charity, humour, respect, tolerance, confidence and joy in their families.

The foregoing are but a few summary illustrations. The point is that the surface of the family, as measured by statistics on truancy, drug use or what have you is but a reflection of the family interior. When extreme families are studied intensively, statistical differences take on greater meaning. In the excellent families, the inner joy and strength is visibly expressed in harmony and happy adjustment. In the troubled or pathological families, pain and chaos may take a variety of forms, all of which visibly reflect disharmony, discontent and a search for elusive meanings and gratifications. Risk-taking drug use by youngsters is to be seen in this light.

Education and
Action

❧ 14 ❧

In this chapter we move away
from research on families to consider a new theme: What can be
done? Our interest remains with the family, but now we consider
new information gathered from parents other than those we have
so far described. We also present information derived from local
community leaders with responsibilities in the drug area. From
what we learned or inferred, we venture to make some recommendations for education and action.

We saw eighty-one middle- and upper-class white parents,
eighty-five blue collar black families, fifty low-income Spanish-
speaking Mexican-American families, and sixty-five community
agents and leaders responsible for work or policies in the area of
youthful drug use. The black and Mexican-American families
were seen during the selected drug census taken as a prelude to
the family study; the white parents were seen in specially arranged
sessions with a PTA group, a Junior League meeting, a Mormon
Ward House parents' meeting, a parents' group at a Jewish
temple, luncheon meeting of university staff and faculty women,
and a gathering of concerned parents enrolled in an adult educa-

285

tion course dealing with drugs. The intention of these interviews was not to gather a representative sample but to learn whether parents were ready to take action vis-à-vis drug risks and to learn what actions might be preferable.

The new sample of parents did not, for the most part consider drug risk a community problem in the sense that everyone is affected, threatened, and required to act. At the community level there were only two concerns which took precedence. One was the belief that crime was associated with drug use and that ordinary citizens were in jeopardy from the nondrug criminality of drug users. The other concern was that drug use signified a moral change or a breakdown of moral standards. In these families, drug use or risk was not a problem. The majority said their children did not use illicit drugs; only one-fourth reported their children had used. Other parents recognized that as long as the environment was full of dangers and temptations, potential personal and family problems existed. Important issues, then, were how to forestall risk, how to combat peer pressures, and a dangerous environment, and how to communicate with their own children.

Drug use was said to be an *individual* problem for the users and for their families, but, as such, it was also a matter of general concern. We asked these parents what problems might arise for individuals in consequence of illicit drug use. They spoke about matters such as personality change, loss of self-respect, apathy, and a narrowing range of interests as one becomes immersed in the drug life. These parents understood the pain of families whose children got in trouble and the distress of the offspring who were sick or rejected or subject to criminal prosecution. They also mentioned how drugs might perpetuate immaturity and inadequacy, lead to feelings of inferiority, encourage disrespect for parents and other authority, and bring about a potential for violence, aggressiveness, impulsiveness, poor judgement, criminality, erratic thought, and failures in personal hygiene. Addiction per se was noted as improbable among their children but important when it did occur. Looking over these possibilities, we see that the emphases are in the personal, social, and moral spheres. Concern with pharmacological reactions, illegality, or medical outcomes are, at most, secondary.

Turning once again to their own family situations, we found that one-half of the parents in this supplemental sample had already felt the need for information or guidance with reference to youthful drug use. This group of parents had most often gone to their child's school to talk with counselors or to get literature, or they had gone to lectures or other educational forums. One-third of the parents had sought assistance elsewhere—most often law enforcement personnel, the mass media, health professionals, or the library. All parents were asked how information ought to be provided. Schools were mentioned most often. Additional sources of information were pastors and church groups, health professionals, mass media, adult education, youth organizations, local government, law enforcement officers, libraries, and pharmacists. We asked parents whose children had used drugs what they, as parents, had done. Typically, most had exploded emotionally, then sought self-control, and finally begun discussing the matter with their children. One-half of the small group who acknowledged illicit drug use by their children felt their interventions had produced the desired effect; one-half of the parents did not feel this way. Thus, only a few parents felt both an urgency of need in the drug risk area and a personal failure in being able to help the child. Similarly, only a few parents said they were lost in the child-rearing arena; most parents seemed self-confident. It was commonly acknowledged, however, that counteracting the disapproved elements of the larger society (peers, change, advertising, and the like) was a challenge in which they would appreciate any help that could be offered. Some parents said they would appreciate assistance in getting trustworthy drug information.

LOW-INCOME MINORITY FAMILIES

Fifty Latin families (usually mothers with their children) and eighty-five black families (usually mothers but sometimes fathers) were interviewed. All families lived in low-income neighborhoods. As we consider their replies, one must remember that priorities of interest and belief among groups differ and that these must be considered as one thinks of action programs. Almost all of the parents were sure that there were serious drug use and drinking problems in their communities. There was general agreement as to why people used drugs and alcohol. However, Spanish-speaking mothers emphasized the fact that drugs were pleasurable or that young people were curious. Black families tended to speak in pathological terms, noting the need to escape, the inability to use free time constructively, and relief from boredom. We asked who should be blamed for local and national drug abuse. Both samples blamed dealers and criminals first. However, the Latins spoke in personal terms, calling attention to the weaknesses or desires of the young people themselves who used these drugs or to the role of the parents and family. The black parents blamed outside institutions which had failed them—the police and the government, for example. The blacks were also likely to emphasize racism and discrimination and economic deprivation—again a projection of blame onto those with power. Both samples placed the schools midway on their list of blameworthy local conditions.

Families were asked to comment on ways to keep young people from getting involved in harmful drug use. There was general agreement, but some interesting differences also occurred. For example, the black sample again emphasized that outside institutions, in this case the school or community, would have to give education. The Spanish-speaking sample gave first priority to a good family life. They also spoke of the importance of seeing to it that youthful friends were wholesome. The black families, however, gave a low rank to the importance of supervision of peers or peer choices. In both the black and the Spanish-speaking group, strict law enforcement was strongly urged.

As regards somewhat extreme circumstances, families were asked how they could prevent their children from becoming drug dealers. Both groups gave priority to good communication within the family, but blacks again spoke highly of drug education as a means of prevention. The Latins spoke first of religious upbringing and instilling moral values. When asked if there were any place where parents could go for help, most blacks said their community did have such facilities. Most Latins (in the neighboring town) said there was no place to go. Parents were then asked what the city might do to help parents and children with drinking or drug problems. Treatment centers had the first priority in both groups, and drug education was also important to both. The Latins emphasized the need for better law enforcement, while the blacks talked of improved education in general.

WELFARE MOTHERS

During 1970, one Bay Area County with a heavy welfare load changed its approach so that no special services were given unless mothers specifically requested them. When that policy was inaugurated, welfare officers and social workers kept a count of the kinds of requests that were made (Cudeback, 1971). The most frequent request of welfare mothers was for help with the drug-using or drug related problems in their youngsters. To get this help, mothers were willing to see counselors, attend classes, or otherwise take the trouble to get guidance. This suggests that at least one portion of a low-income population that produces youth behavior problems and drug risks is alert to drug problems. These mothers are seeking help and are receptive to information and guidance.

RESPONSIBLE COMMUNITY AGENTS

We wondered whether the sixty-five judges, doctors, school personnel, narcotics officers, PTA leaders interviewed in one suburban community were well informed about drug use. Most thought they were fairly well informed; only one claimed ignorance. We asked each person what sources had been useful in obtaining drug information. The majority felt that their own professional experience had taught them the most. Other helpful sources were: (1) sharing experiences with other professionals, (2) learning from those who actually had drug problems, (3) sharing experiences with colleagues in the same profession, (4) reading professional literature, (5) conversing with police personnel or their own children, (6) exploring the work of governmental committees and commissions, and (7) reading articles in the mass media.

We discussed what each person did professionally and asked how much time was spent attending meetings, reading journals, or following other scholarly pursuits. One-third claimed that their daily communication with fellow professionals constituted such learning. Aside from the doctors themselves, most never had exchanges of information with physicians; aside from the lawyers, most never had such exchanges with lawyers. The same held true for the other fields. Aside from law enforcement officers, most of the people never had exchanges with police officers or officials, and, aside from educators, most never had exchanges with teachers or school administrators. About one-half of this group did report attending professional seminars once a month or more and reading professional literature once a month.

We asked these professionals how serious they considered the drug use problem in their community. About one-half considered it extremely or unusually serious; none said it was unimportant. When asked what should be done to prevent young people from getting involved in dangerous drug use, most professionals focused primarily on education. A distant second suggestion was for a good family life with encouragement and help to youngsters. Far down the list were proposals for recreational improvements and strict law enforcement. The majority again proposed some form of drug education to prevent drug dealing.

Each professional was asked what his or her own group could do. Foremost was the belief that groups could best participate in educational improvements and reforms. Doing their own jobs as well as possible was the second proposal. When asked what people in other professions could do, they said that others should educate themselves in the field of drug use or gather information which would help to educate others. Finally, we asked what the federal government should do to help prevent or control illicit drug distribution. The proposals were: (1) support education related to drug abuse prevention; (2) provide money for research; (3) control drug importation and smuggling; (4) change the laws;

(5) provide money for treatment; (6) teach government officials how to recognize the problem; (7) work toward international agreement; (8) avoid making the drug problem a political issue.

WHAT TO DO

The middle-class parents were insightful as to drug issues and effects. For these parents, drug use is mostly a matter that affects others, but, when it strikes home, it is an emotionally charged issue. Even so, these parents try to handle themselves and their children in a rational manner. They have sought information before problems arose, and they tried to encourage communication between themselves and their children. If a problem were to occur, they would first seek self-control and then discuss the problem with their children. If necessary, they would seek help from professionals.

These are active parents, and they probably represent a particularly self-confident and sophisticated group. For them, drug use is an individual, social, moral, and mental issue. Occasionally do they stress medical and pharmacological effects. In shaping programs for these parents, one would first want to listen to their definition of the problem and then focus on matters closest to their concerns. According to these parents, the most reliable route for community action and parent contact is through the schools.

LOW-INCOME MINORITIES

Our interview data lead us to suspect that minority groups can best be approached with methods tailored to their styles and interests. For example, the Latins in our sample (mostly Mexican-American) appear much less political and more family oriented in their views than do other groups. The black families, to the contrary, are apparently more oriented toward the authority of outside institutions than are other groups. The black families tend to view these institutions with ambivalence, however; the schools and police were criticized but also were considered to be major sources of help and success in combating drug problems. For black families, education is particularly important.

Given the results of our family studies it appears that the

Latin parents are generally more realistic than are the black parents. The Latin parents understood that people use drugs for pleasure as well as for escape; they did not invoke political institutions to account for personal conduct, and they emphasized matters such as morals, personality, and family style—all of which influence the degree of drug risk in families. Nonetheless, the Latins are so family-oriented and so disinterested in Anglo institutions that the problem becomes one of reaching those parents whenever community action begins with Anglos. For years, community action people have taught that real involvement is self-involvement and that real community change comes from the grass roots. Yet among some families these roots seemed rather hard to reach and stimulate.

COMMUNITY LEADERS

Community leaders are essentially self-educated men and women in that they have learned about drug use from experience and clinical sources. Very rarely have they used scholarly or scientific sources; however, they are strongly in favor of education as the major solution for community drug problems. They call for self-education as a major requirement. They want governmental leaders to educate themselves; yet, in their own education, they have not pursued that work and reading that is basic for any profession. Perhaps these community leaders should ask themselves whether they are in fact well informed. Since they have great responsibility in the area of drugs, they should expand their knowledge about the complex field of drug use. Whatever responsible community agents do; and whatever the irony in their recommending to others what they do not do themselves, we call attention to their sharing with others the great belief in education as the tool for solving social problems, shaping behavior, relieving community and personal anxiety, and achieving greater competence with children.

WHAT MIGHT BE DONE?

It is clear from our study of families that drug risk conduct on the part of youngsters is intimately related to child rearing practices, family habits, and parental beliefs. The clinical studies show that underlying the statistical differences evident in earlier chapters, the high risk families were more likely than other families to be uncertain, distressed, and otherwise disharmonious. The data from middle class, blue collar, and semiagrarian families, regardless of ethnic group, support the contention that the youth likely to use psychoactive drugs in risky ways comes from a family where parents are at least permissive if not disorganized, where they are at least relativistic if not fundamentally self-doubting, and where they are likely to be dissatisfied if not in acute psychological misery. Also, the strength of the differences obtained, whether tested by sophisticated statistical methods or intensive clinical ones, makes us reasonably confident that the developmental patterns, the family milieu, and the interaction productive of either low or high risk drug conduct can be specified. It follows that, knowing something about the origins of high drug risk, one may hope to intervene to alter influencing conditions in preventive or remedial ways.

When we moved from our comparative study of high and low risk families to queries to other parents and to community leaders we learned, subject to the qualification that we assume but do not know that local views can be generalized to other places, that many citizens recognize youthful drug problems to be personal, social, and moral matters which originate in and primarily affect families; that is, troublesome drug use is not seen to be a broad social problem arising from secondary institutions such as industry and schools. We also learned from our communitywide study that parents and community leaders appear most receptive to approaching drug problem prevention through education. As for intervention, once a troublesome case of youthful drug use is identified, the first line of response is within the family. All these factors together suggest to us that it may be possible to intervene to prevent high risk drug use by attempting to influence families. One ought also to be able to guide responses to already identified troublesome drug use by influencing families as well. Further, the mode of intervention which appears most acceptable is educational, and the place which most parents are ready to go to for guidance is the public school.

Since parents seem most ready to accept educational measures and to utilize schools or other educational facilities, action programs would be most effective when planned according to this parental readiness. That is, programs should be cast in a framework which parents are most ready to accept and utilize. In the same way, one is well advised to present such programs in a manner that is keyed to parental concerns or definitions of the drug issue.

Insofar as our information can be generalized to other communities and groups, this would mean an action program that is (1) geared to parents' concern about youthful drug risk; (2) focused upon individual matters within the family rather than within the community; (3) cognizant of the fact that drug use is most often conceived as a matter of character and morals or mental competence and outlook; (4) designed to offer guidance to parents on how to insulate their children from undesirable peer pressure or other environmental influences; (5) routed via education rather than, say, mental health counseling or police action; and (6) aware of the fact that parents and children are ready to go to school to obtain information and experiences that will help prevent drug problems. Although the public school appears to be the most accessible facility for parental use, programs that comply with the preceding prerequisites can also attract parents in settings such as churches, adult education centers, community centers, trade unions, grange or service organization meeting halls.

DISTINGUISHING BETWEEN FORM AND FUNCTION

We cannot afford to assume that our educational endeavors with parents and children should be like other forms of didactic schooling. It is painfully evident that the forms of child rearing or education that have existed to date have neither prevented nor solved the problems linked to drug risk. It is also apparent that families vary considerably in their needs for preventive or corrective work; they also vary in their flexibility or capabilities for change. In short, the approach one takes must depend upon the parents' situations and capabilities. Because of these factors, we believe that standard programs of information giving are not the answer. Instead, we need a variety of programs geared to family realities.

One must realize that no program—however varied and

responsive—can be expected to attract every parent who is in need. Furthermore, one family might approve of drug behavior that another family would denounce. One family may be able to handle a problem that would force another family to panic and call in outsiders for help. Disorganization, distrust, or self-sufficiency are additional factors that might keep families from participating in preventive or remedial schemes. All of these factors mean that any public program must expect only limited acceptance in a heterogenous community.

Participation will be predictable on the basis of family and socioeconomic characteristics. Banfield's (1970) review of the effectiveness of work with the disorganized poor gives a bleak picture indeed. Social work, settlement houses, area projects, community projects, and community organizations have all reportedly failed. If that is the case, then clearly any family program in the drug field cannot expect to succeed at all levels of society. Even the optimists would probably agree. But this leaves us with an opportunity as well as a dilemma. The opportunity is to reach those who care through public programs in schools, welfare agencies, and churches. The dilemma is that those who do not care, or who cannot undertake the initiative, will go by the board. Yet, sadly, in these groups one expects the most severe youthful drug risks along with a variety of other troubled conduct.

For those who care and can participate, we are optimistic. Those at the other end of the scale will likely remain mired in their drug problems and other disorders—until such time as either new methods of social intervention are devised or the impatient community takes action to coerce family participation in remedial programs. There is no reason to believe that drug risk prevention or remedial endeavors will have more or less success than other programs which work with the same population groups or with correlated problems.

In regard to the method of intervention, we must first state that our scheme is speculative and must be considered experimental until evaluations and modifications have been made. Indeed, we believe a variety of experiments involving laymen and experts are needed. Until such experiments and evaluations are systematically conducted, perhaps the primary function of programs is to reduce immediate anxieties—a measure which is in itself worthwhile.

NONPROBLEM PARENTS

Large numbers of good parents do exist who are flexible and who will seek out and practice appropriate recommendations in the areas of child rearing and drug use. In the closely related field of mental health, Nunnaly (1961) found that "people are unsure of the correctness of their information and will change their opinions readily." J. A. Davis (1965) found that "the general effect of information flow in the U.S. is to increase the agreement between the population and mental health experts, and those persons most exposed to information show the greatest agreement." If we substitute *drug abuse* for *mental health* and retain the analogy, we could conclude that at least the educationally oriented middle-class and blue collar classes are ready for learning and can learn easily.

As regards these good parents, the central task may simply be to keep them from being misled—especially young parents or those young people who are beginning to plan a family. Major goals would be to lend them courage to emulate the excellent families in our intensive study, to avoid the trap of permissiveness, and to maintain their own family as the central institution in their lives. The approach would be to reassure those parents who are already doing well. The purpose would be to create groups of young parents who are willing to support one another and create their own neighborhood family groups. We feel the family institution is capable of surviving in the face of rapid social change and, further, must survive if our society is to continue.

Many good methods could be used to reassure parents who are already competent. One such method is where parents and their children come together weekly to explore both facts and feeling. In such situations, a teacher or expert who tells parents what is right would prove unprofitable. However, a group leader who has an institutional obligation for program work and who serves as guide would be appropriate. Most likely, such roles could be filled by thoughtful laymen who could be trained for program responsibilities. Our concept does not argue against the use of professionals—as long as they apply their skills to building a parental group and guiding parents to facts and feelings.

We believe that it is best if parents seek out and examine facts about child rearing through active learning, analysis, and discussion. One approach would be to make reading lists and libraries available to these parents so they could read and judge for themselves what the researchers, clinicians, and social philosophers in the field of child development have to report. When conflicting opinions are found, the discussion group should proceed to examine the hidden issues and, thus, arrive at a satisfactory resolution. At times, the group may want to bring in a consultant minister, psychiatrist, narcotics officer, child psychologist, or social worker to report his experiences as well. The reading list for this aspect of the program would cover child development, socialization, family studies, and drug use, including alcoholism and associated problems. It is beyond our work here to provide a list of possible readings, but bibliographies do exist.[1] We do recommend, however, that such readings never be more than an appetizer, for intellectual discussions are not the key to self-examination or the development of confidence or change in child rearing. Readings can serve to give structure and content to the early stages of discussion. Many approaches utilize readings,[2] but, since child rearing is a human process, one will want to ensure that the parent programs are human processes too. The foregoing should not be interpreted as a sanction for anarchy or antiintellectualism. Programs require organization and the consideration of issues demands respect for facts. Moreover, the fact is that some people know more than others and some are better parents than others. We believe parent programs will function best when they are neither intellectualized or antiintellectual.

[1] In the drug field, see, for example: *Drug Dependence and Abuse: A Selected Bibliography*, March 1971, Superintendent of Documents, U.S. Gov't. Printing Office, Washington, D.C., 20402. (Price, 60¢)

[2] For illustrations of special approaches, see: Smith and Smith (1964); Wittes and Radin (1969); Patterson and Guillian (1971). For commentary, see: Glasser and Navarre (1967); Lambie and Werkart (1970); Wittes and Radin (1971); Rose (1969).

PROBLEM PARENTS

Problem parents will require much more than reassurance or the development of groups that reaffirm their existing strengths. These parents also require more than familiarization with the scientific findings. What these parents need most is to learn that they are themselves problem parents and that something can be done about it. The excellent families in the intensive clinical study were self-confident, modest, honest, and forgiving of others and themselves. They love and respect those around them, old and young. They have humor and cultivate joy. Alert, they sense the needs and troubles of others. Flexible, they foster individual development, tolerate disagreement, but assure that conflict is constructive. They express tenderness and demonstrate it by example and contact. Firm, they keep the responsibility of parenthood foremost. They show politeness of the heart. How, one asks, do integrity of purpose, charity, joy, love and self-esteem get taught. The answer is that such qualities must be learned through experience, and, if such attributes have not been gained through family life, then they must come through other experiences. These experiences must be warm and supportive; moreover, they must clarify and give directions.

For widespread application, the traditional ways of attaining such corrective life experiences (one-to-one contacts with professional healers, counselors, pastors, or other appropriate models) are too limited. Again, groups of people may be the answer. Here, we advocate the experience of benign interpersonal relations in a group setting that stresses family styles and the importance of being kind to oneself. Each individual must enter into the spirit of interpersonal alertness and support. This means tolerance and encouraging others to strive to be that which one seeks for oneself for the sake of one's family. Self-change for the sake of others is crucial. In this, the program differs from endeavors that emphasize change for the sake of oneself and instead it anticipates the other-centered spirit of a good family. One cannot be sure that such proposals will work. Nevertheless, it is worth a try to see if one can create a means for helping families reduce the risk of unhappy drug outcomes in their children.

EDUCATING CHILDREN INDIRECTLY

The direct education of children in the prevention or origin of drug risk occurs in the home. Indirect education takes place elsewhere—in peer groups, church, or school. For those places where planned indirect education can take place, we suggest that the major endeavors consider the long term. Indeed, such a process might involve teaching children how to be parents. One could start by teaching children principles of child care that would be applicable to their own younger siblings. One could employ Socratic dialogues, age appropriate, about development of moral capabilities (Piaget, 1932). One might also compare child rearing in different societies, noting their different outcomes and encouraging pupils to think about relationships between parental conduct and the children's behavior (Bronfenbrenner, 1970; Mead, 1950; Whiting and Child, 1953). It might be well to stimulate children to reflect on parenthood and to explore the scientific data and social puzzles concerning parental discipline, warmth, permissiveness, and egalitarianism. These suggestions are tentative because we ourselves are not sure that factual teaching will produce the desired outcomes. Another reason for uncertainty in regard to these proposals is our distrust of further secularization of family affairs. Such character-building tasks are best done in the family—not in the schools. We believe that the family should be central; yet an educational program can complement the family process rather than be a substitute for it. We ask that such innovations be considered.

Admittedly, we are by no means qualified to embark on educational criticism. Presumably, the range of educators is like that of parents—some are excellent, and some are poor. Among the good educators, there is sensibility and flexibility, but such educators must learn how to present their material in a manner that is consistent with the content. For example, it would be incongruous to engage in double bind communication while commenting on its ill effects. Similarly, it would be inconsistent to run a permissive classroom while affirming that limits and discipline are essential to character building. It would be ludicrous for affectionless teachers to wax eloquent over the need for warmth in child development. In short, relating the content to the manner of teaching will be a continuing challenge for planners.

Some parents in our several samples had already taken action in regard to their concerns about drugs. For the most part, these were self-educating endeavors. Others had taken no action but had claimed a sense of urgency about drugs, demanding that "something be done." Many parents felt no need to act. Paradoxes can be found within each of these three groups. For example, some of those who sought education found no alleviation from their own or their children's problems. Some of those who demanded urgent action were doing nothing themselves, and, among those who claimed no problems, some were actually in dire need of change. These all too human inconsistencies raise several questions. One might ask whether the presumed widespread public concern over youthful drug use is not in fact overstated or, at least, is misinterpreted? In addition, one might contemplate what real reasons for resisting planned programs are hidden behind the rhetoric. Consider, for example, the fact that we offered every sample family referral and remedial follow-up services. During the several years of our work, we received only three family requests for help of any kind. We offered advice and referrals but, after one year, saw that two of the three families had taken no action. One might also consider the fact that, during the course of our work, in our community, a drug center for teen-agers was established but nearly failed for want of interest and support.

Probably part of the reason for inaction is laziness or an inability to become motivated. But, we also suspect other reasons which ought to be kept in mind by people working with families in the drug field. One reason is parental commitments to permissiveness. Such parents feel it is wrong to interfere with a youngster even if he is dealing drugs and using them heavily. A second reason is parental complicity in, or unconscious approval of, illicit use. Such parents might be living out their own rebelliousness as their child acts delinquently. A third reason is reluctance which stems from the fact that to take action is to admit that something really is wrong. Such parents hope that the problem will go away by itself, or they are ashamed to show themselves as inadequate parents by seeking outside help.

A fourth reason for inaction is anxiety over discussing problems with the child. These parents fear that discussions will lead to further unpleasantness in the household; rather than hear screaming and the stomping of feet, these parents close their eyes and ears, if not their minds. This then becomes denial—or a shutting out of unpleasant awareness. Such denial accounts for the parents' ignorance of their children's conduct. Basically, it is an unwillingness to communicate because the results are so unhappy.

A fifth reason for inaction is the recognition that even if one does confront the child, the parents will be unable to get the child to change his behavior. The issue here is whether there can be concerted action for remedy. This may involve giving up unwholesome companions, stopping LSD use, or going to the local teenage drug center to work through personal problems. In families where real risk is most likely, the chances of parent-child action in concert are slim. Knowing this, parents may feel defeated in advance.

A sixth reason is disillusionment about one's ability to act. Such disheartenment may stem from generalized passivity, abdication, or despair. It can also be part of special conditions such as undernourishment or psychopathology, or it may occur as part of a constellation of socioeconomic deprivation and hopelessness. In any event, a pall of despair is cast over all self-help or reform endeavors. When contacted by outsiders, such families may react by polite lying, honest depression, confessions of confusion, violently angry projections of blame, denials of responsibility, or exploitative manipulations. The catalogue of reactions is not consequential, however. What matters is that family inactivity about about drug problems ought to be understood as a class or environmental problem as well as a family problem.

A seventh reason is distrust or discomfort with any activity which requires strangers to intervene in family affairs or acquire knowledge of intimate matters. When the family is a member of a minority ethnic group and, as such, feels that the dominant majority is at best noncomprehending if not hostile, then the family will be reluctant to seek assistance from strangers and will simply try to make do with its own inner or extended family resources.

A final reason for inaction is the recognition that a drug problem is in fact a symptom of a whole complex of family disagreements, disappointments, and disorders. Drug use may be recognized as the key which will unlock a crushing burden of unacknowledged troubles. If so, one can comprehend why parents and children stick to rhetoric. In such families, the drug issue is a semitransluscent screen behind which grotesque monsters are thought to be discerned. If seeing the drug issue is so painful, who would want to look behind the screen itself? These considerations may help us to understand the phenomenon of family inaction. When we are struck by the discrepancy between what people say and what they do, we must not yield to easy accusations such as laziness, ignorance, or indifference. Instead, we must enquire after the reasons why people resist taking actions that might benefit them greatly in the long run.

COMMUNITY ACTION

Preventive and remedial programs are undertaken in response to parental expressions of concern, civic leaders' demands for action, and the practical experience of individuals who do have drug related problems. These programs may be in the form of clinics or treatment centers, half-way houses, switchboard operations, live-in rehabilitation facilities, or youth centers which are privately or community sponsored. Because of local sponsorship, such developing organizations usually cannot rely on regular governmental funding. Aside from grants-in-aid from the government, they count on citizens to volunteer dollars and labor. Usually created by dedicated individuals (sometimes drug users or ex-users), these organizations come into being and, if sensitively planned, meet a need and begin to dispense services. The community applauds, but the voluntary dollars and workers do not appear. Surprised and disappointed, the organizers of such services are likely to feel betrayed by the very public that expressed interest in their project.

The same resistances which limit individual family action enter in here. To these specific barriers, one must add many general problems that face self-generated endeavors. It is difficult to get other citizens to support one's own programs as enthusiastically as one does oneself. If there is a lesson herein, it is for organizers not to despair but to realize that there will only be a small number of people who will really get the work done. Having the courage, how does one get started? We raise this question because we suspect that at least some readers will be concerned parents or professionals who come to the field without experience. For those who are interested, we recommend first and foremost *A Community Guide to Drug Abuse Action,* published by the National Coordinating Council on Drug Abuse Education and Information, Inc., Suite 212, 1211 Connecticut Avenue N.W., Washington, D.C. 20036. Another useful guide is *Drug Education for Teachers and Parents,* written by John E. Imhof, Coordinator of Drug Education at Lynbrook, New York, 1970. The reader also may wish to consult the *Resource Book for Drug Abuse Education,* prepared in 1969 by the National Clearing House for Mental Health Information of the Department of Health, Education, and Welfare.

A SILVER LINING

Family worries associated with youthful drug use can have positive effects. One positive effect is that drug use is a tracer or key by which one can identify a host of important issues in child rearing. Because of this, we must not accept superficial explanations of the reasons why children use drugs, nor can we stop at remedial programs which serve simply to control the rising rates of experimentation or use of illicit drugs. Instead, we must consider that our national time of troubles is also a time of opportunity. It is crisis which gives people a chance to examine; it opens up possibilities for constructive innovation and motivates people to pursue solutions.

A second positive effect is that a gradual centering on facts comes about, as opposed to centering on fantasies or demonology. All of us are slowly coming to understand what is real and dangerous, and what is not. We are developing a body of scientific data about the pharmacological effects of drugs. We are learning how drugs function psychologically and what their symbolic significance is socially. As this continues, we shall develop an ethic which accommodates drug facts with the examined morals of our society. Today, our values and guidelines are like a plumb line thrown sidewise. The plumb bob will swing erratically and then, progressing from elipse to circle, will slowly narrow its swing until it hangs nearly straight. In our search for child rearing styles and sensible drug-use standards, our society resembles the plumb bob. Presently, we are moving from ellipse to circle as we zero in. It has been and will continue to be a shaky experience but despite new alarms it is our conviction that we shall be settling down. This does not mean eliminating drug risks or family problems altogether, but it does mean that our capabilities for developing healthy, safe, and sensible youngsters can improve.

FINAL COMMENT

If the family is indeed the crucial source of children's behavior, it follows that those interested in controlling youthful drug use will employ themselves most efficiently by strengthening parental confidence and know-how. The primary attention must be given to children and parents, rather than to outside institutions which are, at best, auxiliary resources. Moral authority and the origins of drug use habits rest with the home. Educators must convince the parents of their potency, assist them in fulfilling their function, and, insofar as parents want to begin with facts, give them the evidence as well. However, the parents must not be allowed to forget that drug use is based on standards of conduct and that these standards need to be inculcated. The school can help to orient parents and children, but it cannot be a substitute home.

Many parents view youthful drug use as a symptom of social decay and the end of the family. Perhaps that gloomy perspective is correct, but our work gives us hope, providing that society succeeds in counteracting the trend that downgrades the importance and potency of the family. The family is *the* institution for forming responsible citizens. The peer group, contrary to what is commonly believed, has little or no influence as long as the family remains strong. Peers take over only when parents have abdicated, and parents will tend to abdicate if family life and values are demeaned.

Dissipation of central familial and cultural strengths occurs whenever a new crisis leads us to invent new institutions or overload existing ones. New institutions serve to replace family functions and substitute impersonal outside experts whose efforts, however well-intentioned, undermine family authority and self-determination. If inventions are necessary, they must serve to deepen the positive emotional meaning of the family itself.

An excellent family is the extended clan where grandparents still play an important part. One of the most valuable teaching aids for any parent is the parent's own attitudes and actions toward the grandparents. A parent can give explicit examples of love, understanding, forgiveness, and appreciation through his own interactions with his own parent. Children exposed to such experiences learn to be lenient toward the failings of others and toward their own. In excellent families, grandparents are incarnations both of proud tradition and of personal greatness. They are also repositories of great human and ethical strength. These extended families create an environment which external distractions cannot negate; in short, this is the kind of institution that successfully prevents adolescent misconduct and creates proud citizens.

Let us keep in mind then that drug education does not consist in the mere accumulation of scientific or historical data. These are components, but the essence is faith in a certain way of living. Youth who suffer no drug risks have discovered that the values worth living by are self-respect and respect for others and kindness and responsibility to the family and to oneself. The democratic concepts of freedom, self-expression, individuality, and equality are noble only when they are predicated on the primary injunction to consider "we" and "thou" before "I." When this injunction is not learned or is ignored, these concepts become weapons used by individuals who pursue power and gain. Drug education is then a family process which transmits the age-old wisdom, "Love thy neighbor as thyself."

Bibliography

ACKERMAN, N. W. *Psychodynamics of Family Life.* New York: Basic Books, 1958.

AICHHORN, A. *Wayward Youth.* New York: Viking, 1935.

ALEXANDER, G. J., MILES, B. E., GOLD, G. M., and ALEXANDER, R. B. "LSD: Injection Early in Pregnancy Produces Abnormalities in Offspring of Rats." *Science,* 1967, *157,* 459–460.

ALKIRE, A. A. "Social Power and Communication Within Families of Disturbed and Nondisturbed Preadolescents." *Journal of Personality and Social Psychology,* 1969, *12,* 335–349.

ARONFREED, J. *Conduct and Conscience.* New York: Academic, 1968.

AUERBACH, R. "The Hallucinogens and Embryonic Malformations." *Capsules,* 1971, *3* (2).

AUERBACH, R., and RUGOWSKI, J. A. "Lysergic Acid Diethylamide; Effects in Drosophila." *Science,* 1967, *155,* 1325–1326.

BALDWIN, J. *The Fire Next Time.* New York: Dell, 1963.

BALL, J. C., and CHAMBERS, C. D. *The Epidemiology of Opiate Addiction in the United States.* Springfield, Ill.: Thomas, 1970.

BANFIELD, E. C. *The Unheavenly City.* Boston: Little, Brown, 1970.

BATESON, G., JACKSON, D. D., HALEY, J., and WEAKLAND, J. "Toward a Theory of Schizophrenia." *Behavioral Science,* 1956, *1,* 251–264.

BAUER, R. "Some Trends in Sources of Alienation from the Soviet System." *Public Opinion Quarterly,* 1955, *19,* 275–291.

BAUMRIND, D. "Current Patterns of Parental Authority." *Developmental Psychology Monographs,* 1971, *4* (1, Pt. 2).

BEECHER, H. K. *Measurement of Subjective Responses.* New York: Oxford University Press, 1959.

BENTEL, D. J., and SMITH, D. E. "The Year of the Middle Class Junkie." *California's Health,* 1971, *28* (10), 1–5.

BERG, D. F. *Illicit Use of Dangerous Drugs in the United States: A*

Compilation of Studies, Surveys, and Polls. Drug Sciences Division, Bureau of Narcotics and Dangerous Drugs. U.S. Department of Justice, 1970.

BETTELHEIM, B. *The Empty Fortress. Infantile Autism and the Birth of the Self.* New York: Free, 1967.

BEWLEY, T. H. "An Introduction to Drug Dependence." *British Journal of Hospital Medicine,* 1970 (August), 150–161.

BLACK, D. J., and REISS, A. J., JR. "Police Control of Juveniles." *American Sociological Review,* 1970, *35* (1), 63–77.

BLAKESLEE, A. *What You Can Do About Dangerous Drugs.* New York: Associated, 1971.

BLOOD, R. O., and WOLFE, D. M. *Husbands and Wives.* Glencoe, Ill.: Free, 1960.

BLOS, P. *On Adolescence: A Psychoanalytic Interpretation.* Glencoe, N.Y.: Free, 1962.

BLUM, E. M. "Horatio Alger's Children," in Blum and Associates, *Students and Drugs.* San Francisco: Jossey-Bass, 1969.

BLUM, E. M., and BLUM, R. H. *Alcoholism: Modern Psychological Approaches to Treatment.* San Francisco: Jossey-Bass, 1967.

BLUM, R. H. "Drugs and Violence," in *Crimes of Violence, Vol. 13.* A Staff Report to the National Commission on the Causes and Prevention of Violence. Washington, D.C.: U.S. Gov't. Printing Office, 1969.

BLUM, R. H. *Deceivers and Deceived: Observations on Confidence Men and Their Victims, Informants and Their Quarry, Political and Industrial Spies and Ordinary Citizens.* Springfield, Ill.: Thomas, 1971.

BLUM, R. H., and ASSOCIATES. *Utopiates: The Use and Users of LSD-25.* New York: Atherton, 1964.

BLUM, R. H., and ASSOCIATES. *Society and Drugs.* Vol. I. San Francisco: Jossey-Bass, 1969a.

BLUM, R. H., and ASSOCIATES. *Students and Drugs.* Vol. II. San Francisco: Jossey-Bass, 1969b.

BLUM, R. H., and ASSOCIATES. *The Dream Sellers: Perspectives on Drug Dealers.* San Francisco: Jossey-Bass, 1972a.

BLUM, R. H., and ASSOCIATES. *Drug Dealing: Intervention and Policy Alternatives.* San Francisco: Jossey-Bass, 1972b.

BLUM, R. H., and BLUM, E. M. *Health and Healing in Rural Greece.* Stanford: Stanford University, 1965.

BLUM, R. H., and BLUM, E. M. *The Dangerous Hour.* New York: Scribner's, 1970.

BOEHM, L. "The Development of Independence: A Comparative Study." *Child Development,* 1957, *28,* 85–92.

BOWLBY, J. *Attachment.* New York: Basic Books, 1969.

BOWLBY, J. *Maternal Care and Mental Health.* Geneva: World Health Organization, 1951.

BRAGINSKY, D. "Machiavellianism and Manipulative Interpersonal Behavior in Children. Two Explorative Studies." Unpublished Doctoral Dissertation, University of Connecticut, 1966.

BRAUNSTEIN, L. "Ideologies." Unpublished paper, 1966.

BRAZELTON, T. B. "Effect of Prenatal Drugs on the Behavior of the Neonate." *American Journal of Psychiatry,* 1970, *126,* 95–100.

BREHM, M. L., and BACK, K. W. "Self-Image and Attitudes Towards Drugs." *Journal of Personality,* 1968, *36* (2), 299–314.

BRONFENBRENNER, U. "Socialization and Social Class through Time and Space," in E. Maccoby, T. Newcomb, and E. Hartley (Eds.), *Readings in Social Psychology.* 3rd ed. New York: Henry Holt, 1958.

BRONFENBRENNER, U. "The Changing American Child," in E. Ginsberg (Ed.), *Values and Ideals of American Youth.* New York: Columbia University, 1961a.

BRONFENBRENNER, U. "Some Familial Antecedents of Responsibility and Leadership in Adolescents," in L. Petrullo and B. Bass (Eds.), *Leadership and Interpersonal Behavior.* New York: Holt, 1961b.

BRONFENBRENNER, U. "Toward a Theoretical Model for the Analysis of Parent-Child Relationships in a Social Context," in J. C. Glidewell (Ed.), *Parental Attitudes and Child Behavior.* Springfield, Ill.: Charles C. Thomas, 1961c.

BRONFENBRENNER, U. "Theory and Research in Soviet Character Education," in A. Simerenko (Ed.), *Social Thought in the Soviet Union.* Chicago: Quadrangle Books, 1969.

BRONFENBRENNER, U. *Two Worlds of Childhood: U.S. and U.S.S.R.* New York: Russell Sage, 1970.

BROWN, C. *Man Child in the Promised Land.* New York: Macmillan, 1965.

BUCKNER, H. T. "Flying Saucers Are for People." *Transaction,* 1966, *3,* 10–13.

BUREAU OF CRIMINAL STATISTICS. "Crime and Delinquency in California. Drug Arrests and Disposition in California." State of California, Department of Justice, Division of Law Enforcement, 1969.

CAHALAN, D. *Problem Drinkers: A National Survey.* San Francisco: Jossey-Bass, 1970.

CALEF, V., GRYLER, R., HILLES, L., HOFER, R., KEMPNER, P., PITTEL, S., and

WALLERSTEIN, R. "Impairments of Ego Functions in Psychedelic Drug Users." Paper delivered to Conference on Drug Use and Drug Subcultures, Asilomar Conference, Pacific Grove, Calif., 1970. (To be published in 1971 *Conference Proceedings*.)

CALIFORNIA STATE DEPARTMENT OF EDUCATION. "A Study of More Effective Education Relative to Narcotics, Other Harmful Drugs and Hallucinogenic Substances." Sacramento, 1970.

CERVANTES, L. S. *The Dropout: Causes and Cures.* Ann Arbor: University of Michigan, 1969.

CHAFETZ, M. E. "Alcohol Excess." *Annals of the New York Academy of Sciences,* 1966, *133* (Art. 3), 808–813.

CHEIN, L., GERARD, D. L., LEE, R. S., and ROSENFELD, E. *The Road to H: Narcotics, Delinquency and Social Policy.* New York: Basic Books, 1964.

CHRISTIE, R., and GEIS, F. *Studies in Machiavellianism.* New York: Academic, 1970.

CISIN, I. H., and CAHALAN, D. "American Drinking Practices." Social Research Project, George Washington University. Presented at a symposium on "The Drug Takers" at the University of California at Los Angeles, June 12, 1966.

CLARK, K. *Dark Ghetto.* New York: Harper and Row, 1965.

CLARK, M. *A Community Study: Health in the Mexican-American Culture.* Berkeley and Los Angeles: University of California, 1959.

CLAUSEN, J. A., and KOHN, M. L. "Social Relations and Schizophrenia: A Research Report and Perspective," in D. Jackson (Ed.), *The Etiology of Schizophrenia.* New York: Basic Books, 1960.

COHEN, M., MARINELLO, M., and BLACK, N. "Chromosomal Damage in Human Leukocytes Induced by Lysergic Acid Diethylamide." *Science,* 1967, *155,* 1417.

COLEMAN, J. S. and others. "Equality of Educational Opportunity." Washington, D.C.: Office of Education, Department of Health, Education and Welfare, 1966.

COOPERSTOCK, R., and SIMS, M. "Mood-Modifying Drugs Prescribed in a Canadian City: Hidden Problem." *American Journal of Public Health,* 1971, *61* (5), 1007–1016.

COWDRY, W., and KENISTON, K. Unpublished paper, 1969, cited by S. M. Lipset in "Youth and Politics," in R. K. Bermton and R. Nisbet (Eds.), *Contemporary Social Problems.* New York: Harcourt-Brace-Jovanovich, 1971.

CUDEBACK, D. Personal communication, 1971.

DAVIS, A. "Child Training and Social Class," in R. G. Barker, J. S.

Kounin, and H. F. Wright (Eds.), *Child Behavior and Development*. New York: McGraw-Hill, 1943.

DAVIS, J. A. (Ed.). *Education for Positive Mental Health*. New York: Aldine, 1965.

DISHOTSKY, N. I., LOUGHMAN, W. D., MOGAR, R. G., and LIPSCOMB, W. R. "LSD and Genetic Damage." *Science*, 1971, *172*, 431–440.

DOHRMAN, H. T. *California Cult: A Story of Mankind United*. Boston: Beacon, 1958.

DORSEN, N. (Ed.). *The Rights of Americans: What They Are—What They Should Be*. New York: Pantheon, 1970.

ELIADE, M. "The Yearning for Paradise in Primitive Tradition," in H. A. Murray (Ed.), *Myths and Mythmaking*. New York: George Braziller, 1960.

ERICKSON, E. "Identity and the Life Cycle." *Psychological Issues*, 1959, *1* (1), 116. Monograph I.

ERIKSON, E. H. *Childhood and Society*. New York: Norton, 1950.

ERIKSON, E. H. *Identity: Youth and Crisis*. New York: Norton, 1968.

FARINA, A. "Patterns of Role Dominance and Conflict in Parents of Schizophrenic Patients." *Journal of Abnormal and Social Psychology*, 1960, *61*, 31–38.

FIEDLER, F. E. "An Experimental Approach to Preventive Psychotherapy." *Journal of Abnormal and Social Psychology*, 1949, *44*, 386–393.

FISCHER, R., GRIFFEN, F., and KAPLAN, A. P. "Taste Thresholds, Cigarette Smoking and Food Dislikes." *Medicina Experimentalis* (Basel, Switzerland), 1963, *9*, 151–167.

FLACKS, R. "The Liberated Generation: An Explanation of the Roots of Student Protest." *Journal of Social Issues*, 1967, *23* (3), 52–75.

FRAZIER, E. F. *The Negro in the United States*. New York: Macmillan, 1949.

FRIES, R. H. "Drug Abuse Survey for the County of Monterey." Monterey County, California, Office of Education, 1969.

FULLER, J. L. "Pharmacogenetics." In W. G. Clark and J. del Guidici (Eds.), *Principles of Psychopharmacology*. New York: Academic Press, 1970.

FUNKENSTEIN, D., KING, S. H., and DROLETTE, M. *Mastery of Stress*. Cambridge: Harvard University, 1957.

GARFIELD, E., BOREING, M., and SMITH, J. P. "Marijuana Use on a Campus: Spring, 1969." *International Journal of the Addictions*, 1971, *6* (3), 487–491.

GARFIELD, M. "Illicit Drug Use Among Undergraduates: 1970–1971." Unpublished paper, 1971.

GAY, G. "Changing Drug Patterns in the Haight-Ashbury Subculture." *Journal of Psychedelic Drugs,* 1971, *4* (Spring), 3.

GLASSER, P. H., and NAVARRE, E. L. "The Problems of Families in AFDC Program." In E. Thomas (Ed.), *Behavioral Science for Social Workers.* New York: Free Press, 1967.

GLIDEWELL, J. C. *Parental Attitudes and Child Behavior.* Springfield, Ill.: Thomas, 1961.

GLOVER, E. *The Roots of Crime.* London: Imago, 1960.

GLUECK, S., and GLUECK, E. *Predicting Delinquency and Crime.* Cambridge: Harvard University, 1960.

GOODE, E. *The Marijuana Smokers.* New York: Basic Books, 1970.

GOODE, W. J. *World Revolution and Family Patterns.* New York: Free Press, 1970.

GRINSPOON, L. "Marihuana." *Scientific American,* 1969, *221* (6), 17–25.

GROUP FOR THE ADVANCEMENT OF PSYCHIATRY (GAP). "Integration and Conflict in Family Relations." Report No. 27. Topeka, Kans.: GAP, 1954.

GROUP FOR THE ADVANCEMENT OF PSYCHIATRY. *Normal Adolescence: Its Dynamics and Impact.* New York: Scribner's, 1968.

GURIN, G., VEROFF, J., and FELD, S. *Americans View Their Mental Health.* New York: Basic Books, 1960.

HAIRE, M., and MORRISON, F. "School Children's Perceptions of Labor and Management." *Journal of Social Psychology,* 1957, *46,* 179–197.

HALEY, J. "Family Experiments: A New Type of Experimentation." *Family Process,* 1962, *1,* 265–293.

HARLOW, H. F., and SUOMI, S. J. "Nature of Love: Simplified." *American Psychologist,* 1970, *25* (2), 161–168.

HAWKS, D., MITCHESON, M., OSBORNE, A., and EDWARDS, G. "Abuse of Methylamphetamines." *British Medical Journal,* 1969, *ii,* 715–721.

HERBST, P. G. "Conceptual Framework for Studying the Family," in O. E. Oeser and S. B. Hammond (Eds.), *Social Structure and Family in a City.* London: Routledge and Kegan Paul, 1954.

HESS, R. D., and SHIPMAN, V. "Early Experience and the Socialization of Children." *Child Development,* 1965, *36,* 869–886.

HESS, R. D., and TORNEY, J. V. *The Development of Political Attitudes in Children.* Chicago, Aldine, 1967.

HOFFMAN, M. L. *Techniques and Processes in Moral Development.* Detroit: Merrill-Palmer Institute, 1961.

HOFFMAN, M. L. "Fathers' Absence and Conscience Development." *Developmental Psychology,* 1971, *4,* 400–406.

HOGAN, R., MANKIN, D., CONWAY, J., and FOX, S. "Personality Correlates of Undergraduate Marijuana Use." *Journal of Consulting and Clinical Psychology*, 1970, *35* (1), 58–63.

HUGHES, H. Hearings Before the Committee on Labor and Public Welfare, Subcommittee on Alcoholism and Narcotics. Washington, D.C.: Alderson-Monick, 1971.

IDANPÄÄN-HEIKKILÄ, J. E., SCHOOLAR, J. C., and ALTON, A. "Total Body Inestics and Placental Transfer of Labelled LSD in Mice," in R. T. Harris, W. M. McIsaac, and C. R. Schuster (Eds.), *Drug Dependence*. Austin: University of Texas, 1970.

ILLICH, I. *De-Schooling Society*. New York: Harper and Row, 1971.

IMHOF, J. *Drug Education for Teachers and Parents*. New York: Sadlier, 1970.

Interim Report of the Commission of Inquiry into the Non-Medical Use of Drugs. Ottawa: Information Canada, 1970.

JACKSON, D. D. (Ed.). *The Human Communication Series*. Vol. 1. *Communication, Family and Marriage*. Vol. 2. *Therapy, Communication and Change*. Palo Alto, Calif.: Science and Behavioral Books, 1968.

JACKSON, J. "Family Interaction, Family Homeostasis, and Some Implications for Congruent Family Therapy," in J. Masserman (Ed.), *Individual and Family Dynamics*. New York: Grune and Stratton, 1959.

JACOBSON, C., and MAGYAR, V. "Genetic Evaluation of LSD," in *Clinical Proceedings, Children's Hospital* (Washington, D.C.), 1968, *24* (5), 152–179.

JACOBSON, C. B., ARIAS-BERNAL, L., VOSBECK, E., DEL RIEGO, A., AHERN, K., and MAGYAR, V. "Clinical Reproductive Dangers Inherent in the Use of Hallucinogenic Agents" in F. W. Sunderman and F. W. Sunderman, Jr. (Eds.), *Laboratory Diagnosis of Diseases Caused by Toxic Agents*. St. Louis: Warren Green, 1970.

JAMES, W. *The Varieties of Religious Experience*. New York: Random House, 1902.

JOHNSON, A. "Sanctions for Superego Lacunae of Adolescents," in *Searchlights on Delinquency*. New York: International Universities, 1949.

JOHNSON, A. "Juvenile Delinquency," in *American Handbook of Psychiatry*. Vol. I. New York: Basic Books, 1959.

JOINT COMMISSION ON MENTAL HEALTH OF CHILDREN, FINAL REPORT. "Crisis in Child Mental Health: Challenge for the 1970's." Washington, D.C., 1969.

JONES, M. C. "Personality Correlates and Antecedents of Drinking Patterns in Adult Males." *Journal of Consulting and Clinical Psychology*, 1968, *32* (1), 2–12.

JORDAN, W. D. *White Over Black.* Baltimore: Penguin, 1969.

KALOW, W. "Pharmacogenetics and the Predictability of Drug Response," in G. Wastenhom and R. Porter (Eds.), *Drug Responses in Man.* Boston: Little, Brown, 1967.

KAPLAN, J. *Marijuana: The New Prohibition.* New York and Cleveland: World, 1970.

KARCZMAR, A. G., and KOELLA, W. P. *Neurophysiological and Behavioral Aspects of Psychotropic Drugs.* Springfield, Ill.: Thomas, 1969.

KARDINER, A., and OVESLEY, L. *The Mark of Oppression.* New York: World, 1962.

KENDALL, R. S., and PITTEL, S. "Three Portraits of the Young Drug User: Comparison MMPI Group Profiles." Paper presented at meeting of Western Psychological Association, Los Angeles, April, 1970.

KENISTON, K. *The Uncommitted.* New York: Dell, 1960.

KENISTON, K. "Notes on young radicals." *Change,* 1969, *1*, 25–33.

KERPELMAN, L. C. "Student Political Activism and Ideology: Comparative Characteristics of Activitists and Non-Activists." *Journal of Counseling Psychology,* 1969, *16* (1), 8–13.

KING, S., and HENRY, A. "Aggression and Cardiovascular Reactions Related to Parental Control over Behavior." *Journal of Abnormal and Social Psychology,* 1955, *50*, 206–214.

KLECKNER, J. H. "Personality Differences between Psychedelic Drug Users and Non-Users." *Psychology,* 1968, *5* (2), 66–71.

KLECKNER, J. H. "Family Perceptions and Attitudes of Psychedelic Drug Users." Unpublished, 1970.

KLERMAN, G. L., DIMASCIO, A., GREENBLATT, M., and RINKEL, M. "The Influence of Specific Personality Patterns on the Reactions to Phrenotropic Agents," in J. Masserman (Ed.), *Biological Psychiatry.* New York: Grune and Stratton, 1959.

KNUPFER, G., FINK, R., CLARK, W. D., and GOFFMAN, A. S. "Factors Related to the Amount of Drinking in an Urban Community." California Drinking Practices Study, Report No. 6. California Department of Public Health, Berkeley, 1963.

KOHN, M. L. "Social Class Differences in Personality and Attitude." *American Sociological Review,* 1959, *24*, 352–366.

KOHN, M. L. "Social Class and Parent-Child Relationship." *American Journal of Sociology,* 1963, *68*, 471–480.

KOMAROVSKY, M. *The Unemployed Man and His Family.* New York: Dryden, 1940.

KOOS, E. L. *Families in Trouble.* New York: King's Crown, 1946.

KOOS, E. L. *The Health of Regionville.* New York: Columbia University, 1954.

LAMBERT, W. W., HOHANSSON, G., FRANKENHAUSER, M., and KLACKENBERG, L. "Calecholamine Excretion in Young Children and Their Parents as Related to Behavior." *Scandinavian Journal of Psychology,* 1969, *10,* 306–318.

LAMBIE, D., and WERKART, D. "Ypsilanti Carnegie Infant Education Project." In J. Hellmuth (Ed.), *Disadvantaged Child: Compensatory Education, A National Debate.* New York: Brunner Mozel, 1970.

LANE, R., and SEARS, D. *Public Opinion.* Englewood Cliffs, N.J.: Prentice-Hall, 1964.

LEVENTHAL, T., and SILLS, M. "The Issue of Control in Therapy with Character Problem Adolescents." *Psychiatry,* 1963, *26* (2), 149–167.

LEWIS, O. *Five Families: Mexican Case Studies in the Culture of Poverty.* New York: Basic Books, 1959.

LIEBERMAN RESEARCH. *The Teenager Looks at Cigarette Smoking.* American Cancer Society, 1969.

LINDESMITH, A. R. *Addiction and Opiates.* Chicago: Aldine, 1968.

LIPSET, S. M. "Youth and Politics," in R. K. Merton and R. Nisbet (Eds.), *Contemporary Social Problems.* 3rd ed. New York: Harcourt, Brace, Jovanovich, 1971.

MAAS, H. S. "Some Social Class Differences in the Family Systems and Group Relationships of Pre- and Early-Adolescents." *Child Development,* 1951, *22,* 145–152.

MACFARLANE, J. W., ALLEN, L., and HONZIK, M. P. *A Developmental Study of the Behavior Problems of Normal Children between Twenty-one Months and Fourteen Years.* University of California Publications in Child Development, Vol. II. Berkeley, Calif.: University of California, 1954.

MANHEIMER, D. I., MELLINGER, G. D., and BALTER, M. B. "Marijuana Use among Urban Adults." *Science,* 1969, *166,* 1544–1545.

MARIN, P., and COHEN, A. Y. *Understanding Drug Use: An Adult's Guide to Drugs and the Young.* New York: Harper and Row, 1971.

MARRIS, P., and REIN, M. *Dilemmas of Social Reform.* New York: Atherton, 1967.

MCARTHUR, C., WALDEN, E., and DICKINSON, J. "Psychology of Smoking." *Journal of Abnormal Social Psychology,* 1958, *56,* 267–275.

MCCORD, W., and MCCORD, J. "A Longitudinal Study of the Personality of Alcoholics," in D. J. Pitman and C. R. Snyder (Eds.), *Society, Culture and Drinking Patterns*. New York: Wiley, 1962.

MCGLOTHLIN, W. H., COHEN, S., and MCGLOTHLIN, M. S. "Long Lasting Effects of LSD on Normals." *Archives of General Psychiatry*, 1967, *17* (5), 521–532.

MCGLOTHLIN, W. H., COHEN, S., and MCGLOTHLIN, M. S. "Personality and Attitude Changes in Volunteer Subjects Following Repeated Administration of LSD." Paper presented before Fifth International Congress, Collegium Neuropsychopharmacalogicum, March, 1967.

MEAD, M. *Coming of Age in Samoa*. New York: Morrow, 1928.

MEAD, M. *Sex and Temperament in Three Primitive Societies*. New York: Morrow, 1950.

MEEHL, P. *Clinical vs. Statistical Prediction*. Minneapolis: University of Minnesota, 1954.

MERRILL, M. A. *Problem of Delinquency*. New York: Houghton Mifflin, 1947.

METCALF, A. Personal communication, 1971.

MILLER, D. R., and SWANSON, C. *The Changing American Parent*. New York: Wiley, 1958.

MILLER, D. R., and SWANSON, G. E. *Inner Conflict and Defense*. New York: Holt, Rinehart, and Winston, 1960.

MILLER, W. B. "The Impact of a 'Total-Community' Control Project." *Social Problems*, 1962, *10*, 168–191.

MITCHESON, M., DAVIDSON, J., HAWKS, D. V., HITCHENS, L., and MALONE, S. "Sedative Use by Heroin Addicts." *Lancet*, 1970, *i*, 606–607.

MORRISON, D. F.. *Multivariate Statistical Methods*. McGraw-Hill Series in Probability and Statistics. New York: McGraw-Hill, 1967.

MUTWA, V. C. *Indaba My Children*. New York: Humanities, 1965.

NATIONAL COMMISSION ON THE CAUSES AND PREVENTION OF VIOLENCE. *To Establish Justice, To Insure Domestic Tranquility. Final Report, 1969*. Washington, D.C.: U.S. Gov't. Printing Office, 1970.

NICHOLS, J. R. "A Procedure which Produces Sustained Opiate-Directed Behavior (Morphine Addiction) in the Rat." Paper read at Chicago meeting of the American Psychological Association, September 6, 1960.

NOBLE, P. J. "Drug Taking in Delinquent Boys." *British Medical Journal*, 1970, *i*, 102–105.

NUNNALY, J. C., JR. *Popular Conceptions of Mental Health: Their De-*

velopment and Change. New York: Holt, Rinehart, and Winston, 1961.

ORLANSKY, H. "Infant Care and Personality." Psychological Bulletin, 1949, 46, 1–48.

PACKER, H. The Limits of the Criminal Sanction. Stanford: Stanford University, 1969.

PAINE, R. S., and OPPÉ, T. E. Neurological Examination of Children. The Spastics Society Medical Education and Information Unit in association with William Heinemann Medical Books, 1966.

PATTERSON, G. R., and GUILLIAN, M. E. Living with Children: New Methods for Parents or Teachers. Champaign, Ill.: Research Press, 1971.

PIAGET, J. The Moral Judgment of the Child. New York: Macmillan, 1932.

PITTEL, S. "Psychological Effects of Psychological Drugs: Preliminary Observations and Hypotheses." Paper presented at meeting of the Western Psychological Association, June 21, 1969.

PITTEL, S. M. (Ed.). Drug Use and Drug Subcultures. Washington, D.C.: U.S. Gov't. Printing Office, 1971. In press.

PREBLE, E., and CASEY, J. J., JR. "Taking Care of Business—the Heroin User's Life on the Street." International Journal of the Addictions, 1969, 4 (1), 1–24.

REISS, A. A. The Public and the Police. New Haven: Yale University, 1971.

RINKEL, M. Specific and Non-Specific Factors in Psychopharmacology. New York: Philosophical Library, 1963.

ROBINS, L. N. Deviant Children Grown Up. Baltimore, Maryland: Williams and Wilkins, 1966.

ROBINS, L. N., and MURPHY, G. E. "Drug use in a normal population of young Negro men." American Journal of Public Health, 1967, 57 (9), 1580–1596.

RONEY, J. G., JR., and NALL, M. L. "Medication Practices in a Community: An Exploratory Study." Menlo Park, California: Stanford Research Institute, August, 1966.

ROSE, S. D. "A Behavioral Approach to the Group Treatment of Parents." Social Work, July 4, 1969.

RUDOFF, A. "The Incarcerated Mexican-American Delinquent." Journal of Criminal Law, Criminology and Police Science, 1971, 62, 224–238.

SALTMAN, J. Marijuana and Your Child. New York: Grosset and Dunlap, 1970.

SAN MATEO COUNTY SCHOOL STUDY. "Five Mind Altering Drugs: The

Use of Alcoholic Beverages, Amphetamines, LSD, Marijuana and Tobacco, Reported by High School and Junior High School Students, San Mateo County, California, 1968, 1969, 1970." Prepared at the request of the Narcotic Advisory Committee of the Juvenile Justice Commission.

SCHACHTER, S. "Some Extraordinary Facts about Obese Humans and Rats." *American Psychologist,* 1971, *26* (2), 129–144.

SCOTT, C. H. "Pattern of Child Adjustment," in O. E. Oeser and S. B. Hammon (Eds.), *Social Structure and Family in a City.* London: Routledge, 1954.

SCOTT, P. D., and WILLCOX, D. R. C. "Delinquency and the Amphetamines." *British Journal of Addiction,* 1965, *61,* 9–27.

SEARS, R. R., MACCOBY, E. E., and LEVIN, H. *Patterns of Child Rearing.* New York: Harper and Row, 1957.

SEARS, R. R., RAU, L., and ALPERT, R. *Identification and Child Rearing.* Stanford: Stanford University, 1965.

SELIGMAN, B. *Poverty as a Public Issue.* Glencoe: The Free Press, 1965.

SEWELL, W. H. "Infant Training and the Personality of the Child." *American Journal of Sociology,* 1952, *58,* 150–159.

SHEPPARD, C. W., and GAY, G. R. "The Changing Face of Heroin Addiction in the Haight-Ashbury." *International Journal of the Addictions,* 1971, *6,* 4.

SHOSTAK, A., and GOMBERGUE, W. (Eds.). *New Perspectives on Poverty.* Englewood Cliffs, N.J.: Prentice-Hall, 1965.

SMITH, J., and SMITH, D. *Child Management, A Program for Parents and Teachers.* Ann Arbor, Mich.: Ann Arbor Publishers, 1964.

SMITH, R. *The Marketplace of Speed: Violence and Compulsive Methedrine Abuse.* Chicago. Aldine, 1971.

SPITZ, R. A. "An Inquiry into the Genesis of Psychiatric Conditions in Early Childhood," in *Psychoanalytic Study of the Child.* Vol. I. New York: International Universities, 1945.

STEFFENHAGEN, R. A., MCAREE, C. P., and ZHEUTLIN, L. S. "Some Social Factors in College Drug Usage." *International Journal of Social Psychiatry,* 1969, *15* (2), 92–96.

STEVENSON, G. H. *Drug Addiction in British Columbia.* Vancouver: University of British Columbia, 1956.

STRODBECK, F. "Family Interaction, Values and Achievement," in A. L. Baldwin, U. Bronfenbrenner, D. C. McClelland, and F. Strodbeck (Eds.), *Talent and Society.* Princeton: N.J.: Van Nostrand, 1958.

STUBBS, V., and JACOBSON, C. "LSD and Genetic Damage." *The George*

Washington University Magazine, 1968–69 (December–January), 26–31.

SULLIVAN, H. F. *The Interpersonal Theory of Psychiatry.* New York: Norton, 1953.

SZUREK, S. "The Needs of Adolescents for Emotional Health," in *Modern Perspectives in Child Psychiatry.* Edinburgh: Oliver and Boyd, 1969.

TASK FORCE ON PRESCRIPTION DRUGS. *The Drug Prescribers.* Department of Health, Education, and Welfare. Washington, D.C.: U.S. Gov't. Printing Office, 1968.

TIME. "The American Family: Future Uncertain." December 28, 1970.

ULLMAN, W. *The Individual and Society in the Middle Ages.* Baltimore: Johns Hopkins, 1966.

UNGERLEIDER, J. T., FISHER, D. D., FULLER, M., and CALDWELL, A. "The Bad Trip—the Etiology of the Adverse LSD Reaction." *American Journal of Psychiatry*, 1968, *124* (11), 1483–1490.

WALLERSTEIN, J. S., and WYLE, C. J. "Our Law-Abiding Law Breakers." *Probation*, 1947, *25*, 107–112.

WATZLAWICK, P., BEAVIN, J., and JACKSON, D. V. *Pragmatics of Human Communications.* New York: Norton, 1967.

WEAKLAND, J. H. "The 'Double-Bind' Hypothesis of Schizophrenia and Three Party Interaction," in D. D. Jackson (Ed.), *The Etiology of Schizophrenia.* New York: Basic Books, 1960.

WESTLEY, W. A., and EPSTEIN, N. B. *The Silent Majority.* San Francisco: Jossey-Bass, 1969.

WHITE HOUSE CONFERENCE. Final Report of the Intern Task Force on Drugs for the White House Conference on Youth, 1971.

WHITING, J. W. M., and CHILD, I. L. *Child Training and Personality.* New Haven: Yale University, 1953.

WILSON, R. R. *Sects and Society.* Berkeley: University of California, 1961.

WISEMAN, J. P. *Stations of the Lost.* Englewood Cliffs, N.J.: Prentice-Hall, 1970.

WITKIN, H. A., DYK, R. B., FATERSON, H. F., GOODENOUGH, D. R., and KARP, S. A. *Psychological Differentiation* New York: Wiley, 1962.

WITTES, G., and RADIN, N. *Ypsilanti Home and School Handbook, Helping Your Child Learn.* San Rafael, Calif.: Dimensions, 1969.

WITTES, G., and RADIN, N. "Two Approaches to Group Work with Parents in a Compensatory Preschool Program." *Social Work*, January 16, 1971.

WOLFE, J. "Report on Drug Use Among Boarding and Day Students." Unpublished paper, 1969.

ZELDITCH, M. "Family, Marriage and Kinship," in R. E. Favis (Ed.), *Handbook of Sociology*. Chicago: Rand McNally, 1964.

ZINBERG, N., and WEIL, A. "A Comparison of Marijuana Users and Non-Users." *Nature*, 1970, *226*, 119–123.

Index

A

ACKERMAN, N. W., 14
Adolescents, literature on drug use by, 1–3
Adults: literature on drug use by, 3–5; self-medication among, 4
Affection and discipline in child rearing, 7–12
Age and drug use, 34–35
AHEARN, K., 186
AICHHORN, A., 37
Alcohol use by parents, 36–37
Alcoholism, predictors of, 36–37
ALEXANDER, G. J., 185
ALKIRE, A. A., 21
ALLEN, L., 25
ALPERT, R., 7
ALTON, A., 186
ARIAS-BERNAL, L., 186
ARONFREED, J., 9
AUERBACH, R., 184, 185

B

BACK, K. W., 26
BALDWIN, J., 19
BALL, J. C., 2, 18, 121
BALTER, M. B., 4
BANFIELD, E. C., 18, 27, 32, 33, 295
BATESON, G., 21, 57, 105

BAUER, R., 62
BAUMRIND, D., 12–13, 17
BEAVIN, J., 21
BEECHER, H. K., 40
BENTEL, D. J., 34
BERG, D. F., 2
BEWLEY, T. H., 24
Biochemical-neurophysiological factors in drug use, 28–29
BLACK, D. J., 112
BLACK, N., 185
Black families, 109–116, 140–154; analysis of low and high risk characteristics of, 150–154; children and child-rearing practices in, 143–144; delinquency in, 111–112; and drug scene, 110–112; education on child rearing and drug risk of, 291–292; family organization of, 112, 144–145; fathers in, 142–143; interviewing study of, 114–116; mothers in, 141–142; observations in home of, 145–147; parental concern over drugs in, 287; reports by children in, 147–150
BLAKESLEE, A., 2
BLOOD, R. O., 14
Blue-collar black families. *See* Black families